SOCIOLOGY IS A MARTIAL ART

SOCIOLOGY IS A MARTIAL ART

Political Writings by Pierre Bourdieu

Pierre Bourdieu

Edited by Gisèle Sapiro

Translated by Priscilla Parkhurst Ferguson,
Richard Nice, and Loïc Wacquant

THE NEW PRESS

NEW YORK
LONDON

Requests for permission to reproduce selections from this book should be mailed to:
Permissions Department, The New Press, 38 Greene Street, New York, NY 10013.

Page 309 constitutes an extension of this copyright page.

Published in the United States by The New Press, New York, 2010
Distributed by Perseus Distribution

LIBRARY OF CONGRESS CATALOGING-IN-PUBLICATION DATA

Bourdieu, Pierre, 1930–2002.
[Selections. English. 2010]
    Sociology is a martial art : political writings by Pierre Bourdieu /
Pierre Bourdieu ; edited by Gisèle Sapiro ; translated by Priscilla
Parkhurst Ferguson, Richard Nice, and Loïc Wacquant.
        p.   cm.
    Includes bibliographical references and index.
    ISBN 978-1-59558-543-1 (pbk. : alk. paper)
        1. Sociology—Philosophy. 2. Political sociology. I. Sapiro, Gisèle. II. Ferguson,
Priscilla Parkhurst. III. Nice, Richard W. IV. Wacquant, Loïc J. D. V. Title.
    HM585.B683   2010
    306.2—dc22   2010033466

The New Press was established in 1990 as a not-for-profit alternative to the large,
commercial publishing houses currently dominating the book publishing industry.
The New Press operates in the public interest rather than for private gain, and is
committed to publishing, in innovative ways, works of educational, cultural, and
community value that are often deemed insufficiently profitable.

www.thenewpress.com

Composition by dix!
This book was set in Scala

Printed in the United States of America

10 9 8 7 6 5 4 3 2 1

CONTENTS

Contents

INTRODUCTION

The texts collected in this volume were conceived by Pierre Bourdieu as "interventions." Having achieved high academic recognition, Bourdieu decided to put his symbolic capital at the service of a cause, thus embodying—after Voltaire, Zola, Sartre, and Foucault—the French traditional figure of the public intellectual who engages in political and social matters. According to this model, an intellectual, a scholar, should not remain in an ivory tower; it is his or her duty to be involved in current affairs. His role is to offer a critical perspective and not to serve the political, economic, or religious powers. He must keep autonomous from political organizations and economic interests.

Yet the way Bourdieu envisioned his commitment was different from that of his illustrious predecessors. Sartre's model of the "total intellectual" taking a stand on any and every question was no longer relevant in a context of specialization and fragmentation of knowledge. This is why Foucault developed the idea of the "specific intellectual," who discusses only the matters she masters scientifically.

Critical of the figure of the media intellectual that emerged in the late 1970s with the Nouveaux Philosophes ("New Philosophers")—who illustrate in his view the "negative intellectual" [1]—Bourdieu went one step further in seriously considering the division of scientific labor. He suggested the notion of the "collective intellectual," whose political stands are based on scientific knowledge and on the results of individual or collective research. Like Foucault's "specific intellectual," Bourdieu's "collective intellectual" offers a model of counterexpertise. This stands in contradistinction to the figure of the expert called on by the political and economic forces to provide "neutral" scientific knowledge in order to legitimize policies he has not elaborated or answer problems he has not defined by himself. [2]

Bourdieu materialized this idea in the aftermath of the 1995 social movement in France, which divided the intellectual field between those who supported the neoliberal "reform" of the health policy and those who combated it. Having committed himself in support of the social movement, Bourdieu extended his fight against neoliberalism by founding a committee of scholars, Raisons d'agir (Reasons to act), which later became an association, and by launching a series of books called *Liber-Raisons d'agir*. Published in 1996, *On Television* was the first title in a series in which the two collections of interventions entitled *Contre-feux* also appeared. The English translations of these three books, which are brought together in this volume with some additional interventions and interviews (translated by Richard Nice), were published in the United States by The New Press. *On Television*, translated by Priscilla Ferguson, appeared in 1998. The other two were published in 2009: the first was *Acts of Resistance: Against the Tyranny of the Market*, translated by Richard Nice; the second, *Firing Back: Against the Tyranny of the Market 2*, translated by Loïc Wacquant. These publications extended Bourdieu's audience beyond the academic world in English-speaking countries (all of his former books were published by academic presses), as the attention he received in the *New York Times* and in other newspapers proves (see p. xii).

Translated into twenty-five languages for twenty-seven countries, *On Television* is Bourdieu's most popular book. It had sold more than 200,000 copies as of 2009. With this book, Bourdieu moved from the position of a highly recognized social scientist to that of a "global thinker."[3] Bourdieu was aware that aiming at a larger readership required a simplified and less-specialized discourse. But he considered it an obligation for scholars, especially in the social sciences, "to make the advances of research available to everyone," as he writes. They should think of themselves as "humanity's civil servants," as Edmund Husserl put it (see p. 15).

In *On Television* he addresses the impact of television on society and the symbolic violence it exerts. Bourdieu forged this concept of symbolic violence to designate a kind of violence which is misrecognized as such, and therefore accepted by the dominated because they share with the dominant representations and categories of thinking that are inculcated through the educational system and the media. The role of television in producing and reproducing these representations and categories of thinking is crucial, since it is the most consumed medium. This is all the more true in the context of the crisis of the written press, a crisis which was just beginning when Bourdieu wrote this book, and which has deepened since then with the development of the Internet. Bourdieu was particularly concerned by the depoliticized way television deals with political and social issues. In order to understand the mechanisms underlying this depoliticization of information, one has to understand the specific interests which guide journalists' choices. It is not enough to reduce it to external social conditions, as a Marxist analysis would do. Bourdieu uses the concept of the "field," a concept he forged to describe the functioning of social spaces that have their own rules and within which the agents compete around specific issues. Since its emergence in the nineteenth century, the journalistic field had been structured around the opposition between news and views—between serious information and political commentary. Nowadays, news tends to focus on nonpolitical issues like natural disasters, crime, and stories of human interest. This evolution characterizes journalism more broadly, but television, where entertainment has replaced serious matters under the pretext of the lack of interest of the public as measured through audience ratings, is in large part responsible for it.

This functioning of television has an impact on other fields, namely the political and the intellectual, on which it imposes its own rules. As television tends to depoliticize politics, politicians are more and more concerned about their image in the media and rumors about their private lives. In the intellectual field, television promotes what Bourdieu calls "fast-thinkers," like the French Nouveaux Philosophes, while there is a "negative connection between time pressures and thought" (p. 27). In both cases, the public image of individuals takes the place of content. And the growing power of the media results in an increasing heteronomy within the political and intellectual fields. Far from bridging the gap between the "specialists" and the "nonspecialists," television deepens it by hiding the real issues at stake in favor of a discourse aimed at entertaining or winning over the largest possible audience. Bourdieu compares it to demagogy in politics. Analyzing the sadly famous French case of little Karine, he shows the role the media played in reinstating life imprisonment for her murderer, thus reducing the autonomy of justice. Journalists should be more aware of their symbolic power, Bourdieu argued in a talk he gave in 1992 at a conference of the international association Reporters Without Borders, and which is included in the present volume—namely in their use of words, since language conveys categories of thinking and presuppositions that make up the collective unconscious.

The critical attention *On Television* received in the United States is a sign of Bourdieu's recognition as a "global thinker." The book was praised in the *New York Times* by Cass R. Sunstein, a member of the Federal Advisory Committee on the Public Interest Obligations of Digital Television Broadcasters. For him, Bourdieu's most important assertion is that "television provides far less autonomy, or freedom, than we think."[4] While acknowledging that Bourdieu's purpose was to point out a problem, not to propose remedies, he regretted that he did not address questions about new technologies and did not go further in asking practical questions about the possible solutions. Yet this reaction in itself proves that Bourdieu had reached his aim in provoking a social debate on this issue. And indeed, despite the references to the French context and the use of a scientific vocabulary, Bourdieu's argument was considered by the reviewers to be "interesting and pertinent,"[5] and the message was well understood, as this excerpt from the article in *Publishers Weekly* illustrates:

> Bourdieu's withering critique of television created a furor in France that lasted several months after airing of the two televised lectures that this broadside comprises. The author, a sociology professor in Paris, damns television as an enemy of critical discourse and a tool of social control that reinforces the status quo by decontextualizing events and fostering ignorance and passivity. For American readers, his acid appraisal will provide shudders of recognition, as when he writes: "Our news anchors, our talk show hosts, and our sports announcers have turned into two-bit spiritual guides, representatives of middle-class morality. They are always telling us what we

'should think.' " Tabloid TV journalism, endless trivia and
"human-interest" stories, programs pandering to mass audiences, telejournalists' defining of a narrow agenda of acceptable issues are served up with Gallic intellectualism and a
dollop of structuralist analysis.[6]

The two other collections of interventions address various social,
economic, and political issues. Some of these texts abandon the objective style of the social scientist to adopt polemical or prophetic accents, as in "The Government Finds the People Irresponsible," where
Bourdieu denounces state racism, drawing a parallel between the way
the French administration treats people with an Arab-looking name
and the attitude of the Vichy administration toward the Jews at the
very moment when the French government was expressing its repentance for the latter. Bourdieu does not hesitate to challenge politicians
like the social democrat trio Blair-Schröder-Jospin as well as powerful
figures like Bill Gates, Hans Titmeyer (the president of the German
Bank), or famous "negative intellectuals," like Bernard Henri-Lévy or
the French writer Philippe Sollers, who betrayed the principle of autonomy by agreeing to play the game of the media or by bowing to
politicians.

Until 1995, the interventions focused mainly on French matters, such as the treatment of immigrants or social policy. By 1996,
Bourdieu had become convinced that the right level of analysis for understanding social changes was a global one. Many of these changes
were dictated by the ideology of neoliberalism, which tends to globalize the rule of the free market by reducing the regulatory role of the
state. This ideology had to be combated. The struggle, he thought,
should be organized first in Europe, where there is a tradition of social
struggle and where many organizations such as trade unions and associations already exist. He therefore tried to impel a European social
movement and to create a European public space. Many of his talks
were given and/or published outside of France, first mostly in Germany, but also in Greece, then later on in the United States, Korea,
and Japan, confirming his position as a global thinker. Most of them
were intended for a nonacademic audience: they were published in

newspapers like *Le Monde, Libération, Die Zeit,* or presented at political meetings. The two collections are complemented here with three later pieces: an interview published in the *Revue d'études palestiniennes* (vol. 74/22, in winter 2000) and two speeches he gave in 2001, one of them at a countersummit held on January 27 in Zürich at the same time as the Davos World Economic Forum,[7] and the second one at the People Summit organized on April 4 in Québec by the Continental Social Alliance (an organization gathering representatives of social movements and trade unions from thirty-five American countries) as a protest against the Summit of the Americas which aimed at extending the law of free exchange to the continent.

Neoliberalism, Bourdieu claims, has become a *doxa,* a shared belief that is not put into question. It has succeeded in presenting itself as "self-evident" (p. 108). Politicians, think tanks, experts (especially economists), journalists, and public intellectuals are responsible for this, because they have legitimized it through mathematical equations (economic models) and through words like "globalization" and "flexibility," thereby spreading the idea of its inevitability. Neoliberalism, an ideological construct, has to be deconstructed with intellectual tools.

"Flexibility," for instance, is a euphemistic formula to designate the loss of job security, a strategy which aims not only at increasing the competition between workers from every country but also at preventing a social movement. In his fieldwork on Algerian workers in the late 1950s, Bourdieu showed that rational behavior, which is characterized by the ability to plan, is highly linked to job security.[8] Workers deprived of it are less inclined to political action. In this regard, he considered the movement of the unemployed that arose in France by the end of the 1990s as a social miracle.[9] He was hoping this movement would spread all over Europe, but his scientific findings proved more predictive than his wishful prophecy.

Neoliberal policies undermine the rights workers won after decades of social struggles, denouncing them as archaic, and their defense as conservative, thereby turning the progressive vocabulary against itself. This process, which Bourdieu assimilates to a conservative revolution, happened first in countries where these rights were not protected by the State—namely in the United States under Ronald Reagan and in the United Kingdom under Margaret Thatcher. In the United States, the welfare state has progressively been replaced by the penal state.[10] In France, the implementation of neoliberal policies has led to the dismantling of the welfare state.

Bourdieu's argument relies on the theory of the State he developed at the beginning of the 1990s in a course he gave at the Collège de France,[11] and of which he provides a brief overview in "The Globalization Myth and the Welfare State." Contrary to Marxist theory, which reduces the State to a mere superstructure, Bourdieu conceives it as relatively autonomous from the dominant social and economic forces. From a historical perspective, the State first concentrated physical force (a process the German sociologist Max Weber defined as the monopoly of legitimate violence) and economic force, then cultural capital (with the nationalization of education), and, last, authority. As a consequence of this process, the State is an "ambiguous reality" (p. 111): though not totally independent from the dominant groups, it secures at the same time—in the welfare conception, at least—social rights like work conditions, access to health insurance, the right to education. Bourdieu uses the metaphor of "the right hand and the left hand of the State" to designate political and economic power on one side, the social issues handled by the spending ministries on the other. This opposition is gendered. The "right hand" is very masculine, whereas care, education, and culture have become mainly female occupations. The dominated position of the "left hand" makes it all the more difficult to resist the pressure of the "right" one.

Bourdieu stresses that his defense of the State has nothing to do with nationalism. It concerns the universal functions of the State. The functions can and should be undertaken by supranational organizations. The European Union is of course one of them, but instead of playing this role, it has been the vehicle of neoliberal policies. This explains the nationalist reaction of lower classes to the European construction. In his call "For a New Internationalism," Bourdieu makes some proposals for the organization of a European social movement and the development of a social European policy which would counter the neoliberal trends.

Bourdieu sets this new internationalism in opposition to the concept of "globalization," which is, according to him, merely a "justificatory myth" for breaking through the borders of the welfare state and extending the markets to sectors such as cultural goods, education, and health (the latter was the task of the General Agreement on Trade in Services, or GATS, negotiated during the Uruguay Round, which came into effect in 1995). Neoliberal policy, Bourdieu argues, attacks health "from two directions, by contributing to an increase in the incidence of illness and the number of sick people (through the correlation between poverty and pathology: alcoholism, drugs, delinquency, industrial accidents, etc.) and by reducing medical resources and the provision for care [. . .]" (p. 197). In the intervention titled "Culture Is in Danger," Bourdieu denounces the menace that the merchandising of cultural products represents to creative activity. As he demonstrated in *The Rules of Art*, the fields of cultural production (literature and the arts) have gained autonomy from the political, economic, and religious forces that tried to subordinate them to their interests.[12] This means, for instance, that the value of a literary work cannot be reduced to book sales in the short run. Autonomy is the condition for innovation. It can take some time before an avant-garde work that subverts the cognitive frames is accepted by a larger audience, but it then might become a cultural reference. This long-run process characterizes the economy of symbolic goods. But the large conglomerates that have invested in cultural production are more interested in short-term profit. In the book industry, the concentration of ownership, which accelerated in the 1990s with the merging and buying of firms, has reinforced the commercial constraints on book production.[13] Distribution tends more and more to govern the production process, "imposing a veritable censorship by money," as Bourdieu writes (p. 224). Far from fostering diversity, globalization in the cultural production favors blockbusters and bestsellers, entailing homogeneity and standardization at both the national and international levels.

Globalization is also a myth that hides the unequal power relations between the richest countries and the others. The unification of markets, especially the financial market, reinforces the domination of the former over the latter. The invisible hand is in fact that of an international oligarchy of heads and executives of multinationals that acts through such bodies as the World Bank, the International Monetary Fund, and the World Trade Organization to promote its idea of free exchange, which gives advantage to the dominant (i.e., the multinationals) on the globalized market. The Multilateral Agreement on Investment negotiated between members of the Organisation for Economic Co-operation and Development (OECD) from 1995 to 1998 was an example of the way the richest countries were trying to impose their rule on the poorest. The project was abandoned thanks to a large international protest lead by nongovernmental organisations (NGOs), citizens' groups, and some governments of developing countries.

The United States—where the ideology of neoliberalism found favorable conditions for its development, mainly because of an intellectual tradition which considers the market as being ruled by natural laws and collective entities resulting from individual actions,[14] as Bourdieu explains in an intervention which was not included in the first English version of *Firing Back* and which is published for the first time in English in this volume[15]—played a leading role in the promotion of the idea of globalization. The United States was able to foster this ideology thanks to its dominant position in this world market, a position due, as Bourdieu explains in the piece entitled "Unite and Rule," to an exceptional concentration of various kinds of advantages: financial, economic, political, military, cultural (the high quality of scientific research, the power of lawyers), linguistic (the universality of English), and symbolic (the American lifestyle as a worldwide reference)—a role some American scholars were the first to denounce, as Bourdieu reminds us in his preface to the English translation of *Firing Back*.

Neoliberalism tends to depoliticize politics by presenting the law of the markets as ineluctable. The role of public intellectuals is to undermine neoliberal fatalism and give the social movement tools for deconstructing the neoliberal ideology. Bourdieu suggests, for instance, turning their own weapons against the economists. Economic models never calculate the social costs of rationalization and profit: the consequences of human suffering, sickness, alcohol, drugs, or riots, such as those that arose in the French suburban estates around the big cities (the *banlieues*), and that stem in large part from a neoliberal housing policy implemented by the end of the 1970s that led to social segregation. Introducing these calculations would modify the scientific basis of social policies. More broadly, social scientists should elaborate "realistic utopias" and provide counterexpertise to redefine public policies.

"One wonders what will be left in ten years' time of European experimental cinema if nothing is done to provide avant-garde directors with the means of production and perhaps more importantly distribution," Bourdieu wrote in "The Myth of 'Globalization' and the European Welfare State" (p. 115). More than a decade after their first publication, Bourdieu's interventions sound terribly relevant. Many of his predictions have been confirmed; some have taken a dramatic turn. The economic crisis was in large part the result of the autonomization of the financial field described in "Unite and Rule." In this context, the fiercest adversaries of the State, the financers and bankers, suddenly turned to request its support. His reflections on the role of the welfare state are also relevant to the recent debate on the reform of health care policy in the United States. In the cultural industries, including the media, the economic constraints have tightened.

Some of the other issues and cases Bourdieu raised were premonitory. France is now experiencing the replacement of the welfare state by the penal state—for instance, in its immigration policy, with the harshening of the repressive measures against unauthorized foreigners (the *sans papiers*) through six laws adopted from 2002 to 2010. Bourdieu also warned against the racist and xenophobic reactions after the October 1995 terrorist attack in the Paris subway, citing as an example the debate on the Muslim veil. This debate has become acute in France since the passing, in 2004, of a law forbidding the wearing of religious signs at schools in France. Recently, the Belgian parliament passed a law prohibiting the full veil (burqa and niqab) in the street, while in France, the Conseil d'Etat (Council of State, which provides the government with legal advice) rejected a similar bill, contrasting the argument of "personal autonomy" to that of "personal dignity" evoked in the bill, yet it encouraged the government to forbid it in the public services.

Bourdieu's conception of the critical role of sociology and his commitment were at that time considered by many scholars, including some of those who aspire to play such a role today in France, as incompatible with the axiological neutrality required from a scientist. The constraint of objectivity and neutrality, first adopted by the founders of sociology as a way to free themselves from the dominant moral norms, was imposed on social science after World War II mainly through philanthropic foundations as a requirement of empirical research (following the model of the natural sciences) in opposition to pure theory, especially Marxism. Though this paradigm, which developed in the United States before spreading to Europe, was imported into France in the 1950s, Marxism remained very influential until the mid-1970s.[16] Bourdieu's sociology was both theoretical and deeply anchored in empirical research, combining quantitative and qualitative approaches (against what he calls in the interview "armchair Marxism," p. 268). While rejecting the idea of the neutrality of science as a myth, he did not conceive it as pure ideology. By revealing the social mechanisms of domination, sociology plays a critical role and gives tools to the dominated for their struggle.

The critical perspective is at the core of his sociological approach. In the interview he gave to the *Revue d'études palestiniennes* in 2000, Bourdieu says he has always known that sociology is a "political science" (p. 269). From his very first fieldwork in Algeria to his study of *The Social Structures of the Economy*, through his analyses of the role of the school in the reproduction of social inequalities (*The Inheritors, Reproduction*, and *The State Nobility*) and of the cultural dimension of class domination (*Distinction*), he has always addressed politically "burning" topics and challenged the dominant ideology—denouncing the educational system when the myth of democratization in education was prevailing in the 1960s, defending it when it was attacked by neoliberal ideologists in the 1990s.[17] He kept tracking the changes and developments that occurred after his first surveys on education, and found, as he explained in the interview, that despite the apparent democratization of the French system, the social mechanisms of exclusion had not disappeared but were incorporated within the system itself, producing "excluded insiders."

When the intellectual field was dominated by the figure of the "total intellectual," best illustrated by Sartre, Bourdieu remained critical of it, as he explained in the article he published on Sartre in the *London Review of Books* after his death in 1980.[18] Yet Sartre had kept himself autonomous from political organizations even when he was a fellow traveler of the Communist Party in the 1950s, contrary to the Party intellectuals who surrendered their autonomy of thought. By the end of the 1970s, Bourdieu became more and more concerned about the rise of technocratic power and the closure of the French political field on itself, which dispossessed the citizens of their right to intervene in political matters. The 1981 victory of the Socialist Party modified the relations between intellectuals and political power. The alliance of the new government with many former leftists threatened to leave the critical perspective on politics without a voice. Bourdieu had just been appointed to the Collège de France, the most prestigious scientific institution in France. This was the moment when he endorsed the role of the public intellectual. In December 1981, he wrote a manifesto with Foucault in support of the Polish trade union Solidarnosc, which was confronting severe repression by General Jaruzelski's army with the blessing of the USSR. The manifesto reproached the new French socialist government for deciding not to react. In return, the French minister of culture of the socialist government, Jack Lang, accused these intellectuals of "typically structuralist irresponsibility." In his response, Bourdieu claimed the right to criticize the government and the politicians as a citizen and as an intellectual. He claimed the right to be irresponsible in the face of politicians who claim to be "responsible," which means the right to speak freely on political issues, contrary to intellectuals belonging to a political organization.

Bourdieu not only criticized the existing system, he also took part in several reflection groups or committees to propose reforms. But the autonomy of the expert is limited, since she is not free to define the questions she has to address. Counterexpertise was a means of making a political use of scientific knowledge in an autonomous manner.

Bourdieu's engagement against neoliberalism in the mid-1990s aroused a violent reaction from his political adversaries on the right as well as on the center-left (mainly those close to the Socialist Party, which Bourdieu criticized for applying neoliberal policies). By that time, Bourdieu had become the most famous contemporary sociologist in the world. But no man is a prophet in his own land. Within the French scientific community, his radical stand was used by his opponents to try to dismiss his sociology in a period of apparent depoliticization of the French social sciences (accusing a scholar of being ideological was a way to discredit him scientifically).

This situation has changed since Bourdieu's death. In American sociology, the paradigm of neutrality has been challenged with the debate aroused by the 2004 address of the president of the American Sociological Association, Michael Burawoy, entitled "For Public Sociology."[19] Burawoy mentions French sociologists, including Bourdieu, as a model.[20] In France, the balance has also changed, in a context of repoliticization of the intellectual field under the right-wing government. Bourdieu's commitment has become a model for both his supporters and some of his opponents who now aspire to take his place.[21]

Gisèle Sapiro
Paris, April 2010

SOCIOLOGY IS A MARTIAL ART

Part I

On Journalism and Television

JOURNALISM AND POLITICS

It should go without saying that to reveal the hidden constraints on journalists, which they in turn bring to bear on all cultural producers, is not to denounce those in charge or to point a finger at the guilty parties.[1] Rather, it is an attempt to offer to all sides a possibility of liberation, through a conscious effort, from the hold of these mechanisms, and to propose, perhaps, a program for concerted action by artists, writers, scholars, and journalists—that is, by the holders of the (quasi) monopoly of the instruments of diffusion. Only through such a collaboration will it be possible to work effectively to share the most universal achievements of research and to begin, in practical terms, to universalize the conditions of access to the universal.

What can possibly explain the remarkably violent reactions by so many of France's best-known journalists to this analysis?[2] Surely, with all my disavowals, they can't have felt personally targeted (at least the ones who were cited directly, or indirectly through people who work with them or who are like them). In part, no doubt, their virtuous indignation can be attributed to the *transcription effect*—the elimination by transcription of the nonverbal accompaniment to words such as tone, gestures, and mimicry. An impartial viewer perceives these elements, which make all the difference between a discussion meant to produce understanding and the polemic that most journalists saw in this book.

But the furor is best explained by certain attributes typical of the journalistic vision (the very characteristics that generated so much enthusiasm for a book such as *La Misère du monde* just a few years ago[3]): a tendency to equate what is new with what are usually called "revelations"; an emphasis on that which is most obvious in the social world, meaning individuals, what they do, and especially what they do wrong; and, finally, a readiness to denounce or indict. All of these inclinations hinder an understanding of the invisible structures and mechanisms (here, those of the journalistic field) that influence the actions and thoughts of individuals—an understanding that is likely to lead to sympathetic indulgence rather than to indignant condemnation. Then again, there is a predisposition to focus on an analyst's (supposed) "conclusions" rather than the method by which those conclusions were reached. After the publication of *The State Nobility: Elite Schools in the Field of Power*, the result and summing-up of ten years of my research, I remember vividly a journalist who proposed a debate on the Grandes Écoles: the president of the alumni association would speak "for" and I would speak "against."[4] And he hadn't a clue as to why I refused. In just the same way, the journalistic "big guns" who went after my book simply bracketed my method (in particular the analysis of journalism as a field); without even being aware of what they were doing, they reduced the book to a series of utterly hackneyed positions punctuated by a smattering of polemical outbursts.

But this method is precisely what I want to come back to. Even at the risk of new misunderstandings, I want to try to show how the journalistic field produces and imposes on the public a very particular vision of the political field, a vision that is grounded in the very structure of the journalistic field and in journalists' specific interests produced in and by that field.

In a world ruled by the fear of being boring and anxiety about being amusing at all costs, politics is bound to be unappealing, better kept out of prime time as much as possible. So, insofar as it does have to be addressed, this not very exciting and even depressing spectacle, which is so difficult to deal with, has to be made interesting. This imperative explains why, in the United States as much as in Europe, there is a tendency to shunt aside serious commentators and investigative reporters in favor of the talk show host. It also explains why real information, analysis, in-depth interviews, expert discussions, and serious documentaries lose out to pure entertainment and, in particular, to mindless talk show chatter between "approved" and interchangeable speakers. (In the text that follows, I seem to have committed the unpardonable sin of mentioning a couple of them as examples.) To understand what is said in these staged "exchanges" and, in particular, what *can* be said, would require a detailed analysis of the selection process for these individuals, whom Americans call "panelists." These people are always available—meaning always ready not merely to participate but to play the game—and they answer all the questions journalists ask, no matter how silly or outrageous. They're ready for everything and anything, which means to make any concession (as to the subject under discussion, the other participants, and so on), any compromise, any deal as long as they can be "in" on things and receive the direct and indirect benefits of "media" celebrity—prestige in the media world, big fees on the lecture circuit, and so on. Further, particularly at the pre-interviews conducted by some producers in the United States and increasingly in Europe as well, prospective panelists must present their positions in uncomplicated, clear, and striking terms. Above all, they must avoid the quagmire of intellectual complexity. (As the maxim goes, "The less you know, the better off you are.")

To justify this policy of demagogic simplification (which is absolutely and utterly contrary to the democratic goal of informing or educating people by interesting them), journalists point to the public's expectations. But in fact they are projecting onto the public their own inclinations and their own views. Because they're so afraid of being boring, they opt for confrontations over debates, prefer polemics over rigorous argument, and in general do whatever they can to promote conflict. They prefer to confront individuals (politicians in particular) instead of confronting their arguments, that is, what's really at stake in the debate, whether the budget deficit, taxes, or the balance of trade. Given that their claims to competence are based more on their claims to close contacts in the political realm, including access to insider information (even rumors and malicious gossip), than on the objectivity of their observation and investigation, journalists like to stick to their home territory. They direct attention to the game and its players rather than to what is really at stake, because these are the sources of their interest and expertise. They are more interested in the tactics of politics than in the substance, and more concerned with the political effect of speeches and politicians' maneuverings within the political field (in terms of coalitions, alliances, or individual conflicts) than with the meaning of these. (That is, when they don't simply invent issues,

such as the question during the 1997 French elections of whether the
contest between the Left and the Right was going to take place between
two main contenders—Lionel Jospin, leader of the Socialist opposition, and Alain Juppé, the conservative prime minister—or between
four politicians—Jospin and Robert Hue, his Communist ally, on one
side, and, on the other, Juppé and his centrist ally, François Léotard.
Despite its apparent neutrality, the emphasis given to this question
actually made an overtly political move in favor of the conservatives by
focusing attention on possible splits on the Left, between the leading
candidate Jospin and his minor, Communist ally.)

Journalists occupy an ambiguous position in the political world,
in which they are very influential actors but not full-fledged members.
This position enables them to offer politicians vital symbolic support
that they can't get for themselves. (Except, today, collectively, in publishing, where cronyism ensures favorable reviews for journalists and
their books.) This means that journalists are apt to look at things rather
like Thersites, the ugly, cowardly, "thrower of words" in the *Iliad*, who
abuses everybody and "argues nothing but scandal."[5] Typically they
adopt a spontaneous form of a philosophy of doubt, which leads them
to ascribe the sincerest convictions and most disinterested political positions to interests tied to particular positions within the political field
(such as rivalries within a party, or participation in a "trend").

All of this leads them to a cynical view of politics, which is reflected
in their political arguments, and in their interview questions. For
them, politics becomes an arena full of hyperambitious people with no
convictions but with a clear sense of the competitive situation and of
their opposing interests. (Journalists are certainly encouraged in this
attitude by political consultants and advisers, who help politicians with
this sort of explicitly calculated, though not necessarily cynical, kind of
political marketing. Political success increasingly depends on adapting
to the demands of the journalistic field, which becomes a "caucus" increasingly responsible for "making" both politicians and their reputations.) This exclusive attention to the political "microcosm" and to the
facts and effects that can be attributed to it, tends to produce a break
with the public, or at least with those segments of the public most concerned with the real consequences of these political positions on their

lives and on society at large. This break is duplicated and greatly reinforced, particularly in the case of journalism's big television stars, by
the social distance that comes with high economic and social status. It
is common knowledge that, since the 1960s, in the United States and
in most of Europe, media stars augment their already high salaries—
on the order of $100,000 and more in Europe, and several million dol-
lars on the American side[6]—with often-exorbitant honoraria for talk
show appearances and lectures, remuneration for regular newspaper
collaboration, and fees from various "deals," notably at annual conven-
tions and professional meetings. This is why we see the continuing
increase in the distribution of power and privilege in the journalistic
field. Some journalists act much like small-time capitalistic entrepreneurs who need to preserve, and increase, their symbolic capital—
since their media visibility increases their value on the lecture circuit.
At the same time, we are witnessing the growth of a vast journalistic
subproletariat, forced into a kind of self-censorship by an increasingly
precarious job situation.[7]

To these effects must be added others, on which I will elaborate
in this book, that derive from competition within the journalistic field
itself—the obsession with "scoops" and the unquestioned bias in favor
of the news that is the newest and hardest to get; or the predisposition
to overstatement that comes from attempting to offer the subtlest and
strangest interpretation (which often means the most cynical one); or
again, the predictions game, made possible by a collective amnesia
about current events. Not only are these predictions and diagnoses
easy to make (like bets on sports events) but they can be made with
total impunity, protected as the predictor is by the rapidity with which
the journalistic report is forgotten amid the rapid turnover of events.
(This amnesia explains how, in the space of a few months in 1989,
journalists the world over switched from exalting the dazzling emergence of new democracies to condemning the appalling ethnic wars.)

These mechanisms work in concert to produce a general effect
of depoliticization or, more precisely, disenchantment with politics.
Nothing need be said about current events, since whenever politics
raises an important but unmistakably boring question, the search for
entertainment focuses attention on a spectacle (or a scandal) every

time. "Current events" are reduced to an impassioned recital of entertaining events, which tend to lie about halfway between the human interest story and the variety show. (For an exemplary case, take the O.J. Simpson trial.) The result is a litany of events with no beginning and no real end, thrown together only because they occurred at the same time. So an earthquake in Turkey turns up next to proposed budget cuts, and a championship sports team is featured alongside a big murder trial. These events are reduced to the level of the absurd because we see only those elements that can be shown on television at a given moment, cut off from their antecedents and consequences. There is a patent lack of interest in subtle, nuanced changes, or in processes that, like the continental drift, remain unperceived and imperceptible in the moment, revealing their effects only in the long term. This inattention to nuance both repeats and reinforces the structural amnesia induced by day-to-day thinking and by the competition that equates what's important with what's new—the scoop. This means that journalists—the day laborers of everyday life—can show us the world only as a series of unrelated flash photos. Given the lack of time, and especially the lack of interest and information (research and documentation are usually confined to reading articles that have appeared in the press), they cannot do what would be necessary to make events (say, an outbreak of violence in a high school) really understandable, that is, they cannot reinsert them in a network of relevant relationships (such as the family structure, which is tied to the job market, itself tied to governmental hiring policies, and so on). No doubt, they are encouraged to act as they do by politicians, and especially by government officials (who are in turn encouraged by the politicians), both of whom like to stress the short-term effects of the decisions they make and announce to the public. Clearly, these dramatic "coups" they favor create a climate hostile to action whose effect is visible only over time.

This vision is at once dehistoricized and dehistoricizing, fragmented and fragmenting. Its paradigmatic expression is the TV news and the way it sees the world, as a series of apparently absurd stories that all end up looking the same, endless parades of poverty-stricken countries, sequences of events that, having appeared with no explanation, will disappear with no solution—Zaire today, Bosnia yesterday, the Congo tomorrow. Stripped of any political necessity, this string of events can at best arouse a vague humanitarian interest. Coming one after the other and outside any historical perspective, these unconnected tragedies seem to differ little from natural disasters—the tornadoes, forest fires, and floods that also occupy so much of the news. It's almost a journalistic ritual, and certainly a tradition, to focus on simple events that are simple to cover. As for the victims, they're not presented in any more political a light than those of a train derailment or any other accident. We see nothing that might stimulate any sort of truly political cohesion or revolt.

So, especially as a result of the particular form that competition takes there, and through the routines and habits of thought it imposes, the journalistic field represents the world in terms of a philosophy that sees history as an absurd series of disasters which can be neither understood nor influenced. Journalism shows us a world full of ethnic wars, racist hatred, violence and crime—a world full of incomprehensible and unsettling dangers from which we must withdraw for our own protection. And when its commentators spew ethnocentric or racist contempt (as they often do, especially whenever Africa or the inner city are involved), the journalistic evocation of the world does not serve to mobilize or politicize; on the contrary, it only increases xenophobic fears, just as the delusion that crime and violence are always and everywhere on the rise feeds anxieties and phobias about safety in the streets and at home. The world shown by television is one that lies beyond the grasp of ordinary individuals. Linked to this is the impression that politics is for professionals, a bit like high-level competitive sports with their split between athletes and spectators. Especially among those who are basically apolitical, this worldview fosters fatalism and disengagement, which obviously favors the status quo. It requires blind faith in ordinary individuals' (undeniable but limited) capacity for "resistance" to assume, along with a certain "postmodern cultural criticism," that television viewers' active cynicism (exemplified by channel surfing) can do much to counter the cynicism of its producers, whose mind-set, working conditions, and goals—reaching the biggest public with that "extra something" that "sells"—make them more and more like advertising people. Facility with the games of cultural criticism—their "I know that you know that I know"—is not universal. Nor is the ability to spin out elaborate "readings" of the "ironic and metatextual" messages cynically manipulated by television producers and ad people. Anyone who thinks otherwise has simply surrendered to a populist version of one of the most perverse forms of academic pedantry.

ON TELEVISION[8]

PREFACE

I decided to give these two lectures on television because I wanted to reach beyond the usual audience at the Collège de France. I think that television poses a serious danger for all the various areas of cultural production—for art, for literature, for science, for philosophy, and for law. What's more, contrary to what a lot of journalists—even the most responsible of them—say (and think), undoubtedly in all good faith, I think that television poses no less of a threat to political life and to democracy itself. I shall try to explain these views rapidly—a systematic, in-depth analysis would have taken much more time. I could prove this claim easily. I could analyze how, precisely because its goal is the largest audience possible, television, along with some print journalism, has treated individuals who make jingoistic or racist statements, and/or act accordingly. Then again, I could simply run through all the compromises television makes every day with a narrow and narrowly national, not to say chauvinistic, vision of politics. And lest I be accused of fixing on a situation that is strictly French, I'll remind you of the media's treatment of the O.J. Simpson trial, and of a more recent case in which an ordinary murder got turned into a "sex crime" and brought on a whole series of uncontrollable legal consequences.

But it is a recent if less well-known incident between Greece and Turkey that best illustrates the real dangers that come from the relentless competition for an ever-larger audience share. After a private TV station in Greece issued all kinds of calls to action and belligerent statements about the tiny deserted island of Imia, private radio and television in Greece, egged on by the print media, worked themselves into a nationalistic frenzy. Carried along by the same battle for audience ratings, Turkish TV and newspapers jumped on the bandwagon. Greek soldiers landed on the island, the two fleets moved into position—and war was only just avoided. The key to what is really new in these nationalistic outbursts—in Turkey and Greece, but also in the former Yugoslavia, in France and elsewhere—may well lie in the ways modern media are able to exploit these primal passions.

To keep the promise that I had made to myself about this lecture, which I conceived as an *exchange* within a larger debate, I had to construct my arguments so that they would be clear to everyone. This meant, in more than one instance, that I had to simplify or make do with approximations. To maintain the focus on the crucial element— the lecture itself—and contrary to what usually happens on television I chose, in agreement with the producer, to eliminate effects such as changes in the format or camera angles. I also left out illustrations (selections from broadcasts, reproductions of documents, statistics, and so on). Besides taking up precious time, all of these things undoubtedly would have made it harder to follow my argument. The contrast with regular television—the object of the analysis—was, by design, a way of affirming the independence of analytical and critical discourse, even in the cumbersome, didactic, and dogmatic guise of a large public lecture. Television has gradually done away with this kind of discourse (political debates in the United States are said to allow no one to speak for more than seven seconds). But intellectual discourse remains one of the most authentic forms of resistance to manipulation and a vital affirmation of the freedom of thought.

I am well aware that this sort of talk is only a makeshift solution, a less effective and less amusing substitute for a true critique of images through images—of the sort you find in some of Jean-Luc Godard's films, for example, or those of Pierre Carles. I also know that what I am doing continues, or complements, the constant battle of all professionals who work with images and fight for "the independence of their communication code." I am thinking in particular of the critical reflection on images of which Jean-Luc Godard (once again) gives an exemplary illustration in his analysis of the uses made of the journalist Joseph Kraft's photograph of Jane Fonda in North Vietnam. Indeed, I could have taken Godard's agenda as my own: "This work was a beginning of a political [I would say sociological] questioning of images and sounds, and of their *relations*. It meant no longer saying, 'That's a just image' but 'That's just an image'; no longer saying, 'That's a Union officer on a horse,' but, 'That's an *image* of a horse and an officer.' "9

Though I don't harbor many illusions on this score, I can hope that my analysis will not be taken as an "attack" on journalists and television stemming from some sort of nostalgia for the supposed good old days of cultural television, TV-Sorbonne style, or as a refusal—equally reactive and regressive—of everything that television truly can contribute, whatever its faults (certain documentaries, for example). Even though I have every reason to fear that this discussion will mostly feed into the narcissistic complacency of a journalistic world all too inclined to pseudocriticism, I hope that it will furnish some tools or weapons to all those in the image professions who are struggling to keep what could have become an extraordinary instrument of direct democracy from turning into an instrument of symbolic oppression.

IN FRONT OF THE CAMERA AND BEHIND THE SCENES

I'd like to try and pose here, on television, a certain number of questions about television. This is a bit paradoxical since, in general, I think that you can't say much on television, particularly not about television. But if it's true that you can't say anything on television, shouldn't I join a certain number of our top intellectuals, artists, and writers and conclude that one should simply steer clear of it?

It seems to me that we don't have to accept this alternative. I think that it is important to talk on television *under certain conditions*. Today, thanks to the audiovisual services of the Collège de France, I am speaking under absolutely exceptional circumstances. In the first place, I face no time limit; second, my topic is my own, not one imposed on me (I was free to choose whatever topic I wanted and I can still change it); and, third, there is nobody here, as for regular programs, to bring me into line with technical requirements, with the "public-that-won't-understand," with morality or decency, or with whatever else.

The situation is absolutely unique because, to use out-of-date terms, I have a *control of the instruments of production* which is not at all usual. The fact that these conditions are exceptional in itself says something about what usually happens when someone appears on television.

But, you may well ask, why do people accept such conditions? That's a very important question, and, further, one not asked by most of the researchers, scholars, and writers—not to mention journalists— who appear on television. We need to question this failure to ask questions. In fact, it seems to me that, by agreeing to appear on television shows without worrying about whether you'll be able to say anything, you make it very clear that you're not there to say anything at all but for altogether different reasons, chief among them the desire to be seen. Berkeley said that "to be is to be perceived." For some of our thinkers (and our writers), to be is to be perceived on television, which means, when all is said and done, to be perceived by journalists, to be, as the saying goes, on their "good side," with all the compromises and concessions that implies. And it is certainly true that, since they can hardly count on having their work last over time, they have no recourse but to appear on television as often as possible. This means churning out regularly and as often as possible works whose principal function, as Gilles Deleuze used to say, is to get them on television. So the television screen today becomes a sort of mirror for Narcissus, a space for narcissistic exhibitionism.

This preamble may seem a bit long, but it appears to me desirable that artists, writers, and thinkers ask themselves these questions. This should be done openly and collectively, if possible, so that no one is left alone with the decision of whether or not to appear on television, and, if appearing, of whether to stipulate conditions. What I'd really like (you can always dream) is for them to set up collective negotiations with journalists toward some sort of a contract. It goes without saying that it is not a question of blaming or fighting journalists, who often suffer a good deal from the very constraints they are forced to impose. On the contrary, it's to try to see how we can work together to overcome the threat of instrumentalization.

I don't think you can refuse categorically to talk on television. In certain cases, there can even be something of a *duty* to do so, again under the right conditions. In making this choice, one must take into account the specificities of television. With television, we are dealing with an instrument that offers, theoretically, the possibility of reaching everybody. This brings up a number of questions. Is what I have to say meant to reach everybody? Am I ready to make what I say understandable by everybody? Is it worth being understood by everybody? You can go even further: should it be understood by everybody? Researchers, and scholars in particular, have an obligation—and it may be especially urgent for the social sciences—to make the advances of research available to everyone. In Europe, at least, we are, as Edmund Husserl used to say, "humanity's civil servants," paid by the government to make discoveries, either about the natural world or about the social world. It seems to me that part of our responsibility is to share what we have found. I have always tried to ask myself these questions before deciding whether or not to agree to public appearances. These are questions that I would like everyone invited to appear on television to pose or be forced to pose because the television audience and the television critics pose them: Do I have something to say? Can I say it in these conditions? Is what I have to say worth saying here and now? In a word, what am I doing here?

Invisible Censorship

But let me return to the essential point. I began by claiming that open access to television is offset by a powerful censorship, a loss of independence linked to the conditions imposed on those who speak on television. Above all, time limits make it highly unlikely that anything can be said. I am undoubtedly expected to say that this television censorship—of guests but also of the journalists who are its agents— is political. It's true that politics intervenes, and that there is political control (particularly in the case of hiring for top positions in the radio stations and television channels under direct government control). It is also true that at a time such as today, when great numbers of people are looking for work and there is so little job security in television and radio, there is a greater tendency toward political conformity. Consciously or unconsciously, people censor themselves—they don't need to be called into line. You can also consider economic censorship. It is true that, in the final analysis, you can say that the pressure on television is economic. That said, it is not enough to say that what gets on television is determined by the owners, by the companies that pay for the ads, or by the government that gives the subsidies. If you knew only the name of the owner of a television station, its advertising budget, and how much it receives in subsidies, you wouldn't know much. Still, it's important to keep these things in mind. It's important to know that NBC is owned by General Electric (which means that interviews with people who live near a nuclear plant undoubtedly would be . . . but then again, such a story wouldn't even occur to anyone), that CBS is owned by Westinghouse, and ABC by Disney, that TF1 belongs to Bouygues,[10] and that these facts lead to consequences through a whole series of mediations. It is obvious that the government won't do certain things to Bouygues, knowing that Bouygues is behind TF1. These factors, which are so crude that they are obvious to even the most simpleminded critique, hide other things, all the anonymous and invisible mechanisms through which the many kinds of censorship operate to make television such a formidable instrument for maintaining the symbolic order.

I'd like to pause here. Sociological analysis often comes up against a misconception. Anyone involved as the object of the analysis, in this case journalists, tends to think that the work of analysis, the revelation of mechanisms, is in fact a denunciation of individuals, part of an ad hominem polemic. (Those same journalists would, of course, immediately level accusations of bias and lack of objectivity at any sociologist who discussed or wrote about even a tenth of what comes up anytime you talk with the media about the payoffs, how the programs are manufactured, made up—that's the word they use.) In general, people don't like to be turned into objects or objectified, and journalists least of all. They feel under fire, singled out. But the further you get in the analysis of a given milieu, the more likely you are to let individuals off the hook (which doesn't mean justifying everything that happens). And the more you understand how things work, the more you come to understand that the people involved are manipulated as much as they manipulate. They manipulate even more effectively the more they are themselves manipulated and the more unconscious they are of this.

I stress this point even though I know that, whatever I do, anything I say will be taken as a criticism—a reaction that is also a defense against analysis. But let me stress that I even think that scandals such as the furor over the deeds and misdeeds of one or another television news personality, or the exorbitant salaries of certain producers, divert attention from the main point. Individual corruption only masks the *structural corruption* (should we even talk about corruption in this case?) that operates on the game as a whole through mechanisms such as competition for market share. This is what I want to examine.

So I would like to analyze a series of mechanisms that allow television to wield a particularly pernicious form of symbolic violence. Symbolic violence is violence wielded with tacit complicity between its victims and its agents, insofar as both remain unconscious of submitting to or wielding it. The function of sociology, as of every science, is to reveal that which is hidden. In so doing, it can help minimize the symbolic violence within social relations and, in particular, within the relations of communication.

Let's start with an easy example—sensational news. This has always been the favorite food of the tabloids. Blood, sex, melodrama, and crime have always been big sellers. In the early days of television, a sense of respectability modeled on the printed press kept these attention-grabbers under wraps, but the race for audience share inevitably brings it to the headlines and to the beginning of the television news. Sensationalism attracts notice, and it also diverts it, like magicians whose basic operating principle is to direct attention to something other than what they're doing. Part of the symbolic functioning of television, in the case of the news, for example, is to call attention to those elements which will engage everybody—which offer something for everyone. These are things that won't shock anyone, where nothing is at stake, that don't divide, are generally agreed on, and interest everybody without touching on anything important. These items are basic ingredients of news because they interest everyone, and because they take up time—time that could be used to say something else.

And time, on television, is an extremely rare commodity. When you use up precious time to say banal things, to the extent that they cover up precious things, these banalities become in fact very important. If I stress this point, it's because everyone knows that a very high proportion of the population reads no newspaper at all and is dependent on television as their sole source of news. Television enjoys a de facto monopoly on what goes into the heads of a significant part of the population and what they think. So much emphasis on headlines and so much filling up of precious time with empty air—with nothing or almost nothing—shunts aside relevant news, that is, the information that all citizens ought to have in order to exercise their democratic rights. We are therefore faced with a division, as far as news is concerned, between individuals in a position to read so-called serious newspapers (insofar as they can remain serious in the face of competition from television), and people with access to international newspapers and foreign radio stations, and, on the other hand, everyone else, who get from television news all they know about politics. That is to say, precious little, except for what can be learned from seeing people, how they look, and how they talk—things even the most culturally disadvantaged can decipher, and which can do more than a little to distance many of them from a good many politicians.

Show and Hide

So far I've emphasized elements that are easy to see. I'd like now to move on to slightly less obvious matters in order to show how, paradoxically, television can hide by showing. That is, it can hide things by showing something other than what would be shown if television did what it's supposed to do, provide information. Or by showing what has to be shown, but in such a way that it isn't really shown, or is turned into something insignificant; or by constructing it in such a way that it takes on a meaning that has nothing at all to do with reality.

On this point I'll take two examples from Patrick Champagne's work. In his work in *La Misère du monde*, Champagne offers a detailed examination of how the media represent events in the "inner city." [11] He shows how journalists are carried along by the inherent exigencies

of their job, by their view of the world, by their training and orientation, and also by the reasoning intrinsic to the profession itself. They
select very specific aspects of the inner city as a function of their particular perceptual categories, the particular way they see things. These
categories are the product of education, history, and so forth. The
most common metaphor to explain this notion of category—that is,
the invisible structures that organize perception and determine what
we see and don't see—is eyeglasses. Journalists have special "glasses"
through which they see certain things and not others, and through
which they see the things they see in the special way they see them.

The principle that determines this selection is the search for the
sensational and the spectacular. Television calls for *dramatization*, in
both senses of the term: it puts an event onstage, puts it in images.
In doing so, it exaggerates the importance of that event, its seriousness, and its dramatic, even tragic character. For the inner city, this
means riots. That's already a big word . . . And, indeed, words get the
same treatment. Ordinary words impress no one, but paradoxically,
the world of images is dominated by words. Photos are nothing without words—the French term for the caption is *legend*, and often they
should be read as just that, as legends that can show anything at all.
We know that to name is to show, to create, to bring into existence.
And words can do a lot of damage: Islam, Islamic, Islamicist—is the
headscarf Islamic or Islamicist?[12] And if it were really only a kerchief
and *nothing more*? Sometimes I want to go back over *every* word the
television newspeople use, often without thinking and with no idea of
the difficulty and the seriousness of the subjects they are talking about
or the responsibilities they assume by talking about them in front of
the thousands of people who watch the news without understanding
what they see and without understanding that they don't understand.
Because these words do things, they make things—they create phantasms, fears, and phobias, or simply false representations.

Journalists, on the whole, are interested in the exception, which
means whatever is exceptional *for them*. Something that might be perfectly ordinary for someone else can be extraordinary for them and vice
versa. They're interested in the extraordinary, in anything that breaks
the routine. The daily papers are under pressure to offer a daily dose of

the extra-daily, and that's not easy . . . This pressure explains the attention they give to extraordinary occurrences, usual unusual events like fires, floods, or murders. But the extraordinary is also, and especially, what isn't ordinary for other newspapers. It's what differs from the ordinary and what differs from what other newspapers say. The pressure is dreadful—the pressure to get a "scoop."[13] People are ready to do almost anything to be the first to see and present something. The result is that everyone copies each other in the attempt to get ahead; everyone ends up doing the same thing. The search for exclusivity, which elsewhere leads to originality and singularity, here yields uniformity and banality.

This relentless, self-interested search for the extraordinary can have just as much political effect as direct political prescription or the self-censorship that comes from fear of being left behind or left out. With the exceptional force of the televised image at their disposal, journalists can produce effects that are literally incomparable. The monotonous, drab daily life in the inner city doesn't say anything to anybody and doesn't interest anybody, journalists least of all. But even if they were to take a real interest in what goes on in the inner city and really wanted to show it, it would be enormously difficult. There is nothing more difficult to convey than reality in all its ordinariness. Flaubert was fond of saying that it takes a lot of hard work to portray mediocrity. Sociologists run into this problem all the time: How can we make the ordinary extraordinary and evoke ordinariness in such a way that people will see just how extraordinary it is?

The political dangers inherent in the ordinary use of television have to do with the fact that images have the peculiar capacity to produce what literary critics call a *reality effect*. They show things and make people believe in what they show. This power to show is also a power to mobilize. It can give a life to ideas or images, but also to groups. The news, the incidents and accidents of everyday life, can be loaded with political or ethnic significance liable to unleash strong, often negative feelings, such as racism, chauvinism, the fear–hatred of the foreigner, or xenophobia. The simple report, the very fact of reporting, of *putting on record* as a reporter, always implies a social construction of reality that can mobilize (or demobilize) individuals or groups.

Another example from Patrick Champagne's work is the 1986 high school student strike. Here you see how journalists acting in all good faith and in complete innocence—merely letting themselves be guided by their interests (meaning what interests them), presuppositions, categories of perception and evaluation, and unconscious expectations—still produce reality effects and effects in reality. Nobody wants these effects, which, in certain cases, can be catastrophic. Journalists had in mind the political upheaval of May 1968 and were afraid of missing "a new 1968." Since they were dealing with teenagers who were not very politically aware and who had little idea of what to say, reporters went in search of articulate representatives or delegates (no doubt from among the most highly politicized).

Such commentators are taken seriously and take themselves seriously. One thing leads to another, and, ultimately television, which claims to record reality, creates it instead. We are getting closer and closer to the point where the social world is primarily described—and in a sense prescribed—by television. Let's suppose that I want to lobby for retirement at age fifty. A few years ago, I would have worked up a demonstration in Paris, there'd have been posters and a parade, and we'd have all marched over to the Ministry of National Education. Today—this is just barely an exaggeration—I'd need a savvy media consultant. With a few mediagenic elements to get attention—disguises, masks, whatever—television can produce an effect close to what you'd have from fifty thousand protesters in the streets.

At stake today in local as well as global political struggles is the capacity to impose a way of seeing the world, of making people wear "glasses" that force them to see the world divided up in certain ways (the young and the old, foreigners and the French . . .). These divisions create groups that can be mobilized, and that mobilization makes it possible for them to convince everyone else that they exist, to exert pressure and obtain privileges, and so forth. Television plays a determining role in all such struggles today. Anyone who still believes that you can organize a political demonstration without paying attention to television risks being left behind. It's more and more the case that you have to produce demonstrations for television so that they interest television types and fit their perceptual categories. Then, and only then, relayed and amplified by these television professionals, will your demonstration have its maximum effect.

The Circular Circulation of Information

Until now, I've been talking as if the individual journalist were the subject of all these processes. But "the journalist" is an abstract entity that doesn't exist. What exists are journalists who differ by sex, age, level of education, affiliation, and "medium." The journalistic world is a divided one, full of conflict, competition, and rivalries. That said, my analysis remains valid in that journalistic *products* are much more alike than is generally thought. The most obvious differences, notably the political tendencies of the newspapers—which, in any case, it has to be said, are becoming less and less evident . . . —hide the profound similarities. These are traceable to the pressures imposed by sources and by a whole series of mechanisms, the most important of which is competition. Free market economics holds that monopoly creates uniformity and competition produces diversity. Obviously, I have nothing against competition, but I observe that competition homogenizes when it occurs between journalists or newspapers subject to identical pressures and opinion polls, and with the same basic cast of commentators (note how easily journalists move from one news medium or program to another). Just compare the weekly newsmagazine covers at two-week intervals and you'll find nearly identical headlines. Or again, in the case of a major network radio or television news, at best (or at worst) the order in which the news is presented is different.

This is due partly to the fact that production is a collective enterprise. In the cinema, for example, films are clearly the collective products of the individuals listed in the credits. But the collectivity that produces television messages can't be understood only as the group that puts a program together, because, as we have seen, it encompasses journalists as a whole. We always want to know who the subject of a discourse is, but here no one can ever be sure of being the subject of what is said . . . We're a lot less original than we think we are. This is particularly true where collective pressures, and particularly competitive pressures, are so strong that one is led to do things that one wouldn't do if the others didn't exist (in order, for example, to be first). No one reads as many newspapers as journalists, who tend to think that everybody reads all the newspapers (they forget, first of all, that lots of people read no paper at all, and second, that those who do read read only one. Unless you're in the profession, you don't often read *Le Monde, Le Figaro,* and *Libération* in the same day). For journalists a daily review of the press is an essential tool. To know what to say, you have to know what everyone else has said. This is one of the mechanisms that renders journalistic products so similar. If *Libération* gives headlines to a given event, *Le Monde* can't remain indifferent, although, given its particular prestige, it has the option of standing a bit apart in order to mark its distance and keep its reputation for being serious and aloof. But such tiny differences, to which journalists attach great importance, hide enormous similarities. Editorial staff spend a good deal of time talking about other newspapers, particularly about "what they did and we didn't do" ("we really blew that one") and what should have been done (no discussion on that point)—since the other paper did it. This dynamic is probably even more obvious for literature, art, or film criticism. If X talks about a book in *Libération,* Y will have to talk about it in *Le Monde* or *Le Nouvel Observateur* even if he considers it worthless or unimportant. And vice versa. This is the way media success is produced, and sometimes as well (but not always) commercial success.

This sort of game of mirrors reflecting one another produces a formidable effect of mental closure. Another example of this becomes clear in interviews with journalists: to put together the television news at noon, you have to have seen the headlines of the eight o'clock news the previous evening as well as the daily papers; to put together the headlines for the evening news, you must have read the morning papers. These are the tacit requirements of the job—to be up on things and to set yourself apart, often by tiny differences accorded fantastic importance by journalists and quite missed by the viewer. (This is an effect typical of the field: you do things for competitors that you think you're doing for consumers.) For example, journalists will say—and this is a direct quote—"we left TF1 in the dust." This is a way of saying that they are competitors who direct much of their effort toward being different from one another. "We left TF1 in the dust" means that these differences are meaningful: "they didn't have the sound, and we did." These differences completely bypass the average viewer, who could perceive them only by watching several networks at the same time. But these differences, which go completely unnoticed by viewers, turn out to be very important for producers, who think that they are not only seen but boost ratings. Here is the hidden god of this universe who governs conduct and consciences. A one-point drop in audience ratings, can, in certain cases, mean instant death with no appeal. This is only one of the equations—incorrect in my view—made between program content and its supposed effect.

In some sense, the choices made on television are choices made by no subject. To explain this proposition, which may appear somewhat excessive, let me point simply to another of the effects of the circular circulation to which I referred above: the fact that journalists—who in any case have much in common, profession of course, but also so-cial origin and education—meet one another daily in debates that al-ways feature the same cast of characters. All of which produces the closure that I mentioned earlier, and also—no two ways about it—censorship. This censorship is as effective—more even, because its principle remains invisible—as direct political intervention from a central administration. To measure the closing-down effect of this vi-cious informational circle, just try programming some unscheduled news, events in Algeria or the status of foreigners in France, for ex-ample. Press conferences or releases on these subjects are useless; they are supposed to bore everyone, and it is impossible to get analy-sis of them into a newspaper unless it is written by someone with a big name—that's what sells. You can only break out of the circle by breaking and entering, so to speak. But you can only break and enter through the media. You have to grab the attention of the media, or at least one "medium," so that the story can be picked up and amplified by its competitors.

If you wonder how the people in charge of giving us information get their own information, it appears that, in general, they get it from other informers. Of course, there's Agence France-Presse or Associ-ated Press, and there are agencies and official sources of information (government officials, the police, and so on) with which journalists necessarily enter into very complex relationships of exchange. But the really determining share of information, that is, the *information about information* that allows you to decide what is important and therefore worth broadcasting, comes in large part from other informers. This leads to a sort of leveling, a homogenization of standards. I remember one interview with a program executive for whom everything was absolutely obvious. When I asked him why he scheduled one item before another, his reply was, simply, "It's obvious." This is undoubtedly the reason that he had the job he had: his way of seeing things was perfectly adapted to the objective exigencies of his position. Of course, occupying as they do different positions within journalism, different journalists are less likely to find obvious what he found so obvious. The executives who worship at the altar of audience ratings have a feeling of "obviousness" which is not necessarily shared by the freelancer who proposes a topic only to be told that it's "not interesting." The journalistic milieu cannot be represented as uniform. There are small fry, newcomers, subversives, pains-in-the-neck who struggle desperately to add some small difference to this enormous, homogeneous mishmash imposed by the (vicious) circle of information circulating in a circle between people who—and this you can't forget—are all subject to audience ratings. Even network executives are ultimately slaves to the ratings.

Audience ratings—Nielsen ratings in the United States—measure the audience share won by each network. It is now possible to pinpoint the audience by the quarter hour and even—a new development—by social group. So we know very precisely who's watching what, and who's not. Even in the most independent sectors of journalism, ratings have become the journalist's Last Judgment. Aside from *Le Canard enchaîné* [a satirical weekly], *Le Monde diplomatique* [a distinguished, left liberal journal similar to *Foreign Affairs*], and a few small avant-garde journals supported by generous people who take their "irresponsibilities" seriously, everyone is fixated on ratings. In editorial rooms, publishing houses, and similar venues, a "rating mind-set" reigns. Wherever you look, people are thinking in terms of market success. Only thirty years ago, and since the middle of the nineteenth century—since Baudelaire and Flaubert and others in avant-garde milieux of writers' writers, writers acknowledged by other writers or even artists acknowledged by other artists—immediate market success was suspect. It was taken as a sign of compromise with the times, with money . . . Today, on the contrary, the market is accepted more and more as a legitimate means of legitimation. You can see this in another recent institution, the bestseller list. Just this morning on the radio I heard an announcer, obviously very sure of himself, run through the latest bestseller list and decree that "philosophy is hot this year, since *Le Monde de Sophie* sold eight hundred thousand copies."[14] For him this verdict was absolute, like a final decree, provable by the number of copies sold. Audience ratings impose the sales model on cultural products. But it is important to know that, historically, all of the cultural productions that I consider (and I'm not alone here, at least I hope not) the highest human products—math, poetry, literature, philosophy—were all produced against market imperatives. It is very disturbing to see this ratings mind-set established even among avant-garde publishers and intellectual institutions, both of which have begun to move into marketing, because it jeopardizes works that may not necessarily meet audience expectations but, in time, can create their own audience.

Working Under Pressure and Fast-Thinking

The phenomenon of audience ratings has a very particular effect on television. It appears in the pressure to get things out in a hurry. The competition among newspapers, like that between newspapers and television, shows up as competition for time—the pressure to get a scoop, to get there first. In a book of interviews with journalists, Alain Accardo shows how, simply because a competing network has "covered" a flood, television journalists have to "cover" the same flood and try to get something the other network missed. In short, stories are pushed on viewers because they are pushed on the producers; and they are pushed on producers by competition with other producers. This sort of cross pressure that journalists force on each other generates a whole series of consequences that translates into programming choices, into absences and presences.

At the beginning of this talk, I claimed that television is not very favorable to the expression of thought, and I set up a negative connection between time pressures and thought. It's an old philosophical topic—take the opposition that Plato makes between the philosopher, who has time, and people in the *agora*, in public space, who are in a hurry and under pressure. What he says, more or less, is that you can't think when you're in a hurry. It's a perspective that's clearly aristocratic, the viewpoint of a privileged person who has time and doesn't ask too many questions about the privileges that bestow this time. But this is not the place for that discussion. What is certain is the connection between thought and time. And one of the major problems posed by television is that question of the relationships between time and speed. Is it possible to think fast? By giving the floor to thinkers who are considered able to think at high speed, isn't television doomed to never have anything but *fast-thinkers*, thinkers who think faster than a speeding bullet . . . ?

In fact, what we have to ask is why these individuals are able to respond in these absolutely particular conditions, why and how they can think under these conditions in which nobody can think. The answer, it seems to me, is that they think in clichés, in the "received ideas" that Flaubert talks about—banal, conventional, common ideas that are received generally. By the time they reach you, these ideas have already been received by everybody else, so reception is never a problem. But whether you're talking about a speech, a book, or a message on television, the major question of communication is whether the conditions for reception have been fulfilled: Does the person who's listening have the tools to decode what I'm saying? When you transmit a "received idea," it's as if everything is set, and the problem solves itself. Communication is instantaneous because, in a sense, it has not occurred; or it only seems to have taken place. The exchange of commonplaces is communication with no content other than the fact of communication itself. The "commonplaces" that play such an enormous role in daily conversation work because everyone can ingest them immediately. Their very banality makes them something the speaker and the listener have in common. At the opposite end of the spectrum, thought, by definition, is subversive. It begins by taking apart "received ideas" and then presents the evidence in a demonstration, a logical proof. When Descartes talks about demonstration, he's talking about a logical chain of reasoning. Making an argument like this takes time, since you have to set out a series of propositions connected by "therefore," "consequently," "that said," "given the fact that . . ." Such a deployment of *thinking* thought, of thought in the process of being thought, is intrinsically dependent on time.

If television rewards a certain number of *fast-thinkers* who offer cultural "fast food"—predigested and prethought culture—it is not only because those who speak regularly on television are virtually on call (that, too, is tied to the sense of urgency in television news production). The list of commentators varies little (for Russia, call Mr. or Mrs. X, for Germany, it's Mr. Y). These "authorities" spare journalists the trouble of looking for people who really have something to say, in most cases younger, still-unknown people who are involved in their research and not much for talking to the media. These are the people who should be sought out. But the media mavens are always right on hand, set to churn out a paper or give an interview. And, of course, they are the special kind of thinkers who can "think" in these conditions where no one can do so.

Debates Truly False or Falsely True

Now we must take on the question of televised debates. First of all, there are debates that are entirely bogus, and immediately recognizable as such. A television talk show with Alain Minc and Jacques Attali, or Alain Minc and Guy Sorman, or Luc Ferry and Alain Finkielkraut, or Jacques Julliard and Claude Imbert is a clear example, where you know the commentors are birds of a feather.[15] (In the United States, some people earn their living just going from campus to campus in duets like these . . .) These people know each other, lunch together, have dinner together. Guillaume Durand once did a program about elites.[16] They were all on hand: Attali, Sarkozy, Minc . . . At one point, Attali was talking to Sarkozy and said, "Nicolas . . . Sarkozy," with a pause between the first and last name. If he'd stopped after the first name, it would've been obvious to the French viewer that they were cronies, whereas they are called on to represent opposite sides of the political fence. It was a tiny signal of complicity that could easily have gone unnoticed. In fact, the milieu of television regulars is a closed world that functions according to a model of permanent self-reinforcement. Here are people who are at odds but in an utterly conventional way; Julliard and Imbert, for example, are supposed to represent the Left and the Right. Referring to someone who twists words, the Kabyles say, *"he put my east in the west."* Well, these people put the Right on the Left. Is the public aware of this collusion? It's not certain. It can be seen in the wholesale rejection of Paris by people who live in the provinces (which the fascist criticism of Parisianism tries to appropriate). It came out a lot during the strikes last November: "All that is just Paris blowing off steam." People sense that something's going on, but they don't see how closed in on itself this milieu is, closed to their problems and, for that matter, to them.

There are also debates that seem genuine, but are falsely so. One quick example only, the debate organized by Cavada during those November strikes.[17] I've chosen this example because it looked for all the world like a democratic debate. This only makes my case all the stronger. (I shall proceed here as I have so far, moving from what's most obvious to what's most concealed.) When you look at what happened during this debate, you uncover a string of censorship.

First, there's the moderator. Viewers are always stuck by just how interventionist the moderator is. He determines the subject and decides the question up for debate (which often, as in Durand's debate over "should elites be burned?" turns out to be so absurd that the responses, whatever they are, are absurd as well). He keeps debaters in line with the rules of the game, even and especially because these rules can be so variable. They are different for a union organizer and for a member of the Académie Française. The moderator decides who speaks, and he hands out little tokens of prestige. Sociologists have examined the nonverbal components of verbal communication, how we say as much by our looks, our silences, our gestures, imitations and eye movements, and so on, as we do with our words. Intonation counts, as do all manner of other things. Much of what we reveal is beyond our conscious control (this ought to bother anyone who believes in the truth of Narcissus's mirror). There are so many registers of human expression, even on the level of the words alone—if you keep pronunciation under control, then it's grammar that goes down the tubes, and so on—that no one, not even the most self-controlled individual, can master everything, unless obviously playing a role or using terribly stilted language. The moderator intervenes with another language, one that he's not even aware of, which can be perceived by listening to how the questions are posed, and their tone. Some of the participants will get a curt call to order, "Answer the question, please, you haven't answered my question," or "I'm waiting for your answer. Are you going to stay out on strike or not?" Another telling example is all the different ways to say "thank you." "Thank you" can mean "Thank you ever so much, I am really in your debt, I am awfully happy to have your thoughts on this issue"; then there's the "thank you" that amounts to a dismissal, an effective "OK, that's enough of that. Who's next?" All of this comes out in tiny ways, in infinitesimal nuances of tone, but the discussants are affected by it all, the hidden semantics no less than the surface syntax.

The moderator also allots time and sets the tone, respectful or disdainful, attentive or impatient. For example, a preemptory "yeah, yeah, yeah" alerts the discussant to the moderator's impatience or lack of interest . . . In the interviews that my research team conducts it has become clear that it is very important to signal our agreement and interest; otherwise the interviewees get discouraged and gradually stop talking. They're waiting for little signs—a "yes, that's right," a nod that they've been heard and understood. These imperceptible signs are manipulated by him, more often unconsciously than consciously. For example, an exaggerated respect for high culture can lead the moderator, as a largely self-taught person with a smattering of high culture, to admire false great personages, academicians and people with titles that compel respect. Moderators can also manipulate pressure and urgency. They can use the clock to cut someone off, to push, to interrupt. Here, they have yet another resource. All moderators turn themselves into representatives of the public at large: "I have to interrupt you here,

I don't understand what you mean." What comes across is not that the moderator is dumb—no moderator will let that happen—but that the average viewer (dumb by definition) won't understand. The moderator appears to be interrupting an intelligent speech to speak for the "dummies." In fact, as I have been able to see for myself, it's the people in whose name the moderator is supposedly acting who are the most exasperated by such interference.

The result is that, all in all, during a two-hour program, the union delegate had exactly five minutes to speak (even though everybody knows that if the union hadn't been involved, there wouldn't have been any strike, and no program either, and so on). Yet, on the surface—and this is why Cavada's program is significant—the program adhered to all the formal signs of equality.

This poses a very serious problem for democratic practice. Obviously, all discussants in the studio are not equal. You have people who are both professional talkers and television pros, and, facing them, you have the rank amateurs (the strikers might know how to talk on their home turf but . . .). The inequality is patent. To reestablish some equality, the moderator would have to be inegalitarian, by helping those clearly struggling in an unfamiliar situation—much as we did in the interviews for *La Misère du monde*. When you want someone who is not a professional talker of some sort to say something (and often these people say really quite extraordinary things that individuals who are constantly called upon to speak couldn't even imagine), you have to help people talk. To put it in nobler terms, I'll say that this is the Socratic mission in all its glory. You put yourself at the service of someone with something important to say, someone whose words you want to hear and whose thoughts interest you, and you work to help get the words out. But this isn't at all what television moderators do: not only do they not help people unaccustomed to public platforms but they inhibit them in many ways—by not ceding the floor at the right moment, by putting people on the spot unexpectedly, by showing impatience, and so on.

But these are still things that are up-front and visible. We must look to the second level, to the way the group appearing on a given talk show is chosen. Because these choices determine what happens and how. And they are not arrived at onscreen. There is a backstage process of shaping the group that ends up in the studio for the show, beginning with the preliminary decisions about who gets invited and who doesn't. There are people whom no one would ever think of inviting, and others who are invited but decline. The set is there in front of viewers, and what they see hides what they don't see—and what they don't see, in this constructed image, are the social conditions of its construction. So no one ever says, "hey, so-and-so isn't there." Another example of this manipulation (one of a thousand possible examples): during the strikes, the *Cercle de minuit* talk show had two successive programs on intellectuals and the strikes. Overall, the intellectuals were divided into two main camps. During the first program, the intellectuals against the strikes appeared on the right side of the set. For the second, follow-up program the setup had been changed. More people were added on the right, and those in favor of the strikes were dropped. The people who appeared on the right during the first program appeared on the left during the second. Right and left are relative, by definition, so in this case, changing the arrangement on the set changed the message sent by the program.

The arrangement of the set is important because it is supposed to give the image of a democratic equilibrium. Equality is ostentatiously exaggerated, and the moderator comes across as the referee. The set for the Cavada program discussed earlier had two categories of people. On the one hand, there were the strikers themselves; and then there were others, also protagonists but cast in the position of observers. The first group was there to *explain themselves* ("Why are you doing this? Why are you upsetting everybody?" and so on), and the others were there to *explain things*, to make a metadiscourse, a talk about talk.

Another invisible yet absolutely decisive factor concerns the arrangements agreed upon with the participants prior to the show. This groundwork can create a sort of screenplay, more or less detailed, that the guests are obliged to follow. In certain cases, just as in certain games, preparation can almost turn into a rehearsal. This prescribed scenario leaves little room for improvisation, no room for an offhand, spontaneous word. This would be altogether too risky, even dangerous, both for the moderator and the program.

The model of what Ludwig Wittgenstein calls the language game is also useful here. The game about to be played has tacit rules, since television shows, like every social milieu in which discourse circulates, allow certain things to be said and proscribe others. The first, implicit assumption of this language game is rooted in the conception of democratic debates modeled on wrestling. There must be conflicts, with good guys and bad guys . . . Yet, at the same time, not all holds are allowed: the blows have to be clothed by the model of formal, intellectual language. Another feature of this space is the complicity between professionals that I mentioned earlier. The people I call "fast-thinkers," specialists in throwaway thinking—are known in the industry as "good guests." They're the people whom you can always invite because you know they'll be good company and won't create problems. They won't be difficult and they're smooth talkers. There is a whole world of "good guests" who take to the television format like fish to water—and then there are others who are like fish on dry land.

The final invisible element in play is the moderator's unconscious. It has often happened to me, even with journalists who are pretty much on my side, that I have to begin all my answers by going back over the question. Journalists, with their special "glasses" and their peculiar categories of thought, often ask questions that don't have anything to do with the matter at hand. For example, on the so-called "inner city problem," their heads are full of all the phantasms I mentioned earlier. So, before you can even begin to respond, you have to say, very politely, "Your question is certainly interesting, but it seems to me that there is another one that is even more important . . ." Otherwise, you end up answering questions that shouldn't be even asked.

Contradictions and Tensions

Television is an instrument of communication with very little autonomy, subject as it is to a whole series of pressures arising from the characteristic social relations between journalists. These include *relations of competition* (relentless and pitiless, even to the point of absurdity) and *relations of collusion*, derived from objective common interests. These interests in turn are a function of the journalists' position

in the field of symbolic production and their shared cognitive, perceptual, and evaluative structures, which they share by virtue of common
social background and training (or lack thereof). It follows that this
instrument of communication, as much as it appears to run free, is in
fact reined in. During the 1960s, when television appeared on the cultural scene as a new phenomenon,[18] a certain number of "sociologists"
(quotation marks needed here) rushed to proclaim that, as a "means of
mass communication," television was going to "massify" everything.
It was going to be the great leveler and turn all viewers into one big,
undifferentiated mass. In fact, this assessment seriously underestimated viewers' capacity for resistance. But, above all, it underestimated television's ability to transform its very producers and the other
journalists that compete with it and, ultimately, through its irresistible
fascination for some of them, the ensemble of cultural producers. The
most important development, and a difficult one to foresee, was the
extraordinary extension of the power of television over the whole of
cultural production, including scientific and artistic production.

Today, television has carried to the extreme, to the very limit, a contradiction that haunts every sphere of cultural production. I am referring to the contradiction between the economic and social conditions
necessary to produce a certain type of work and the social conditions of
transmission for the products obtained under these conditions. I used
math as an obvious example, but my argument also holds for avant-
garde poetry, philosophy, sociology, and so on, works thought to be
"pure" (a ridiculous word in any case), but which are, let's say, at least
relatively independent of the market. There is a basic, fundamental
contradiction between the conditions that allow one to do cutting-edge
math or avant-garde poetry, and so on, and the conditions necessary to
transmit these things to everybody else. Television carries this contradiction to the extreme to the extent that, through audience ratings and
more than all the other milieux of cultural production, it is subject to
market pressures.

By the same token, in this microcosm that is the world of journalism, tension is very high between those who would like to defend
the values of independence, freedom from market demands, freedom

from made-to-order programs, and from managers, and so on, and those who submit to this necessity and are rewarded accordingly . . . Given the strength of the opposition, these tensions can hardly be expressed, at least not onscreen. I am thinking here of the opposition between the big stars with big salaries who are especially visible and especially rewarded, but who are also especially subject to all these pressures, and the invisible drones who put the news together, do the reporting, and who are becoming more and more critical of the system. Increasingly well trained in the logic of the job market, they are assigned to jobs that are more and more pedestrian, more and more insignificant—behind the microphones and the cameras you have people who are incomparably more cultivated than their counterparts in the 1960s. In other words, this tension between what the profession requires and the aspirations that people acquire in journalism school or in college is greater and greater—even though there is also anticipatory socialization on the part of people really on the make . . . One journalist said recently that the midlife crisis at forty (which is when you used to find out that your job isn't everything you thought it would be) has moved back to thirty. People are discovering earlier the terrible requirements of this work and in particular, all the pressures associated with audience ratings and other such gauges. Journalism is one of the areas where you find the greatest number of people who are anxious, dissatisfied, rebellious, or cynically resigned, where very often (especially, obviously, for those on the bottom rung of the ladder) you find anger, revulsion, or discouragement about work that is experienced as or proclaimed to be "not like other jobs." But we're far from a situation where this spite or these refusals could take the form of true resistance, and even farther from the possibility of collective resistance.

To understand all this—especially all the phenomena that, in spite of all my efforts, it might be thought I was blaming on the moderators as individuals—we must move to the level of global mechanisms, to the structural level. Plato (I am citing him a lot today) said that we are god's puppets. Television is a universe where you get the impression that social actors—even when they seem to be important, free, and independent, and even sometimes possessed of an extraordinary aura (just take a look at the television magazines)—are the puppets of a necessity that we must understand, of a structure that we must unearth and bring to light.

INVISIBLE STRUCTURES AND THEIR EFFECTS

To move beyond a description, however meticulous, of what happens in a television studio, in order to try and grasp the explanatory mechanisms of journalistic practice, I have to introduce a somewhat technical term—the idea of the journalistic field. Journalism is a microcosm with its own laws, defined both by its position in the world at large and by the attractions and repulsions to which it is subject from other such microcosms. To say that it is independent or autonomous, that it has its own laws, is to say that what happens in it cannot be understood by looking only at external factors. That is why I did not want to explain what happens in journalism as a function of economic factors. What happens on TF1 cannot be explained simply by the fact that it is owned by the Bouygues holding company. Any explanation that didn't take this fact into account would obviously be inadequate, but an explanation based solely on it would be just as inadequate—more inadequate still, perhaps, precisely because it would seem adequate. This half-baked version of materialism, associated with Marxism, condemns without shedding light anywhere and ultimately explains nothing.

Market Share and Competition

To understand what goes on at TF1, you have to take into account everything that TF1 owes to its location in a universe of objective relations between the different, competing television networks. You also have to recognize that the form this competition takes is defined invisibly by unperceived power relations that can be grasped through indicators like market share, the weight given to advertising, the collective capital of high-status journalists, and so on. In other words, not only are there interactions between these news media—between people who do or do not speak to each other, people who influence each other and read each other's work, everything on which I've touched up to now—there are also completely invisible power relations. These invisible relations mean that, in order to understand what goes on at TF1 or Arte, you have to take into account the totality of the objective power relations that structure the field. In the field of economic enterprises, for example, a very powerful company has the power to alter virtually the entire economic playing field. By lowering its prices and setting up a sort of entry barrier, it can forestall the entry into the market of new enterprises. These effects are not necessarily deliberate or intended. TF1 transformed television simply by accumulating a set of specific powers that influence this universe and are translated into an increased share of the market. Neither the viewers nor the journalists are able to see this structure. Journalists see its effects, but they don't see the extent to which the relative weight of the institution for which they work weighs on them, on their place within it and their own ability to affect this same institution. To try and understand what journalists are able to do, you have to keep in mind a series of parameters: first, the relative position of the particular news medium, whether it's TF1 or *Le Monde*; and second, the positions occupied by journalists themselves within the space occupied by their respective newspapers or networks.

A field is a structured social space, a field of forces, a force field. It contains people who dominate and others who are dominated. Constant, permanent relationships of inequality operate inside this space, which at the same time becomes a space in which the various actors struggle for the transformation or preservation of the field. All the individuals in this universe bring to the competition all the (relative) power at their disposal. It is this power that defines their position in the field and, as a result, their strategies. Economic competition between networks or newspapers for viewers, readers, or for market share, takes place concretely in the form of a contest between journalists. This contest has its own, specific stakes—the scoop, the "exclusive," professional reputations, and so on. This kind of competition is neither experienced nor thought of as a struggle purely for economic gain, even though it remains subject to pressures deriving from the position the news medium itself occupies within a larger set of economic and symbolic power relations. Today, invisible but objective relations connect people and parties who may never meet—say, the very serious monthly *Le Monde diplomatique*, at one extreme, and the TF1 television channel, at the other. Nevertheless, in everything these entities do, they are led, consciously or unconsciously, to take into account the same pressures and effects, because they belong to the same world. In other words, if I want to find out what one or another journalist is going to say or write, or will find obvious or unthinkable, normal or worthless, I have to know the position that journalist occupies in this space. I need to know, as well, the specific power of the news medium in question. This impact can be measured by indicators such as the economic weight it pulls, that is, its share of the market. But its symbolic weight also comes into play, and that is much more difficult to quantify. (In fact, to be complete, the position of the national media field within the global media field would have to be taken into account. We'd also have to bring in the economic-technical, and especially, the symbolic dominance of American television, which serves a good many journalists as both a model and a source of ideas, formulas, and tactics.)

To understand this structure better in its current form, it's a good idea to go back over how it was established. During the 1950s, in France, television was barely a factor in the journalistic field. Hardly anyone thought about TV. Television workers were doubly dominated: culturally and symbolically, in terms of prestige, because they were suspected of being dependent on the political powers-that-be; and economically, because they were dependent on government subsidies and therefore much less efficient and much less powerful than their autonomous private counterparts. With time (the process warrants detailed examination) this relationship was completely reversed, so that television now dominates the journalistic field both economically and symbolically. The general crisis faced by newspapers today makes this domination particularly conspicuous. Some newspapers are simply folding, and others are forced to spend every minute worrying about their very survival, about getting their audience, or getting it back. The most threatened, at least in France, are the papers that used to specialize in human interest stories or sports: they simply don't have much to offer against television programming that focuses more and more on sports and human interest stories, circumventing the rules set by serious journalism (which puts, or used to put, on the front page foreign affairs, politics, even political analysis, giving lesser placement to human interest stories and sports).

Of course, this description is a rough one. It would be necessary to go into much more detail to provide a social history of the evolving relationships between the different media (as opposed to histories of a single newspaper or other news medium)—something that unfortunately doesn't exist. It's on this level of structural history that the most important things appear. What counts in a field is relative weight, relative impact. A newspaper can remain absolutely the same, not lose a single reader, and yet be profoundly altered because its relative importance in the field has changed. For example, a newspaper ceases to dominate the field when it loses the power to lay down the law. It can certainly be said that *Le Monde* used to lay down the law in France in the world of print journalism. A field already existed, divided between the poles recognized by all historians of journalism, consisting of newspapers that give *news*—stories and events—and newspapers that give *views*—opinions and analysis; between mass circulation newspapers such as *France Soir* and newspapers with relatively small circulation that are nonetheless endowed with a semiofficial authority. *Le Monde* was in a good position on both counts: it had a large enough circulation to draw advertisers, and it had enough symbolic capital to be an authority. It held both factors of power in the field simultaneously.

Such "newspapers of opinion and analysis" appeared in France at the end of the nineteenth century as a reaction to the mass circulation sensational press. Educated readers have always viewed the sensational papers with fear or distrust or both. Television—the mass medium par excellence—is therefore unprecedented only in its scope. Here I'll make an aside. One of the great problems faced by sociologists is how to avoid falling into one or the other of two symmetrical illusions. On the one hand, there is the sense of something that has never been seen before. (There are sociologists who love this business, and it's very much the thing, especially on television, to announce the appearance of incredible phenomena or revolutions.) And, on the other hand (mostly from conservative sociologists), there's the opposite, "the way it always has been," "there's nothing new under the sun," "there'll always be people on top and people on the bottom," "the poor are always with us; and the rich too . . ." The already-great risk of falling into such traps is all the greater because historical comparison is extremely difficult. Comparisons can only be made from structure to structure, and there is always the chance that you will make a mistake and describe as extraordinary something that is totally banal, simply because you don't know any better. This is one of the things that can make journalists dangerous. Since they're not always very educated, they marvel at things that aren't very marvelous and don't marvel at things that are in fact extraordinary . . . History is indispensable to sociologists. Unfortunately, in a good many areas, especially for the history of the present, the available studies are inadequate. This is particularly true in the case of new phenomena, such as journalism.

Making Everything Ordinary

To return to the problem of television's effects, it is true that the opposition between news and analysis existed before, but never with this intensity. (You see here that I'm steering between "never-been-seen-before" and "the-way-it-always-has-been.") Television's power of diffusion means that it poses a terrible problem for the print media and for culture generally. Next to it, the mass circulation press that sent so many shudders up educated spines in earlier times doesn't seem like much at all. (Raymond Williams argued that the entire romantic revolution in poetry was brought about by the horror that English writers felt at the beginnings of the mass circulation press.) [19] By virtue of its reach and exceptional power, television produces effects which, though not without precedent, are completely original.

For example, the evening news on French TV brings together more people than all the French newspapers together, morning and evening editions included. When the information supplied by a single news medium becomes a universal source of news, the resulting political and cultural effects are clear. Everybody knows the "law" that if a newspaper or other news vehicle wants to reach a broad public, it has to dispense with sharp edges and anything that might divide or exclude readers (just think about *Paris-Match* or, in the United States, *Life* magazine). It must attempt to be inoffensive, not to "offend anyone," and it must never bring up problems—or, if it does, only problems that don't pose any problem. People talk so much about the weather in day-to-day life because it's a subject that cannot cause trouble. Unless you're on vacation and talking with a farmer who needs rain, the weather is the absolutely ideal *soft* subject. The farther a paper extends its circulation, the more it favors such topics that interest "everybody" and don't raise problems. The object—news—is constructed in accordance with the perceptual categories of the receiver.

The collective activity I've described works so well precisely because of this homogenization, which smooths over things, brings them into line, and depoliticizes them. And it works even though, strictly speaking, this activity is without a subject, that is, no one ever thought of or wished for it as such. This is something that is observed frequently in social life. Things happen that nobody wants but seem somehow · to have been willed. Herein lies the danger of simplistic criticism. It takes the place of the work necessary to understand phenomena such as the fact that, even though no one really wished it this way, and without any intervention on the part of the people actually paying for it, we end up with this very strange product, the "TV news." It suits everybody because it confirms what they already know and, above all, leaves their mental structures intact. There are revolutions, the ones we usually talk about, that aim at the material bases of a society—take the nationalization of Church property after 1789—and then there are symbolic revolutions effected by artists, scholars, or great religious or (sometimes, though less often) political prophets. These affect our mental structures, which means that they change the ways we see and think. Manet is an example: his painting upset the fundamental structure of all academic teaching of painting in the nineteenth century, the opposition between the contemporary and the traditional.[20] If a vehicle as powerful as television were oriented even slightly toward this kind of symbolic revolution, I can assure you that everyone would be rushing to put a stop to it . . .

But it turns out that, without anyone having to ask television to work this way, the model of competition and the mechanisms outlined above ensure that television does nothing of the sort. It is perfectly adapted to the mental structures of its audience. I could point to television's moralizing, telethon side, which needs to be analyzed from this perspective. André Gide used to say that worthy sentiments make bad literature. But worthy sentiments certainly make for good audience ratings. The moralizing bent of television should make us wonder how cynical individuals are able to make such astoundingly conservative, moralizing statements. Our news anchors, our talk show hosts, and our sports announcers have turned into two-bit spiritual guides, representatives of middle-class morality. They are always telling us what we "should think" about what they call "social problems," such as violence in the inner city or in the schools. The same is true for art and literature, where the best-known of the so-called literary programs serve the establishment and ever-more obsequiously promote social conformity and market values.[21]

Journalists—we should really say the journalistic field—owe their importance in society to their de facto monopoly on the large-scale informational instruments of production and diffusion of information. Through these, they control the access of ordinary citizens but also of other cultural producers such as scholars, artists, and writers, to what is sometimes called "public space," that is, the space of mass circulation. (This is the monopoly that blocks the way whenever an individual or member of a group tries to get a given piece of news into broad circulation.) Even though they occupy an inferior, dominated position in the fields of cultural production, journalists exercise a very particular form of domination, since they control the means of public expression. They control, in effect, public existence, one's ability to be recognized as a *public figure*, obviously critical for politicians and certain intellectuals. This position means that at least the most important of these figures are treated with a respect that is often quite out of proportion with their intellectual merits . . . Moreover, they are able to use part of this power of consecration to their own benefit. Even the best-known journalists occupy positions of structural inferiority vis-à-vis social categories such as intellectuals or politicians—and journalists want nothing so much as to be part of the intellectual crowd. No doubt, this structural inferiority goes a long way to explain their tendency toward anti-intellectualism. Nevertheless, they are able to dominate members of these "superior" categories on occasion.

Above all, though, with their permanent access to public visibility, broad circulation, and mass diffusion—an access that was completely unthinkable for any cultural producer until television came into the picture—these journalists can impose on the whole of society their vision of the world, their conception of problems, and their point of view. The objection can be raised that the world of journalism is divided, differentiated, and diversified, and as such can very well represent all opinions and points of view or let them be expressed. (It is true that to break through journalism's protective shield, you can to a certain extent and provided you possess a minimum of symbolic capital on your own, play journalists and media off against one another.) Yet it remains true that, like other fields, the journalistic field is based on a set of shared assumptions and beliefs, which reach beyond differences of position and opinion. These assumptions operate within a particular set of mental categories; they reside in a characteristic relationship to language, and are visible in everything implied by a formulation such as "it's just *made* for television." These are what supplies the principle that determines what journalists select both within social reality and among symbolic productions as a whole. There is no discourse (scientific analysis, political manifesto, whatever) and no action (demonstration, strike) that doesn't have to face this trial of journalistic selection in order to catch the public eye. The effect is *censorship*, which journalists practice without even being aware of it. They retain only the things capable of *interesting* them and "keeping their attention," which means things that fit their categories and mental grid; and they reject as insignificant or remain indifferent to symbolic expressions that ought to reach the population as a whole.

Another consequence, one more difficult to grasp, of television's increased (relative) power in the space of the means of diffusion and of the greater market pressures on this newly dominant medium, shows up in the shift from a national cultural policy, which once worked through television, to a sort of spontaneous demagoguery. While this change affects television in particular, it has also contaminated supposedly serious newspapers—witness the greater and greater space given over to letters to the editor and op-ed pieces. In the 1950s, television in France was openly "cultural": it used its monopoly to influence virtually every product that laid claim to high cultural status (documentaries, adaptations of the classics, cultural debates, and so forth) and to raise the taste of the general public. In the 1990s, because it must reach the largest audience possible, television is intent on exploiting and pandering to these same tastes. It does so by offering viewers what are essentially raw products, of which the paradigmatic program is the talk show with its "slices of life." These lived experiences come across as unbuttoned exhibitions of often extreme behavior aimed at satisfying a kind of voyeurism and exhibitionism. (TV game shows, which people are dying to get on, if only as a member of the studio audience, just to have a moment of visibility, are another example.) That said, I don't share the nostalgia professed by some people for the paternalistic-pedagogical television of the past, which I see as no less opposed to a truly democratic use of the means of mass circulation than populist spontaneism and demagogic capitulation to popular tastes.

Struggles Settled by Audience Ratings

So you have to look beyond appearances, beyond what happens in the studio, and even beyond the competition inside the journalistic field. To the extent that it decides the very form of onscreen interactions, one must understand the power relationship between the different news media. To understand why we continually see the same debates between the same journalists, we have to consider the position of the various media that these journalists represent and their position within those media. Similarly, both of these factors have to be kept in mind if we want to understand what a reporter for *Le Monde* can and cannot write. What are actually positional pressures are experienced as ethical interdictions or injunctions: "that's not the practice at *Le Monde*" or "that doesn't fit with *Le Monde*'s culture," or again, "that just isn't done here," and so on. All these experiences, presented as ethical precepts, translate the structure of the field through an individual who occupies a particular position in this space.

Competitors within a given field often have polemical images of one another. They produce stereotypes about one another and insults as well. (In the world of sports, for example, rugby players routinely refer to soccer players as "armless wonders.") These images are often strategies that take into account and make use of power relationships, which they aim to transform or preserve. These days, print journalists, in particular those who occupy a dominated position within this sphere (that is, those who write for lesser newspapers and are in lesser positions), are elaborating a discourse that is highly critical of television.

In fact, these images themselves take a stand, which essentially gives expression to the position occupied by the individual who, with greater or lesser disclaimers, articulates the view in question. At the same time, these strategies aim to transform the position this individual occupies in the field. Today, the struggle over television is central to the journalistic milieu, and its centrality makes it very difficult to study. Much pseudo-scholarly discourse on television does no more than record what TV people say about TV. (Journalists are all the more inclined to say that a sociologist is good when what he says is close to what they think. Which means—and it's probably a good thing, too—that you haven't a prayer of being popular with TV people if you try to tell the truth about television.) That said, there are indicators that, relative to television, print journalism is in gradual retreat. Witness the increasing space given to TV listings in newspapers, or the great store set by journalists in having their stories picked up by television, as well as, obviously, being seen on television. Such visibility gives them greater status in their newspaper or journal. Any journalist who wants power or influence has to have a TV program. It is even possible for television journalists to get important positions in the printed press. This calls into question the specificity of writing, and, for that matter, the specificity of the entire profession. The fact that a television news anchor can become the editor of a newspaper or newsmagazine from one day to the next makes you wonder just what the specific competence required of a journalist might be.

Then there is the fact that television more and more defines what Americans call the *agenda* (the issues up for discussion, the subjects of the editorials, important problems to be covered). In the circular circulation of information I've described, television carries decisive weight. If the printed press should happen to raise an issue—a scandal or a debate—it becomes central only when television takes it up and gives it full orchestration, and, thereby, political impact. This dependence on television threatens the position of print journalists, and this too calls the specificity of the profession into question. Of course, all of this needs to be documented and verified. What I'm giving here is simultaneously a balance sheet based on a number of studies and a program for further research. These are very complicated matters about which knowledge cannot really advance without significant empirical work. This doesn't prevent the practitioners of "mediology," self-designated specialists in a science that doesn't exist, from drawing all sorts of peremptory conclusions about the state of media in the world today before any study has been conducted.

But the most important point is that through the increased symbolic power of television overall, and, among the competing kinds of television, the increased influence of the most cynical and most successful seekers after anything sensational, spectacular, or extraordinary, a certain vision of the news comes to take over the whole of the journalistic field. Until recently, this conception of the news had been relegated to the tabloids specializing in sports and human interest stories. Similarly, a certain category of journalists, recruited at great cost for their ability immediately to fulfill the expectations of the public that expects the least—journalists who are necessarily the most cynical, the most indifferent to any kind of structural analysis, and even more reluctant to engage in any inquiry that touches on politics—tends to impose on all journalists its "values," its preferences, its ways of being and speaking, its "human ideal." Pushed by competition for market share, television networks have greater and greater recourse to the tried and true formulas of tabloid journalism, with emphasis (when not the entire newscast) devoted to human interest stories or sports. No matter what has happened in the world on a given day, more and more often the evening news begins with French soccer scores or another sporting event, interrupting the regular news. Or it will highlight the most anecdotal, ritualized political event (visits of foreign heads of state, the president's trips abroad, and so on), or the natural disasters, accidents, fires and the like. In short, the focus is on those things which are apt to arouse curiosity but require no analysis, especially in the political sphere.

As I've said, human interest stories create a political vacuum. They depoliticize and reduce what goes on in the world to the level of anecdote or scandal. This can occur on a national or international scale, especially with film stars or members of royal families, and is accomplished by fixing and keeping attention fixed on events without political consequences, but which are nonetheless dramatized so as to "draw a lesson" or be transformed into illustrations of "social problems." This is where our TV philosophers are called in to give meaning to the meaningless, anecdotal, or fortuitous event that has been artificially brought to stage center and given significance—a headscarf worn to school, an assault on a schoolteacher or any other "social fact" tailor-made to arouse the pathos and indignation of some commentators or the tedious moralizing of others. This same search for sensational news, and hence market success, can also lead to the selection of stories that give free rein to the unbridled constructions of demagoguery (whether spontaneous or intentional) or can stir up great excitement by catering to the most primitive drives and emotions (with stories of kidnapped children and scandals likely to arouse public indignation). Purely sentimental and therapeutic forms of mobilizing feelings can come into play, but, with murders of children or incidents tied to stigmatized groups, other forms of mobilization can also take place, forms that are just as emotional but aggressive enough almost to qualify as symbolic lynching.

It follows that the printed press today faces a choice: Should it go in the direction of the dominant model, which means publishing newspapers that resemble TV news, or should it emphasize its difference and engage instead in a strategy of product differentiation? Should it compete, and run the risk of losing on both fronts, not reaching a mass public while losing the one that remains faithful to the strict definition of the cultural message? Or, once again, should it stress its difference? The same problem exists inside the television field itself, which is, of course, a subfield within the larger journalistic field. From my observations so far, I think that, unconsciously, those in charge, who are themselves victims of the "audience ratings mind-set," don't really choose. (It is regularly observed that major social decisions aren't made by anyone. If sociologists always disturb things, it's because they force us to make conscious things that we'd rather leave unconscious.) I think that the general trend is for old-style means of cultural production to lose their specificity and move onto a terrain where they can't win. Thus, the cultural network Channel 7 (now Arte) moved from a policy of intransigent, even aggressive, esotericism to a more or less disreputable compromise with audience ratings. The result is programming that makes concessions to facile, popular programming during prime time and keeps the esoteric fare for late at night. *Le Monde* (like other serious newspapers throughout the world) currently faces the same choice. I think I've said enough to show the move from the analysis of invisible structures—a bit like the force of gravity, things that nobody sees but have to be accepted for us to understand what's going on—to individual experience, and how the invisible power relations are translated into personal conflicts and existential choices.

The journalistic field has one distinguishing characteristic: it is much more dependent on external forces than the other fields of cultural production, such as mathematics, literature, law, science, and so on. It depends very directly on demand, since, and perhaps even more than the political field itself, it is subject to the decrees of the market and the opinion poll. The conflict of "pure" versus "market" can be seen in every field. In the theater, for example, it turns up in the opposition between big, popular shows and avant-garde theater, between Broadway musicals and off-Broadway experimental theater. In the media, it's the difference between TF1 and *Le Monde*. All reflect the same opposition between catering to a public that is more educated, on the one hand, less so on the other, with more students for the one, more businessmen for the other. But if this opposition is ubiquitous, it's particularly brutal in the journalistic field, where the market weighs particularly heavily. Its intensity is unprecedented and currently without equal. Furthermore, the journalistic field has no equivalent of the sort of immanent justice in the scientific world that censures those individuals who break certain rules and rewards those who abide by them with the esteem of their peers (as manifested most notably in citations and references). Where are the positive or negative sanctions for journalism? The only criticism consists of satirical spoofs such as that on the Puppets.[22] As for the rewards, there is little more than the possibility of having one's story "picked up" (copied by another journalist), but this indicator is infrequent, not very visible, and ambiguous.

The Power of Television

The world of journalism in itself is a field, but one that is subject to great pressure from the economic field via audience ratings. This very heteronomous field, which is structurally very strongly subordinated to market pressures, in turn applies pressure to all other fields. This structural, objective, anonymous, and invisible effect has nothing to do with what is visible or with what television usually gets attacked for, namely, the direct intervention of one or another individual . . . It is not enough, it should not be enough, to attack the people in charge. For example, Karl Kraus, the great Viennese satirist early in this century, launched violent attacks on a man who was the equivalent of the editor of *Le Nouvel Observateur*. He denounced the cultural conformism so destructive of culture and the complacency of minor or measly writers whom he saw as discrediting pacifist ideas by championing them hypocritically . . . As a general rule, critics are concerned with individuals. But when you do sociology, you learn that men and women are indeed responsible, but that what they can or cannot do is largely determined by the structure in which they are placed and by the positions they occupy within that structure. So polemical attacks on this or that journalist, philosopher, or philosopher-journalist are not enough . . . Everyone has a favorite whipping boy, and I'm no exception. Bernard-Henri Lévy has become something of a symbol of the writer-journalist and the philosopher-journalist. But no sociologist worthy of the name talks about Bernard-Henri Lévy.[23] It is vital to understand that he is only a sort of structural epiphenomenon, and that, like an electron, he is the expression of a field. You can't understand anything if you don't understand the field that produces him and gives him his parcel of power.

This understanding is important both to remove the analysis from the level of drama and to direct action rationally. I am in fact convinced (and this presentation on television bears witness to this conviction) that analyses like this can perhaps help to change things. Every science makes this claim. Auguste Comte, the founder of sociology, proclaimed that "science leads to foresight, and foresight leads to action." Social science has as much right to this aspiration as any other science. By describing a space such as journalism, investing it from the beginning with drives, feelings, and emotions—emotions and drives that are glossed over by the work of analysis—sociologists can hope to have some effect. Increasing awareness of the mechanisms at work, for example, can help by offering a measure of freedom to those manipulated by these mechanisms, whether they are journalists or viewers. Another aside: I think (or at least I hope) that if they really listen to what I am saying, journalists who might initially feel attacked will feel that, by spelling out things they know vaguely but don't really want to know too much about, I am giving them instruments of freedom with which to master the mechanisms I discuss.

In fact, it might be possible to create alliances between news media that could cancel out certain of the structural effects of competition that are most pernicious, such as the race for the scoop. Some of these dangerous effects derive from the structural effects shaping the competition, which produces a sense of urgency and leads to the race for the scoop. This means that news which might prove dangerous to those involved can be broadcast simply to beat out a competitor, with no thought given to the danger. To the extent that this is true, making these mechanisms conscious or explicit could lead to an arrangement that would neutralize competition. In a scenario somewhat like what sometimes happens now in extreme cases, as when children are kidnapped, for example, one could imagine—or dream—that journalists might agree to forget about audience ratings for once and refuse to open their talk shows to political leaders known for and by their xenophobia. Further, they could agree not to broadcast what these characters say. (This would be infinitely more effective than all the so-called refutations put together.)

All of this is utopian, and I know it. But to those who always tax the sociologist with determinism and pessimism, I will only say that if people became aware of them, conscious action aimed at controlling the structural mechanisms that engender moral failure would be possible. As we have seen, this world characterized by a high degree of cynicism has a lot of talk about morality. As a sociologist, I know that morality only works if it is supported by structures and mechanisms that give people an interest in morality. And, for something like a moral anxiety to occur, that morality has to find support, reinforcement, and rewards in this structure. These rewards could also come from a public more enlightened and more aware of the manipulations to which it is subject.

I think that all the fields of cultural production today are subject to structural pressure from the journalistic field, and not from any one journalist or network executive, who are themselves subject to control by the field. This pressure exercises equivalent and systematic effects in every field. In other words, this journalistic field, which is more and more dominated by the market model, imposes its pressures more and more on other fields. Through pressure from audience ratings, economic forces weigh on television, and through its effect on journalism, television weighs on newspapers and magazines, even the "purest" among them. The weight then falls on individual journalists, who little by little let themselves be drawn into television's orbit. In this way, through the weight exerted by the journalistic field, the economy weighs on all fields of cultural production.

In a very interesting paper in a special issue on journalism of *Actes de la recherche en sciences sociales*, Remi Lenoir shows how, in the juridical world, a certain number of hard-hitting judges—not always the most respectable according to the norms internal to the juridical field—made use of television to change the power relations inside their field: essentially, they short-circuited internal hierarchies. This might be fine in some cases, but it can also endanger a stage of collective rationality that is achieved only with difficulty. Or, more precisely, it calls into question everything that has been acquired and guaranteed by the autonomy of a juridical world able to set its model of rationality against intuitive senses of justice and juridical common sense, both of which often give in to appearances or emotion. Whether expressing their vision and their own values or claiming, in all good faith, to represent "popular feeling," journalists can influence judges, sometimes very directly. This has led to talk of a veritable transfer of the power to judge. An equivalent could also be found in science, where, as shown in the "scandals" analyzed by Patrick Champagne, the demagogic model—precisely the model of audience ratings—takes precedence over that of internal criticism.[24]

All this may appear quite abstract. In each field, the university, history, whatever, there are those who dominate and those who are dominated according to the values internal to that field. A "good historian" is someone good historians call a good historian. The whole business is circular by definition. But heteronomy—the loss of autonomy through subjection to external forces—begins when someone who is not a mathematician intervenes to give an opinion about mathematics, or when someone who is not recognized as a historian (a historian who talks about history on television, for instance) gives an opinion about historians—and is listened to. With the "authority" conferred by television, Mr. Cavada tells you that Mr. X is the greatest French philosopher. Can you imagine a referendum or a debate between two parties chosen by a talk show host like Cavada settling an argument between two mathematicians, two biologists, or two physicists? But the media never fail to offer their verdicts. The weekly magazines love this sort of thing—summing up the decade, giving the hit parade of the "in" "intellectuals" of the year, the month, the week—the intellectuals who count, the ones on their way up or on their way down . . .

Why does this tactic meet with such success? Because these instruments let you play the intellectual stock market. They are used by intellectuals—who are the shareholders in this enterprise (often small shareholders to be sure, but powerful in journalism or publishing)—to increase the value of their shares. Encyclopedias and dictionaries (of philosophers, of sociologists or sociology, of intellectuals, whatever) are and have always been instruments of power and consecration. One of the most common strategies is to include individuals who (according to field-specific criteria) could or should be excluded, or to exclude others who could or should be included. Or again, to modify the structure of the judgments being rendered in this "hit parade," you can put side by side, say, Claude Lévi-Strauss and Bernard-Henri Lévy—that is, someone whose value is indisputable and someone whose value is indisputably disputable. But newspapers intervene as well, posing problems that are then immediately taken up by the journalist-intellectuals. Anti-intellectualism, which is (very understandably) a structural constant in the world of journalism, pushes journalists periodically to impute errors to intellectuals or to initiate debates that will mobilize only other journalist-intellectuals, and frequently often exist only to give these TV intellectuals their media existence.

These external demands are very threatening. In the first place, they can deceive outsiders, who necessarily matter, at least to the extent that cultural producers need listeners, viewers, and readers who buy books and, through sales, affect publishers, and so determine future possibilities of publication. Given the tendency of the media today to celebrate market products designed for the bestseller lists—and their obliging accommodation to backscratching between writer-journalists and journalist-writers—young poets, novelists, sociologists, and historians who sell three hundred copies of their books are going to have a harder and harder time getting published. I think that, paradoxically, sociology, and most particularly the sociology of intellectuals, has made its own contribution to the state of the French intellectual field today—quite unintentionally, of course. Sociology can in fact be used in two contrary modes. The first, *cynical* mode uses knowledge of the laws of a given milieu to maximize the effect of one's own strategies; the other, which can be called *clinical*, uses the knowledge of these laws or tendencies in order to challenge them. My conviction is that a certain number of cynics—the prophets of transgression, TV's "fast-thinkers," the historian-journalists who edit encyclopedias or spout summaries of contemporary thought—deliberately use sociology (or what they think is sociology) to engineer coups d'état within the intellectual field. You could say as much about the genuinely critical thought of Guy Debord. Touted as the great thinker of the "society of the spectacle," today Debord is used to vindicate a fake, cynical radicalism that ends up cancelling out his thought altogether.

Collaboration

But journalistic forces and manipulation can also act more subtly. Like the Trojan horse, they introduce heteronomous agents into autonomous worlds. Supported by external forces, these agents are accorded an authority they cannot get from their peers. These writers for nonwriters or philosophers for nonphilosophers and the like, have television value, a journalistic weight that is not commensurate with their particular weight in their particular world. It's a fact: in certain disciplines, media credentials are now taken more and more into account—even in the review committees of the Centre National de la Recherche Scientifique. Any producer of a TV or radio program who invites a researcher onto a show gives that individual a form of recognition that, until quite recently, was taken as a sign of corruption or decline. Barely thirty years ago, Raymond Aron was seen as deeply suspect, in spite of his hardly debatable merits as a scholar, simply because he was associated with the media as a columnist for Le Figaro.[25] Today, the power relationships between fields have changed to the extent that, more and more, external criteria of evaluation—appearing on Bernard Pivot's popular TV book show,[26] being endorsed or profiled by the weekly newsmagazines—are more important than peer evaluation. This occurs even in the purest universe of the hard sciences. (It would be more complicated for the social sciences because sociologists talk about the social world, in which everyone has a stake and an interest, which means that people have their good and bad sociologists for reasons that have nothing to do with sociology.) In the case of apparently more independent disciplines, such as history or anthropology, biology or physics, media mediation becomes more and more important to the degree that subsidies and grants may depend on a notoriety in which one is hard put to distinguish what is owed to media validation from what is due to peer evaluation. This may seem excessive. Unfortunately, however, I could give all kinds of examples of media intrusion—or, rather the intrusion of economic pressures as relayed by the media—even in the "purest" science. This is why the question of deciding whether or not to appear on television is absolutely central, and why I'd like the scientific community to think about it carefully. Such reflection could increase awareness of the mechanisms I have described, and perhaps could even lead to collective attempts to protect the autonomy crucial to scientific progress against the growing power of television.

For the media to exert power on worlds such as science, the field in question must be complicitous. Sociology enables us to understand this complicity. Journalists often take great satisfaction in noting how eagerly academics rush into the arms of the media, soliciting book reviews and begging for invitations to talk shows, all the while protesting against the oblivion to which they are relegated. Listening to their stories, one comes to have real doubts about the subjective autonomy of writers, artists, and scholars. This dependence has to be put on record. Above all, we must attempt to understand its reasons, or its causes. In some sense, we are seeking to understand who collaborates. I use this word advisedly. A recent issue of the *Actes de la recherche en sciences sociales* contained an article by Gisèle Sapiro on the French literary field during the Occupation. The goal of this fine analysis was not to say who was or was not a collaborator, nor was it a retrospective settling of accounts; rather, working from a certain number of variables, it attempted to understand why, at a given moment, writers chose one camp and not another. In short, her analysis shows that the more people are recognized by their peers, and are therefore rich in specific capital, the more likely they are to resist. Conversely, the more heteronomous they are in their literary practices, meaning drawn to market criteria (like Claude Farrère, a bestselling author of exotic novels at the time, whose counterparts are easily found today), the more inclined they are to collaborate.

But I have to explain better what "autonomous" means. A highly autonomous field, mathematics for example, is one in which producers' sole consumers are their competitors, that is, individuals who could have made the discovery in question. (I dream of sociology becoming like this, but, unfortunately, everyone wants to get in on the act. Everybody thinks they know what sociology is, and Alain Peyrefitte thinks he has to give me sociology lessons.[27] Well, why not? you may ask, since there are plenty of sociologists or historians only too happy to talk things over with him . . . on television . . .). Autonomy is achieved by constructing a sort of "ivory tower" inside of which people judge, criticize, and even fight each other, but with the appropriate weapons—properly scientific instruments, techniques, and methods. I happened to be on the radio one day with one of my colleagues in history. Right on the air, he says to me, "my dear colleague, I redid your factor analysis (a method of statistic analysis) for the managers, and I didn't get at all what you got." And I thought, "Terrific! Finally, here's someone who is really criticizing me . . ." But it turned out that he'd used a different definition of management and had eliminated bank directors from the population under study. All that had to be done to bring us together was to restore the bank directors (a choice that entailed important theoretical and historical choices). The point is, true scientific agreement or disagreement requires a high degree of agreement about the bases for disagreement and about the means to decide the question. People are sometimes astonished to see on television that historians don't always agree with each other. They don't understand that very often these discussions bring together individuals who have nothing in common and who have no reason even to be talking with one another (somewhat as if you brought together—in just the sort of encounter bad journalists love—an astronomer and an astrologist, a chemist and an alchemist, or a sociologist of religion and a religious cult leader).

From the choices made by French writers under the Occupation can be derived a more general law: The more a cultural producer is autonomous, rich in specific capital from a given field and exclusively integrated into the restricted market in which the only audience is competitors, the greater the inclination to resist. Conversely, the more producers aim for the mass market (like some essayists, writer-journalists, and popular novelists), the more likely they are to collaborate with the powers that be—State, Church, or Party, and, today, journalism and television—and to yield to their demands or their orders.

This law also applies to the present. The objection will be raised that collaborating with the media is not at all the same thing as collaborating with the Nazis. That's true, of course, and obviously, I do not condemn out of hand every kind of collaboration with newspapers, radio, or television. But, from the viewpoint of factors inclining the individual to collaboration, understood as unconditional submission to pressures destructive of the norms of autonomous fields, the analogy is striking. If the fields of science, politics, or literature are threatened by the power of the media, it's because of the presence within them of "heteronomous individuals," people from the outside who have little authority from the viewpoint of the values specific to the field. To use the language of everyday life, these people are already, or are about to become, "failures," which means that they have an interest in heteronomy. It is in their interest to look outside the field for their authority and the rewards (however precipitate, premature, and ephemeral) they did not get inside the field. Moreover, journalists think well of these individuals because they aren't afraid (as they are of more autonomous authors) of people who are ready to accept whatever is required of them. If it seems to me indispensable to combat these heteronomous intellectuals, it's because they constitute the Trojan horse through which heteronomy—that is, the laws of the market and the economy—is brought into the field.

The political field itself enjoys a certain autonomy. Parliament, for example, is an arena within which, in accordance with certain rules, debate and votes resolve disputes between individuals who supposedly articulate divergent or even antagonistic interests. Television produces in this field effects analogous to those it produces in other fields, the juridical field in particular. It challenges the rights of the field to autonomy. To show this mechanism at work, let us examine a story reported in the same issue of *Actes de la recherche en sciences sociales* on the power of journalism, the story of Karine. Karine is a little girl in the south of France who was murdered. The local newspaper reported all the facts, the indignant protests of her father and her uncle, who organized small, local demonstrations, which were carried first by one paper, then a whole string of papers. Everyone said, "How awful! a little kid! We have to reinstate the death penalty." Local political leaders, people close to the National Front, got especially worked up.[28] A conscientious journalist from Toulouse tried to issue a warning: "Watch out! This is a lynching. Take your time, think about what you're doing." Lawyers' groups got involved, denouncing the appeal to vigilante justice . . . Pressure mounted, and when things finally settled down, life imprisonment without parole had been reinstated.

This film run fast forward shows clearly how a perverse form of direct democracy can come into play when the media act in a way that is calculated to mobilize the public. Such "direct democracy" maximizes the effect both of the pressures working upon the media and of collective emotion. The usual buffers (not necessarily democratic) against these pressures are linked to the relative autonomy of the political field. Absent this autonomy, we are left with a revenge model, precisely the model against which the juridical and even political model of justice was established in the first place. It happens on occasion that, unable to maintain the distance necessary for reflection, journalists end up acting like the fireman who sets the fire. They help create the event by focusing on a story (such as the murder of one young Frenchman by another young man, who is just as French but "of African origin"), and then denounce everyone who adds fuel to the fire that they lit themselves. In this case, I am referring, of course, to the National Front, which, obviously, exploits or tries to exploit "the emotions aroused by events." This in the words of the very newspapers and talk shows that started the whole business by writing the headlines in the first place, and by rehashing events endlessly at the beginning of every evening news program. The media then appear virtuous and humane for denouncing the racist moves of the very figure [LePen] they helped create and to whom they continue to offer his most effective instruments of manipulation.

Entry Fee and Exit Duty

I'd now like to say a few words about the relations between esotericism and elitism. This has been a problem since the nineteenth century.

Mallarmé, for example—the very symbol of the esoteric, a pure writer, writing for a few people in language unintelligible to ordinary mortals—was concerned throughout his whole life with giving back what he had mastered through his work as a poet. If the media today had existed in full force at the time, he would have wondered: "Shall I appear on TV? How can I reconcile the exigency of 'purity' inherent in scientific and intellectual work, which necessarily leads to esotericism, with the democratic interest in making these achievements available to the greatest number?" Earlier, I pointed out two effects of television. On the one hand, it lowers the "entry fee" in a certain number of fields—philosophical, juridical, and so on. It can designate as sociologist, writer, or philosopher people who haven't paid their dues from the viewpoint of the internal definition of the profession. On the other hand, television has the capacity to reach the greatest number of individuals. What I find difficult to justify is the fact that the extension of the audience is used to legitimate the lowering of the standards for entry into the field. People may object to this as elitism, a simple defense of the besieged citadel of big science and high culture, or even, an attempt to close out ordinary people (by trying to close off television to those who, with their honoraria and showy lifestyles, claim to be representatives of ordinary men and women, on the pretext that they can be understood by these people and will get high audience ratings). In fact, I am defending the conditions necessary for the production and diffusion of the highest human creations. To escape the twin traps of elitism or demagogy we must work to maintain, even to raise the requirements for the *right of entry*—the entry fee—into the fields of production. I have said that this is what I want for sociology, a field that suffers from the fact that the entry fee is too low—and we must reinforce the *duty to get out*, to share what we have found, while at the same time improving the conditions and the means for doing so.

Someone is always ready to brandish the threat of "leveling" (a recurrent theme of reactionary thought found, for one example, in the work of Heidegger). Leveling can in fact come from the intrusion of media demands into the fields of cultural production. It is essential to defend both the inherent esotericism of all cutting-edge research and the necessity of de-esotericizing the esoteric. We must struggle to achieve both these goals under good conditions. In other words, we have to defend the conditions of production necessary for the progress of the universal, while working to generalize the conditions of access to that universality. The more complex an idea—because it has been produced in an autonomous world—the more difficult it is to present to the larger world. To overcome this difficulty, producers in their little citadels have to learn how to get out and fight collectively for optimum conditions of diffusion and for ownership of the relevant means of diffusion. This struggle has to take place as well with teachers, with unions, voluntary associations, and so on, so that those on the receiving end receive an education aimed at raising their level of reception. The founders of the French Republic in the late nineteenth century used to say something that is forgotten all too often: The goal of teaching is not only the reading, writing, and arithmetic needed to make a good worker; the goal of education is to offer the means of becoming a good citizen, of putting individuals in a position to understand the law, to understand and to defend their rights, to set up unions . . . We must work to universalize the conditions of access to the universal.

The audience rating system can and should be contested in the name of democracy. This appears paradoxical, because those who defend audience ratings claim that nothing is more democratic (this is a favorite argument of advertisers, which has been picked up by certain sociologists, not to mention essayists who've run out of ideas and are happy to turn any criticism of opinion polls—and audience ratings—into a criticism of universal suffrage). You must, they declare, leave people free to judge and to choose for themselves ("all those elitist intellectual prejudices of yours make you turn your nose up at all this"). The audience rating system is the sanction of the market and the economy, that is, of an external and purely market law. Submission to the requirements of this marketing instrument is the exact equivalent for culture of what poll-based demagogy is for politics. Enslaved by audience ratings, television imposes market pressures on the supposedly free and enlightened consumer. These pressures have nothing to do with the democratic expression of enlightened collective opinion or public rationality, despite what certain commentators would have us believe. The failure of critical thinkers and organizations charged with articulating the interests of dominated individuals to think clearly about this problem only reinforces the mechanisms I have described.

THE OLYMPICS—AN AGENDA FOR ANALYSIS[29]

What exactly do we mean when we talk about the Olympics? The apparent referent is what "really" happens. That is to say, the gigantic spectacle of sport in which athletes from all over the world compete under the sign of universalistic ideals; as well as the markedly national, even patriotic ritual of the parades by various national teams, and the award ceremonies replete with flying flags and blaring anthems. But the hidden referent is the television show, the ensemble of representations of the first spectacle, as it is filmed and broadcast by television in selections which, since the competition is international, appear unmarked by national bias. The Olympics, then, are doubly hidden: no one sees all of it, and no one sees that they don't see it. Every television viewer can have the illusion of seeing *the* (real) Olympics.

It may seem simply to record events as they take place, but in fact, given that each national television network gives more airplay to athletes or events that satisfy national pride, television transforms a sports competition between athletes from all over into a confrontation between champions, that is, officially selected competitors from different countries.

To understand this process of symbolic transformation, we would first have to analyze the social construction of the entire Olympic spectacle. We'd have to look at the individual events and at everything that takes place around them, such as the opening and closing parades. Then we'd have to look at the production of the televised image of this spectacle. Inasmuch as it is a prop for advertising, the televised event is a commercial, marketable product that must be designed to reach the largest audience and hold on to it the longest. Aside from the fact that these events must be timed to be shown on prime time in economically dominant countries, these programs must be tailored to meet audience demand. The expectations of different national publics and their preferences for one or another sport have to be taken into account. The sports given prominence and the individual games or meets shown must be carefully selected to showcase the national teams most likely to win events and thereby gratify national pride. It follows that the relative importance of the different sports within the international sports organizations increasingly depends on their television popularity and the correlated financial return they promise. More and more, as well, the constraints of television broadcasting influence the choice of sports included in Olympic competition, the site and time slot awarded to each sport, and even the ways in which matches and ceremonies take place. This is why (after negotiations structured by tremendous financial considerations), the key final events at the Seoul Olympics were scheduled to coincide with prime time in the United States.

All of which means that to understand the games, we would have to look at the whole field of production of the Olympics as a *televised show* or, in marketing terms, as a "means of communication." That is to say, we would have to assess all the objective relations between the agents and institutions competing to produce and sell the images of, and commentary about, the Olympics. These would include first the International Olympic Committee (IOC), which has gradually become a vast commercial enterprise with an annual budget of $20 million, dominated by a small, closed group of sports executives and representatives from major companies (Adidas, Coca-Cola, and so on). The IOC controls transmission rights (which were estimated, for Barcelona, at $633 billion), sponsorship rights, and the Olympic city selection. Second, we would need to turn our attention to the big (especially American) television networks competing for transmission rights (divided up by country or by language). Third would be the large multinational corporations (Coca-Cola, Kodak, Ricoh, Philips, and so on) competing for exclusive world rights to promote their products in connection with the Games (as "official sponsors").[30] Finally, we cannot forget the producers of images and commentary for television, radio, and newspapers (some ten thousand at Barcelona), since it is their competition that conditions the construction of the representation of the Olympics by influencing how these images are selected, framed, and edited, and how the commentary is elaborated. Another important consideration is the intensified competition between countries that is produced by the globalization of the Olympic spectacle. The effects of this competition can be seen in official *sports policies* to promote international sports success, maximizing the symbolic and financial rewards of victory and resulting in the *industrialization of the production of sports* that implies the use of drugs and authoritarian forms of training.[31]

A parallel can be seen in artistic production. The individual artist's directly visible actions obscure the activity of the other actors—critics, gallery owners, museum curators, and so on—who, in and through their competition, collaborate to produce the meaning and the value of both the artwork and the artist. Even more important, they produce the very belief in the value of art and the artist that is the basis of the whole art game.[32] Likewise, in sports, the champion runner or javelin thrower is only the obvious subject of a spectacle that in some sense is produced twice.[33] The first production is the actual event in the stadium, which is put together by a whole array of actors, including athletes, trainers, doctors, organizers, judges, goalkeepers, and masters of the ceremonies. The second show reproduces the first in images and commentary. Usually laboring under enormous pressure, those who produce on the second show are caught up in a whole network of objective relationships that weighs heavily on each of them.

As a collectivity, the participants in the event we call "the Olympics" might conceivably come to control the mechanisms that affect them all. But they would be able to do so only by undertaking a serious investigation to bring to light the mechanisms behind this *two-step social construction*, first of the sports event, then of the media event. Only with the conscious control of these mechanisms that can be gained from such a process of research and reflection would this collectivity be able to maximize the potential for universalism—today in danger of extinction—that is contained within the Olympic Games.[34]

THE POWER OF JOURNALISM[35]

My objective here is not "the power of journalists"—and still less of journalism as a "fourth estate"—but, rather, the hold that the *mechanisms* of a journalistic field increasingly subject to market demands (through readers and advertisers) have *first on journalists* (and on journalist-intellectuals) and then, in part through them, on the various fields of cultural production—the juridical field, the literary field, the artistic field, and the scientific field. Accordingly, we must examine how the structural pressure exerted by the journalistic field, itself dominated by market pressures, more or less profoundly modifies power relationships within other fields. This pressure affects what is done and produced in given fields, with very similar results within these otherwise very different worlds. We must avoid, however, falling into one or the other of two opposite errors: the illusion of the "never-been-seen-before" and its counterpart, "the-way-it-always-has-been."

The power exerted by the journalistic field, and through it the market, on other fields of cultural production, even the most autonomous among them, is not radically new. It wouldn't be difficult to find nineteenth-century texts describing similar effects of the market on these protected worlds.[36] But it is essential not to overlook the specificity of the current situation, which, while in some ways homologous to past situations, is characterized by elements that are indeed new. In their intensity and scope, the effects television produces in the journalistic field and through it, on all other fields of cultural production, are incomparably more significant than those of the rise of so-called industrial literature—with the mass press and the serial novel—which roused nineteenth-century writers to indignation or revolt and led, according to Raymond Williams, to modern definitions of "culture."[37]

The journalistic field brings to bear on the different fields of cultural production a group of effects whose form and potency are linked to its own structure, that is, to the position of the various media and journalists with respect to their autonomy vis-à-vis external forces, namely, the twin markets of readers and advertisers. The degree of autonomy of a news medium is no doubt measured by the percentage of income that it derives from advertising and state subsidies (whether indirectly through program promotion or direct subvention) and also by the degree of concentration of its advertisers. As for the autonomy of an individual journalist, it depends first of all on the degree to which press ownership is concentrated. (Concentration of the press augments job insecurity by reducing the number of potential employers.) Next, the individual journalist's autonomy depends on the position occupied by his newspaper within the larger space of newspapers, that is, its specific location between the "intellectual" and the "market" poles. Then, the journalist's own position within that newspaper or news medium (as reporter, freelancer, and so forth) determines statutory guarantees (largely a function of reputation) as well as salary (which makes the individual less vulnerable to the "soft" forms of public relations and less dependent on writing for money, potboilers and the like—both of which essentially relay the financial interests of sponsors). Finally, the journalist's own capacity for autonomous production of news must be taken into account. (Certain writers, such as popularizers of science or economic journalists, are in a state of particular dependence.) It is clear that the authorities, the government in particular, influence the media not only through the economic pressure that they bring to bear but also through their monopoly on legitimate information—government sources are the most obvious example. First of all, this monopoly provides governmental authorities (juridical, scientific, and other authorities as much as the police) with weapons for manipulating the news or those in charge of transmitting it. For its part, the press attempts to manipulate these "sources" in order to get a news exclusive. And we must not ignore the exceptional symbolic power given to state authorities to define, by their actions, their decisions, and their entry into the journalistic field (interviews, press conferences, and so on), the journalistic agenda and the hierarchy of importance assigned to events.

SOME CHARACTERISTICS OF THE JOURNALISTIC FIELD

The journalistic field tends to reinforce the "commercial" elements at the core of all fields to the detriment of the "pure." It favors those cultural producers most susceptible to the seductions of economic and political powers, at the expense of those intent on defending the principles and the values of their professions. To understand how this happens, it is necessary to see that the whole journalistic field is structured like other fields, and also that the market weighs much more heavily on it than on other fields.

The journalistic field emerged as such during the nineteenth century around the opposition between newspapers offering "news," preferably "sensational" or better yet, capable of creating a sensation, and newspapers featuring analysis and "commentary," which marked their difference from the other group by loudly proclaiming the values of "objectivity."[38] Hence, this field is the site of an opposition between two models, each with its own principle of legitimation: that of peer recognition, accorded individuals who internalize most completely the internal "values" or principles of the field; or that of recognition by the public at large, which is measured by numbers of readers, listeners, or viewers, and therefore, in the final analysis, by sales and profits. (Considered from this point of view, a political referendum expresses the verdict of the market.)

Like the literary field or the artistic field, then, the journalistic field is the site of a specific, and specifically cultural, model that is imposed on journalists through a system of overlapping constraints and the controls that each of these brings to bear on the others. It is respect for these constraints and controls (sometimes termed a code of ethics) that establishes reputations of professional morality. In fact, outside perhaps the "pick-ups" (when one's work is picked up by another journalist), the value and meaning of which depend on the positions within the field of those who do the taking up and those who benefit from it, there are relatively few indisputable positive sanctions. And negative sanctions, against individuals who fail to cite their sources for example, are practically nonexistent. Consequently, there is a tendency not to cite a journalistic source, especially from a minor news medium, except when necessary to clear one's name.

But, like the political and economic fields, and much more than the scientific, artistic, literary, or juridical fields, the journalistic field is permanently subject to trial by market, whether directly, through advertisers, or indirectly, through audience ratings (even if government subsidies offer a certain independence from immediate market pressures). Furthermore, journalists are no doubt all the more inclined to adopt "audience rating" standards in the production process ("keep it simple," "keep it short") or when evaluating products and even producers ("that's just made for TV," "this will go over really well"), to the extent that those who better represent these standards occupy higher positions (as network heads or editors-in-chief) in news media more directly dependent on the market (that is, commercial television as opposed to PBS). Conversely, younger and less established journalists are more inclined to invoke the principles and values of the "profession" against the more "realistic," or more cynical, stipulations of their "elders." [39]

In the case of a field oriented toward the production of such a highly perishable good as the news, competition for consumers tends to take the form of competition for the newest news ("scoops"). This is increasingly the case, obviously, the closer one gets to the market pole. Market pressure is exercised only through the effect of the field: actually, a high proportion of the scoops so avidly sought in the battle for customers is destined to remain unknown as such to readers or viewers. Only competitors will see them, since journalists are the only ones who read all the newspapers . . . Imprinted in the field's structure and operating mechanisms, this competition for priority calls for and favors professionals inclined to place the whole practice of journalism under the sign of speed (or haste) and permanent renewal.[40] This inclination is continually reinforced by the temporality of journalistic practice, which assigns value to news according to how new it is (or how "catchy"). This pace favors a sort of permanent amnesia, the negative obverse of the exaltation of the new, as well as a propensity to judge producers and products according to the opposition between "new" or "out-of-date."[41]

Another effect of competition on the field, one that is completely paradoxical and utterly inimical to the assertion of either collective or individual autonomy, is the permanent surveillance (which can turn into mutual espionage) to which journalists subject their competitors' activities. The object is to profit from competitors' failures by avoiding their mistakes, and to counter their successes by trying to borrow the *supposed* instruments of that success, such as themes for special issues that "must" be taken up again, books reviewed elsewhere that "you can't not talk about," guests you "must have," subjects that "have to be covered" because others discovered them, and even big-name journalists who have to appear. This "borrowing" is a result as much of a determination to keep competitors from having these things as from any real desire to have them. So here, as in other areas, rather than automatically generating originality and diversity, competition tends to favor *uniformity*. This can easily be verified by comparing the contents of the major weekly magazines, or radio and television stations aimed at a general audience. But this very powerful mechanism also has the effect of insidiously imposing on the field as a whole the "choices" of those instruments of diffusion most directly and most completely subject to the market, like television. This, in turn, means that all production is oriented toward preserving established values. This conservatism can be seen, for example, in the way that the periodic "hit parades"—through which journalist-intellectuals try to impose their vision of the field (and, via mutual "back-scratching," gain and confer peer recognition . . .)—almost always feature the authors of highly perishable cultural goods; these goods are nonetheless destined, with the help of the media, for the bestseller list, along with authors recognized both as a "sure value," capable of validating the good taste of those who validate them, and as bestsellers in the long run. Which is to say that even if the actors have an effect as individuals, it is the *structure* of the journalistic field that determines the intensity and orientation of its mechanisms, as well as their effects on other fields.

THE EFFECTS OF INTRUSION

In every field, the influence of the journalistic field tends to favor those actors and institutions closer to the market. This effect is all the stronger in fields that are themselves structurally more tightly subordinated to this market model, as well as wherever the journalistic field exercising this power is also more subordinated to those external pressures that have a structurally stronger effect on it than on other fields of cultural production. But we see today that internal sanctions are losing their symbolic force, and that "serious" journalists and newspapers are also losing their cachet as they suffer under the pressure to make concessions to the market, to the marketing tactics introduced by commercial television, and to the new principle of legitimacy based on ratings and "visibility." These things, marketing and media visibility, become the—seemingly more democratic—substitute for the internal standards by which specialized fields once judged cultural and even political products and their producers. Certain "analyses" of television owe their popularity with journalists—especially those most susceptible to the effects of audience ratings—to the fact that they confer a *democratic legitimacy* to the market model by posing in *political* terms (as, for example, a referendum), what is a problem of *cultural* production and diffusion.[42]

Thus, the increased power of a journalistic field itself increasingly subject to direct or indirect domination by the market model threatens the autonomy of other fields of cultural production. It does so by supporting those actors or enterprises at the very core of these fields that are most inclined to yield to the seduction of "external" profits precisely because they are less rich in capital specific to the field (scientific, literary, or other) and therefore less assured of the specific rewards the field is in a position to guarantee in the short or longer term.

The journalistic field exercises power over other fields of cultural production (especially philosophy and the social sciences) primarily through the intervention of cultural producers located in an uncertain site between the journalistic field and the specialized fields (the literary or philosophical, and so on). These journalist-intellectuals use their dual attachments to evade the requirements specific to each of the worlds they inhabit, importing into each the capabilities they have more or less completely acquired in the other. In so doing, they exercise two major effects.[43] On the one hand, they introduce new forms of cultural production, located in a poorly defined intermediary position between academic esotericism and journalistic "exotericism." On the other hand, particularly through their critical assessments, they impose on cultural products evaluative principles that validate market sanctions by giving them a semblance of intellectual authority and reinforcing the spontaneous inclination of certain categories of consumers to *allodoxia*. So that, by orienting choices (editors' choices, for one) toward the least demanding and most commercially viable products, these journalist-intellectuals reinforce the impact of audience ratings or the bestseller list on the reception of cultural products and ultimately if indirectly, on cultural production itself.[44]

Moreover, they can count on the support of those who equate "objectivity" with a sort of social savoir-vivre and an eclectic neutrality with respect to all parties concerned. This group puts middlebrow cultural products in the avant-garde or denigrates avant-garde work (and not only in art) in the name of common sense. But this group in its turn can count on the approval or even the complicity of consumers who, like them, are inclined to *allodoxia* by their distance from the "center of cultural values" and by their self-interested propensity to hide from themselves the limits of their own capacities of appropriation—following the model of self-deception that is expressed so well by readers of popularizing journals when they assert that "this is a high-level scientific journal that anybody can understand."

In this way, achievements made possible by the autonomy of the field and by its capacity to resist social demands can be threatened. It was with these dynamics in mind, symbolized today by audience ratings, that writers in the last century objected vehemently to the idea that art (the same could be said of science) should be subject to the judgments of universal suffrage. Against this threat there are two possible strategies, more or less frequently adopted according to the field and its degree of autonomy. One may firmly delimit the field and endeavor to restore the borders threatened by the intrusion of journalistic modes of thought and action. Alternatively, one may quit the ivory

tower (following the model Émile Zola inaugurated during the Dreyfus Affair) to impose the values nurtured in that tower and to use all
available means, within one's specialized field and without, and also
within the journalistic field itself, to try to impose on the outside the
achievements and victories that autonomy made possible.

There are economic and cultural conditions of access to enlightened scientific judgment. There can be no recourse to universal suffrage (or opinion polls) to decide properly scientific problems (even
though this is sometimes done indirectly, with no one the wiser) without annihilating the very conditions of scientific production, that is,
the entry barrier that protects the scientific (or artistic) world against
the destructive invasion of external, therefore inappropriate and misplaced, principles of production and evaluation. But it should not be
concluded that the barrier cannot be crossed *in the other direction*, or
that it is intrinsically impossible to work for a democratic redistribution of the achievements made possible by autonomy—on the condition that it clearly be seen that every action aimed at disclosing the
rarest achievements of the most advanced scientific or artistic work
assumes a challenge to the *monopoly of the instruments of diffusion* of
this scientific or artistic information, that is, to the monopoly held by
the journalistic field. We must also question the representation of the
general public's expectations as constructed by the market demagogy
of those individuals in a position to set themselves between cultural
producers (today, this applies to politicians as well) and the great mass
of consumers (or voters).

The distance between professional cultural producers (or their
products) and ordinary consumers (readers, listeners, or viewers, and
voters as well) relates to the autonomy of the field in question and
varies according to field. It will be greater or lesser, more or less difficult to cross, and more or less unacceptable from the point of view of
democratic principles. And, contrary to appearances, this distance also
exists in politics, whose declared principles it contradicts. Like those
in the journalistic field, actors in the political field are in a competitive
relationship of continual struggle. Indeed, in a certain way, the journalistic field is part of the political field on which it has such a powerful
impact. Nevertheless, these two fields are both very directly and very

tightly in the grip of the market and the referendum. It follows that the power wielded by the journalistic field reinforces the tendencies of political actors to accede to the expectations and the demands of the largest majority. Because these demands are sometimes highly emotional and unreflective, their articulation by the press often turns them into claims capable of mobilizing groups.

Except when it makes use of the freedoms and critical powers assured by autonomy, the press, especially the televised (commercial) press, acts in the same way as polls (with which it, too, has to contend). While polls can serve as an instrument of rationalistic demagogy which tends to reinforce the self-enclosure of the political field, their primary function is to set up a direct relationship with voters, a relationship *without mediation* which eliminates from the game all individual or collective actors (such as political parties or unions) socially mandated to elaborate and propose considered solutions to social questions. This unmediated relationship takes away from all self-styled spokemen and delegates the claim (made in the past by all the great newspaper editors) to a monopoly on legitimate expression of "public opinion." At the same time, it deprives them of their ability to elaborate critically (and sometimes collectively, as in legislative assemblies) their constituents' actual or assumed will.

For all of these reasons, the ever-increasing power of a journalistic field itself increasingly subject to the power of the market model to influence a political field haunted by the temptation of demagogy (most particularly at a time when polls offer the means for a rationalized exercise of demagogic action) weakens the autonomy of the political field. It weakens as well the powers accorded representatives (political and other) as a function of their competence as *experts* or their authority as *guardians of collective values.*

Finally, how can one not point to the judges who, at the price of a "pious hypocrisy," are able to perpetuate the belief that their decisions are based not in external, particularly economic constraints, but in the transcendent norms of which they are the guardians? The juridical field is not what it thinks it is. It is not a pure world, free of concessions to politics or the economy. But its image of purity produces absolutely real social effects, first of all, on the very individuals whose job it is to declare the law. But what would happen to judges, understood as the more or less sincere incarnations of a collective hypocrisy, if it became widely accepted that, far from obeying transcendent, universal verities and values, they are thoroughly subject, like all other social actors, to constraints such as those placed on them, irrespective of judicial procedures and hierarchies, by the pressures of economic necessity or the seduction of media success?

ON THE UNINTENDED EFFECTS
OF THE RIGHT TO INFORMATION

It is possible to get an idea of the contribution of journalism to the genesis of an "active and effective public opinion" by following the chronological development of a quite ordinary case, that of "little Karine," which would have remained confined to a short report in a regional newspaper, but was gradually transformed into a regular matter of state by the constitution of collective, public and legitimate opinion, and finally ratified by a law providing for life imprisonment.

This started with the Perpignan *Indépendant* reporting the disappearance of a little girl on 15 September 1993, the "emotional appeal" of her mother (16 September), the accusation of a "suspect," a family friend who had "already been condemned twice by the assize court" (20 September), and the confession of the murderer (22 September). Then, on 23 September, came a change of tone: a declaration by the victim's father appealing for the restoration of the death penalty, a similar declaration by Karine's godfather, and an editorial suggesting that the facts leading up to the murder "should have led to definite measures to prevent further recidivism." On the twenty-fifth, an appeal from the family for a demonstration in support of a draft law increasing sentences for the rape and murder of children, the announcement of the creation of an Association des Amis des Parents de Karine in a small neighbouring village, and an appeal to the minister of the interior from another village. On the twenty-sixth, a demonstration with banners demanding the restoration of the death penalty or at least life imprisonment. *La Dépêche de Toulouse* closely followed the same movement, though an editorial on the twenty-sixth spoke of "a man who remains one of us" and called for moderation. On 27 September,

L'Indépendant announced that the government would bring to the Assembly in the autumn session a draft law to increase sentences for the murder of children. A number of politicians spoke at this point, first of all members of the Front National, then from other parties (in particular, the Socialist mayor of Perpignan).

From this point on, the debate moved into the national arena. *L'Indépendant* announced on 6 October that the Association Karine, which now had the services of a lawyer, would be represented throughout the case, and that it had called for a demonstration and for people to write to deputies; on 8 October the association met with the minister of justice; on the ninth it called for a rally; on the tenth a demonstration for "genuine life imprisonment" was held. On the sixteenth, a further demonstration at Montpellier; on the twenty-fifth, a meeting attended by 2,700 people. The twenty-eighth, new visit to the minister of justice. The thirtieth, 137 right-wing deputies demand the restoration of the death penalty. On 17 November, television forcefully intervenes, Charles Villeneuve presenting a program titled "Le Jury d'Honneur" on which "Karine's mother and Maître Nicolas" appear, as well as the minister of justice, representatives of various associations and lawyers, on the subject: "What should we do with child killers?" a question in which every word is an appeal to vengeful identification. The Paris newspapers only get involved rather belatedly, and not very strongly. Except *Le Figaro*, which from the end of September has a piece by a lawyer, the author of *Ces enfants qu'on assassine*, who demands an end to indulgence and appeals for a referendum, making several subsequent appearances in favour of reforming the law (as does *Le Quotidien de Paris*). The announcement on 4 November that the Council of Ministers has decided to present a law establishing life imprisonment triggers resistance from the main organizations of magistrates, and an advocates' association notes that "by pursuing a media goal, the project goes against the serenity of legislative work" (*La Croix*, 4 November).[46]

In the first month of the case, therefore, journalists played a determining role. By offering it the possibility of access to public expression, they transformed a wave of private indignation that would have remained impotent into a public—*published*—appeal, licit and legitimate, for revenge and mobilization, which then served as the basis for a public and organized movement of public protest (demonstrations, petitions, etc.). The brevity of the time span, less than four months, between the death of the young girl and the legislative decision restoring life imprisonment, has the merit of making clear the effects that journalists are able to produce, each time that, by the simple act of *publication,* i.e., a disclosure that implies ratification and making something official, they stoke up or mobilize popular impulses. And as for the intervention of television in this affair, its subjection to audience ratings and the logic of competition for market shares leads to fawning on the most widespread expectations, thus strengthening the propensity to let the unknown effects of publication have free rein, or even multiplying them by the demagogic excitation of basic passions. The responsibility of journalists certainly lies in a laissez-faire irresponsibility that lets them have unpredictable effects in the name of a right to information, which, constituted into a sacrosanct principle of democracy, sometimes provide demagogy with its best alibi.

QUESTIONS OF WORDS⁴⁷

A MORE MODEST VIEW OF THE ROLE OF JOURNALISTS

I do not want what I am going to say to be taken as a critique of journalism, at least in the sense that is generally given to this term, i.e., an "attack" on an activity and those who practice it.

My intention is simply to contribute to a process of self-reflection that journalists are themselves conducting. And to do so first of all by recalling the limits that such self-reflection necessarily comes up against. Every group produces a representation of what it is and what it wants to be; and this is particularly true for the specialized agents of cultural production. This representation clearly owes a great deal to the interests, conscious and unconscious, of those who produce it, and who notably sin by omission or by indulgence towards themselves. If Marx said that "mankind only poses problems that it can solve," one could say here that "groups only pose the problems that they can stand." They have escape strategies, especially that of posing extreme problems bound up with limit situations, in order to avoid everyday problems. The debate about medical ethics is an example of this: to pose the problem of euthanasia is a way of avoiding that of the nurses, of daily life in the hospitals, etc. I would warn therefore against the danger to which a group such as the one here is exposed: we shall speak a great deal about the Gulf War, a situation in which journalistic freedom was reduced almost to zero, and avoid raising those problems where the freedom of journalists is weak but still real. The first step toward ethical reflection consists in defining the zones of freedom where genuine responsibilities and real possibilities of action are involved.

How can one raise these ordinary problems that consideration of extraordinary problems tends to obscure? How can we avoid shifting discussion from those regions of practice that depend on us—as the

Stoics put it—toward those that do not depend on us, so that we are exempt by definition from any responsibility and any action? We must start by returning to a far more modest view of the role of journalists. What actually does lie in their power? Among those things that do depend on them, there is the handling of words. It is thus by controlling their use of words that they can limit the effects of symbolic violence that they may exert willy-nilly. Symbolic violence is a violence practiced in and through ignorance, and all the more readily in that those who practice it are unaware they are doing so, and those experiencing it unaware they are experiencing it.

This statement has an abstract air, but here is a concrete example. This morning I heard a trailer for a program by Jean-Marie Cavada, in the course of which a philosophy of the social history of relations between the sexes was put forward as if this could simply be taken for granted: 1970s, sexual liberation; 1980s, moralism; 1990s, the return of sentiment—something like that. When I hear things of this kind—and God knows how many one hears every day, it's "the return of the subject," "the end of structuralism," "the return to democracy," "the end of history," etc.—I always wonder: "How do they know?" In the world of journalists, however, which is the site par excellence of the production, reproduction, and circulation of this vulgate, the strange fact is that no one asks this question. You read on the front page of *Le Nouvel Observateur* about "the return of sentiment," or in a headline of *Le Quotidien de Paris* "the end of the sexual revolution." These media coups are symbolic coups de force that are struck in all innocence, and all the more effective for being unconscious. There is a sense in which this can only be done because the people who practice this violence are themselves victims of the violence that they practice, and this is where we get the false science of the half-educated that likes to give the appearance of scientific ratification to the intuitions of common sense (we could call this the "Cofremca[48] effect"): typologies based on projecting the social unconscious of these new magicians link up with the unconscious of those who commission such things (businessmen or politicians) and those who receive their commissions (journalists). And the responsibility of journalists comes from their involvement in this circulation of unconscious material.

This is an example of those symbolic effects that often take the form of the well-known paralogism: "The king of France is bald." When someone says "The king of France is bald," two senses of the verb "to be" are involved, and an existential proposition (there is a king of France) is hidden by a predicative statement (the king of France has the property of being bald). Attention is attracted to the fact that the king is bald, while in reality, the idea that there is a king of France is smuggled in as self-evident. I could cite countless statements about the social world that are all of this type, especially those that have collective nouns as their subject: "France is fed up," "The people will not accept," "The French support the death penalty," etc. In the opinion polls, instead of asking first: "Do you think there is a moral crisis at the present time," and then: "Is it serious, very serious, etc.?" people are simply asked: "Is the present moral crisis serious, very serious, etc.?"

Among the most powerful tacit propositions are all those that bear on those oppositions, that are principles of vision and division, such as rich/poor, bourgeois/common people, on which the struggle of the workers' movement was based and which are still present in the unconscious of the majority of us; but also today, oppositions like nationals/foreigners, indigenous/immigrants, us/them, etc. This is a tremendous change. People might take completely different positions on what should be done about immigrants, but even those with opposing views tacitly agree—consensus within dissent—that the opposition between indigenous and immigrants has predominance and priority over every other kind of opposition, starting with that between rich and poor—within which there can of course also be indigenous and foreigners. This realizes the dream of all bourgeoisies, to have a bourgeoisie without a proletariat. From the point that there are only nationals, rich and poor together, everything is well sorted out, at least for the rich. A number of words that we use without even thinking about them, and particularly all these pairs of adjectives, are categories of perception, principles of vision and division that are historically transmitted and socially produced and reproduced, principles that organize our perception of the social world, and especially of conflicts; and political struggle essentially aims at maintaining or transforming these principles, reinforcing or changing our view of the social world.

Journalists therefore play a central role, because among the producers of discourse it is they who wield the most powerful means for circulating and imposing these. They thus occupy a privileged position in the symbolic struggle to make things seen and believed. This is why intellectuals have an ambiguous position toward them. They are envied by some intellectuals who would like to be seen ("did you see me?"), and envied also by less garish intellectuals who would like to be heard. Those who know something about the social world would certainly like to be able to say it, but they come up against those who control access to the means of communication, and are therefore in a position to select who can have access to a mass audience.

To sum up, I would say that the strongest part of communication is its unconscious aspect, the underlying communication between unconsciouses—which in Aristotle's sense are particularly those "things with which we communicate, but about which we never communicate," those fundamental oppositions that make discussion possible, yet are never the object of discussion. What I am preaching here is the necessity of communication about the unconscious of communication. If this is not simply to remain a pious wish, we would need to conceive and create a critical instance able to sanction and punish—at least by means of ridicule—those who overstep the limits. I know that I am indulging in utopia, but I would like to imagine a critical program bringing together scholars and artists, singers and satirists, with the aim of putting to the test of satire and laughter those journalists, politicians, and media "intellectuals" who fall in too glaring a fashion into abuse of symbolic power.

Part II

Acts of Resistance:
Against the Tyranny of the Market

TO THE READER

The texts that follow were written or spoken as contributions to movements and moments of resistance, and it is because I believe that the dangers that provoked them are neither isolated nor occasional that I decided to bring them together for publication. Although they are more exposed than methodically controlled texts to the inconsistencies stemming from the diversity of circumstances, I hope that they can still provide useful weapons to all those who are striving to resist the scourge of neoliberalism.[1]

I do not have much inclination for prophetic interventions and I have always been wary of occasions in which the situation or a sense of solidarity could lead me to overstep the limits of my competence. So I would not have engaged in public position-taking if I had not, each time, had the—perhaps illusory—sense of being forced into it by a kind of legitimate rage, sometimes close to something like a sense of duty.

The ideal of the collective intellectual, to which I have tried to conform whenever I could make common cause with others on some particular point, is not always easy to put into effect.[2] And if, to be effective, I have sometimes had to commit myself in my own person and my own name, I have always done it in the hope—if not of triggering a mobilization, or even one of those debates without object or subject which arise periodically in the world of the media—at least of breaking the appearance of unanimity which is the greater part of the symbolic force of the dominant discourse.

THE LEFT HAND AND THE
RIGHT HAND OF THE STATE

Interview of Pierre Bourdieu (PB) with R. P. Droit and T. Ferenczi, published in *Le Monde*, 14 January 1992.

Q: *A recent issue of the journal that you edit was devoted to the theme of suffering.*[3] *It includes several interviews with people whose voices are not much heard in the media: young people on deprived estates, small farmers, social workers. The head teacher of a secondary school in difficulty, for example, expresses his bitterness. Instead of overseeing the transmission of knowledge, he has become, against his will, the superintendent of a kind of police station. Do you think that individual and anecdotal testimonies of that kind can cast light on a collective malaise?*

PB: In the survey we are conducting on social suffering, we encounter many people who, like that head teacher, are caught in the contradictions of the social world, which are experienced in the form of personal dramas. I could also cite the project leader, responsible for coordinating all the work on a "difficult estate" in a small town in northern France. He is faced with contradictions which are the extreme case of those currently experienced by all those who are called "social workers": family counsellors, youth leaders, rank-and-file magistrates, and also, increasingly, secondary and primary teachers. They constitute what I call the left hand of the state, the set of agents of the so-called spending ministries which are the trace, within the state, of the social struggles of the past. They are opposed to the right hand of the state, the technocrats of the Ministry of Finance, the public and private banks and the ministerial *cabinets*. A number of social struggles that we are now seeing (and will see) express the revolt of the minor state nobility against the senior state nobility.[4]

Q: *How do you explain that exasperation, those forms of despair, and those revolts?*

PB: I think that the left hand of the state has the sense that the right hand no longer knows, or, worse, no longer really wants to know what the left hand does. In any case, it does not want to pay for it. One of the main reasons for all these people's despair is that the state has withdrawn, or is withdrawing, from a number of sectors of social life for which it was previously responsible: social housing, public service broadcasting, schools, hospitals, etc., which is all the more stupefying and scandalous, in some of these areas at least, because it was done by a Socialist government, which might at least be expected to be the guarantor of public service as an open service available to all, without distinction . . . What is described as a crisis of politics, antiparliamentarianism, is in reality despair at the failure of the state as the guardian of the public interest.

If the Socialists had simply not been as socialist as they claimed, that would not shock anyone—times are hard and there is not much room for maneuver. But what is more surprising is that they should have done so much to undermine the public interest, first by their deeds, with all kinds of measures and policies (I will only mention the media . . .) aimed at liquidating the gains of the welfare state, and above all, perhaps, in their words, with the eulogy of private enterprise (as if one could only be enterprising within an enterprise) and the encouragement of private interest. All that is somewhat shocking, especially for those who are sent into the front line to perform so-called "social" work to compensate for the most flagrant inadequacies of the logic of the market, without being given the means to really do their job. How could they not have the sense of being constantly undermined or betrayed?

It should have been clear a long time ago that their revolt goes far beyond questions of salary, even if the salary granted is an unequivocal index of the value placed on the work and the corresponding workers. Contempt for a job is shown first of all in the more or less derisory remuneration it is given.

Q: *Do you think that the politicians' room for maneuver is really so limited?*

PB: It is no doubt less limited than they would have us think. And in any case there remains one area where governments have considerable scope: that of the symbolic. Exemplary behavior ought to be de rigueur for all state personnel, especially when they claim to belong to a tradition of commitment to the interests of the least advantaged. But it is difficult not to have doubts when one sees not only examples of corruption (sometimes quasiofficial, with the bonuses given to some senior civil servants) or betrayal of public service (that word is no doubt too strong—I am thinking of *pantouflage*)[5] and all the forms of misappropriation, for private purposes, of public property, profits or services—nepotism, cronyism (our leaders have many "personal friends" . . .),[6] clientelism . . .

And I have not even mentioned symbolic profits! Television has probably contributed as much as bribery to the degradation of civic virtue. It has invited and projected on to the political and intellectual stage a set of self-promoting personalities concerned above all to get themselves noticed and admired, in total contradiction with the values of unspectacular devotion to the collective interest which once characterized the civil servant or the activist. It is the same self-serving attention seeking (often at the expense of rivals) which explains why "headline grabbing"[7] has become such a common practice. For many ministers, it seems, a measure is only valid if it can be announced and regarded as achieved as soon as it has been made public. In short, large-scale corruption which causes a scandal when it is uncovered because it reveals the gap between professed virtues and real behavior is simply the extreme case of all the ordinary little "weaknesses," the flaunting of luxury and the avid acceptance of material or symbolic privileges.

Q: *Faced with the situation you describe, how, in your view, do the citizens react?*

PB: I was recently reading an article by a German author on ancient Egypt. He shows how, in a period of crisis of confidence in the state and in the public good, two tendencies emerged: among the rulers, corruption, linked to the decline in respect for the public interest; and, among those they dominated, personal religiosity, associated with despair concerning temporal remedies. In the same way, one has the sense now that citizens, feeling themselves ejected from the state (which, in the end, asks of them no more than obligatory material contributions, and certainly no commitment, no enthusiasm), reject the state, treating it as an alien power to be used so far as they can to serve their own interests.

Q: *You referred to the considerable scope that governments have in the symbolic domain. This is not just a matter of setting an example of good behavior. It is also about words, ideals that can mobilize people. How do you explain the current vacuum?*

PB: There has been much talk of the silence of the intellectuals. What strikes me is the silence of the politicians. They are terribly short of ideals that can mobilize people. This is probably because the professionalization of politics and the conditions required of those who want to make a career in the parties increasingly exclude inspired personalities. And probably also because the definition of political activity has changed with the arrival of a political class that has learned in its schools (of political science) that, to appear serious, or simply to avoid appearing old-fashioned or archaic, it is better to talk of management than self-management, and that they must, at any rate, take on the appearances (that is to say the language) of economic rationality.

Locked in the narrow, short-term economism of the IMF worldview which is also causing havoc, and will continue to do so, in North-South relations, all these half-wise economists fail, of course, to take account of the real costs, in the short and more especially the long term, of the material and psychological wretchedness which is the only certain outcome of their economically legitimate Realpolitik: delinquency, crime, alcoholism, road accidents, etc. Here too, the right hand, obsessed by the question of financial equilibrium, knows nothing of the problems of the left hand, confronted with the often very costly social consequences of "budgetary restrictions."

Q: *Are the values on which the actions and contributions of the state were once founded no longer credible?*

PB: The first people to flout them are often the very ones who ought to be their guardians. The Rennes Congress[8] and the amnesty law[9] did more to discredit the Socialists than ten years of antisocialist campaigning. And a "turncoat" activist does more harm than ten opponents. But ten years of Socialist government have completed the demolition of belief in the state and the demolition of the welfare state that was started in the 1970s in the name of liberalism. I am thinking in particular of housing policy.[10] The declared aim has been to rescue the petite bourgeoisie from publicly owned housing (and thereby from "collectivism") and facilitate their move into ownership of a house or apartment. This policy has in a sense succeeded only too well. Its outcome illustrates what I said a moment ago about the social costs of some economies. That policy is probably the major cause of social segregation and consequently of the problems referred to as those of the "*banlieues.*"[11]

Q: *So if one wants to define an ideal, it would be a return to the sense of the state and of the public good. You don't share everybody's opinion on this.*

PB: Whose opinion is everybody's opinion? The opinion of people who write in the newspapers, intellectuals who advocate the "minimal state" and who are rather too quick to bury the notion of the public and the public's interest in the public interest . . . We see there a typical example of the effect of shared belief which removes from discussion ideas which are perfectly worth discussing. One would need to analyze the work of the "new intellectuals," which has created a climate favorable to the withdrawal of the state and, more broadly, to submission to the values of the economy. I'm thinking of what has been called the "return of individualism," a kind of self-fulfilling prophecy which tends to destroy the philosophical foundations of the welfare state and in particular the notion of collective responsibility (toward industrial accidents, sickness or poverty) which has been a fundamental achievement of social (and sociological) thought. The return to the individual is also what makes it possible to "blame the victim," who is entirely responsible for his or her own misfortune, and to preach the gospel of self-help, all of this being justified by the endlessly repeated need to reduce costs for companies.

The reaction of retrospective panic provoked by the crisis of 1968, a symbolic revolution which alarmed all the small holders of cultural capital (subsequently reinforced by the unforeseen collapse of the Soviet-style regimes), created conditions favorable to a cultural restoration, the outcome of which has been that "Sciences-Po thought"[12] has replaced the "thought of Chairman Mao." The intellectual world is now the site of a struggle aimed at producing and imposing "new intellectuals," and therefore a new definition of the intellectual and the intellectual's political role, a new definition of philosophy and the philosopher, henceforward engaged in the vague debates of a political philosophy without technical content, a social science reduced to journalistic commentary for election nights, and uncritical glossing of unscientific opinion polls. Plato had a wonderful word for all these people: *doxosophers*. These "technicians of opinion who think themselves wise" (I'm translating the triple meaning of the word) pose the problems of politics in the very same terms in which they are posed by businessmen, politicians, and political journalists (in other words the very people who can afford to commission surveys . . .).

Q: *You have just mentioned Plato. Is the attitude of the sociologist close to that of the philosopher?*

PB: The sociologist is opposed to the doxosopher, like the philosopher, in that she questions the things that are self-evident, in particular those that present themselves in the form of questions, her own as much as other people's. This profoundly shocks the doxosopher, who sees a political bias in the refusal to grant the profoundly political submission implied in the unconscious acceptance of *commonplaces*, in Aristotle's sense—notions or theses *with* which people argue, but *over* which they do not argue.

Q: *Don't you tend in a sense to put the sociologist in the place of a philosopher-king?*

PB: What I defend above all is the possibility and the necessity of the critical intellectual, who is firstly critical of the intellectual *doxa* secreted by the doxosophers. There is no genuine democracy without genuine opposing critical powers. The intellectual is one of those, of the first magnitude. That is why I think that the work of demolishing the critical intellectual, living or dead—Marx, Nietzsche, Sartre, Foucault, and some others who are grouped together under the label Pensée 68[13]—is as dangerous as the demolition of the public interest and that it is part of the same process of restoration.

Of course I would prefer it if intellectuals had all, and always, lived up to the immense historical responsibility they bear and if they had always invested in their actions not only their moral authority but also their intellectual competence—like, to cite just one example, Pierre Vidal-Naquet, who has engaged all his mastery of historical method in a critique of the abuses of history.[14] Having said that, in the words of Karl Kraus, "between two evils, I refuse to choose the lesser." While I have little indulgence for "irresponsible" intellectuals, I have even less respect for the "intellectuals" of the political-administrative establishment, polymorphous polygraphs who polish their annual essays between two meetings of boards of directors, three publishers' parties, and miscellaneous television appearances.

Q: *So what role would you want to see for intellectuals, especially in the construction of Europe?*

PB: I would like writers, artists, philosophers, and scientists to be able to make their voice heard directly in all the areas of public life in which they are competent. I think that everyone would have a lot to gain if the logic of intellectual life, that of argument and refutation, were extended to public life. At present, it is often the logic of political life, that of denunciation and slander, "sloganization" and falsification of the adversary's thought, which extends into intellectual life. It would be a good thing if the "creators" could fulfill their function of public service and sometimes of public salvation.

Moving to the level of Europe simply means rising to a higher degree of universalization, reaching a new stage on the road to a universal state, which, even in intellectual life, is far from having been achieved. We will certainly not have gained much if eurocentrism is substituted for the wounded nationalisms of the old imperial nations. Now that the great utopias of the nineteenth century have revealed all their perversion, it is urgent to create the conditions for a collective effort to reconstruct a universe of realist ideals, capable of mobilizing people's will without mystifying their consciousness.

Paris, December 1991

SOLLERS *TEL QUEL*

This text was published in *Libération*, 27 January 1995, following the publication of an article by Philippe Sollers, entitled "Balladur tel quel," in *L'Express*, 12 January 1995.

Sollers *tel quel*, Sollers as such, at last . . . [15] There is a curious Spinozan pleasure of truth revealing itself, necessity being accomplished, in the confession of a title: "Balladur tel quel," the concentrate, with high symbolic density, almost too sublime to be true, of a whole trajectory: from *Tel Quel* to Balladur,[16] from the fake avant-garde of literature (and politics) to the authentic political rearguard.

Nothing very remarkable about that, some will say—those who know, and have long known, that what Philippe Sollers has thrown at the feet of the presidential candidate, in a gesture unprecedented since the time of Napoleon III, is not literature, still less the avant-garde, but the imitation of literature, and of the avant-garde. But the counterfeit is calculated to take in the audience for whom he intends it, all those the cynical courtier wants to flatter, the Balladurians and the Balladurophile *énarques*,[17] with enough culture from Sciences-Po for dissertations in two points and embassy dinners; and also all the masters of pretense who have clustered at one time or another around *Tel Quel*—the pretense of being a writer, or a philosopher, or a linguist, or all of those at once, without being any of them or knowing anything about all that; when one "knows the tune" of culture but not the words, when one only knows how to *mimic* the gestures of the great writer, and even, for a while, make terror reign in the world of letters. Thus, in so far as this unscrupulous Tartuffe of the religion of art succeeds in his imposture, he mocks, humiliates, and degrades the whole heritage of two centuries of struggle for autonomy of the literary microcosm by casting it at the feet of the culturally and politically[18] most abject power; and with himself he prostitutes all the often heroic authors—Voltaire, Proust, or Joyce—with whom he claims allegiance in his role as literary correspondent[19] for semiofficial magazines and journals. The cult of transgression without risk which reduces libertinism to its erotic dimension leads him to make cynicism one of the Fine Arts. Turning the postmodern principle "anything goes" into a rule of life, and claiming the right to say anything and its opposite, simultaneously or successively, he is able to have his cake and eat it—to criticize the society of the spectacle and to play the media personality,[20] to glorify Sade and revere Pope John Paul II, to make revolutionary pronouncements and intervene in defense of traditional spelling, to deify the writer and to murder literature (I am thinking of his novel *Femmes*).

This man who presents and sees himself as an incarnation of freedom has always floated at the whim of the forces of the field. Preceded and authorized by all the political slippages of the era of Mitterrand, who may have been to politics, and more precisely to socialism, what Sollers has been to literature, and more precisely to the avant-garde, he has been carried along by all the political and literary illusions and disillusions of the age. And his trajectory, which appears to him as an *exception*,[21] is in fact statistically modal, that is to say banal, and as such is exemplary of the career of the writer without qualities of a period of political and literary *restoration*: he is the ideal-typical incarnation of the individual and collective history of a whole generation of writers of ambition, of all those who, having moved, in less than thirty years, from Maoist or Trotskyist terrorism to positions of power in banks, insurance companies, politics or journalism, will readily grant him their indulgence.

His originality—for there is one—is that he has made himself the theorist of the virtues of recantation and betrayal, and so, in a prodigious self-justificatory reversal, has managed to define all those who refuse to recognize themselves in the new, liberated, "been there, done that" style as dogmatic, archaic, even terrorist. His countless public interventions are so many exaltations of inconsistency, or, more exactly, of *double inconsistency*—calculated to reinforce the bourgeois vision of artistic revolt—the one which, by a double U-turn, a double half-revolution, leads back to the point of departure, the fluttering sycophancies of the young provincial bourgeois, for whom Mauriac and Aragon wrote prefaces.

Paris, January 1995

THE STATUS OF FOREIGNERS:
A SHIBBOLETH

This text, published in *Libération*, 3 May 1995, signed by Jean-Pierre Alaux and myself, presents the findings of the survey which the GE-PEF carried out in March 1995, in which eight candidates for the presidential election were invited to "discuss their proposals regarding the situation of foreigners in France," a subject practically absent from the election campaign.

The question of the status that France gives to foreigners is not a "detail." It is a false problem which has regrettably come to the forefront as a terribly ill-formulated central question in the political battle.

The Groupe d'Examen des Programmes Électoraux sur les Étrangers en France (GEPEF), convinced that it was essential to force the constitutional candidates[22] to make their views clear on this issue, has carried out an experiment whose findings deserve to be made known. With the exception of Robert Hue,[23] and of Dominique Voynet,[24] who has made it one of the central themes of her campaign, with the abrogation of the Pasqua laws,[25] the regularization of the status of persons not subject to expulsion and the concern to protect the rights of minorities, the candidates side-stepped the attempt to ask them a set of questions. Edouard Balladur sent a letter setting out generalities unrelated to our twenty-six questions. Jacques Chirac did not respond to our request for an interview. Lionel Jospin mandated Martine Aubry and Jean-Christophe Cambadélis to answer for him, but they were as uninformed as they were uninformative about the positions of their favorite.

You don't need a degree in political science to discover in their silences and in their discourse that they do not have much to set against the xenophobic discourse which, for some years now, has been working to generate hatred out of the misfortunes of society—unemployment, delinquency, drug abuse, etc. Perhaps for lack of convictions, perhaps for fear of losing votes by expressing them, they have ended up no longer talking about this false problem, which is always present and always absent, except in conventional stereotypes and more or less shame-faced innuendos, with their references for example to "law and order," the need to "reduce entries to the lowest possible level" or to clamp down on "clandestine immigration" (with occasional references, to give a progressive tinge, to "the role of traffickers and employers" who exploit it).

All these vote-catching calculations, only encouraged by the logic of a political and media universe fascinated by opinion polls, are based on a series of presuppositions which are without foundation—or with no other foundation in any case than the most primitive logic of magical participation, contamination by contact and verbal association. To take one of countless examples: how can one speak of "immigrants" to refer to people who have not "emigrated" from anywhere and who are moreover described as "second-generation"? Similarly, one of the major functions of the adjective "clandestine" which fastidious souls concerned for their progressive image link with the term "immigrants" is surely to create a verbal and mental identification between the undetected crossing of frontiers by people and the necessarily fraudulent and therefore clandestine smuggling of objects that are forbidden (on both sides of the frontier) such as drugs or weapons. This is a criminal confusion which causes the people concerned to be thought of as criminals.

These are beliefs which politicians end up believing to be universally shared by their electors. Their vote-catching demagogy is based on the assumption that "public opinion" is hostile to "immigration," to foreigners, to any kind of opening of the frontiers. The verdicts of the "pollsters"—the modern-day astrologers—and the advice of the spin-doctors who make up for their lack of competence and conviction, urge them to strive to "win votes from Le Pen." But, to limit ourselves to just one argument, though a fairly strong one, the very score which Le Pen now obtains, after two years of the Pasqua laws and of language and measures directed towards law and order, suggests that the more the rights of foreigners are reduced, the bigger the electorate of the Front

National grows (this is obviously something of a simplification, but no more so than the idea often put forward that any measure aimed at improving the legal status of foreigners on French territory would have the effect of increasing Le Pen's vote). What is certain, in any case, is that before imputing the electoral score of the Front National solely to xenophobia, one should consider some other factors, such as the corruption scandals that have besmirched the mediopolitical world.

When all that has been said, one still needs to rethink the question of the status of the foreigner in modern democracies, in other words of the frontiers which can legitimately be imposed on the movement of persons in worlds which, like our own, derive so much advantage from the circulation of persons and goods. One should at least, in the short term, if only in the logic of enlightened self-interest, evaluate the costs for the country of the law-and-order policy associated with the name of Mr. Pasqua—the costs resulting from discrimination in and through police checks, which can only tend to create or reinforce "social fracture," and from the increasingly widespread violation of fundamental rights, costs for the prestige of France and its particular tradition as defender of human rights, etc.

The question of the status accorded to foreigners is indeed the decisive criterion, the shibboleth[26] enabling one to judge the capacity of the candidates to take a position, in all their choices, against the narrow-minded, regressive, security-minded, protectionist, conservative, xenophobic France, and in favor of the open, progressive, internationalist, universalist France. That is why the choice of the elector-citizens ought to fall on the candidate who most clearly makes a commitment to perform the most radical and most total break with the present policy of France as regards the "reception" of foreigners. It ought to be Lionel Jospin . . . But will he want it?

Paris, May 1995

ABUSE OF POWER BY THE
ADVOCATES OF REASON

Intervention at the public discussion organized by the International Parliament of Writers at the Frankfurt Book Fair, 15 October 1995.

[. . .] From deep inside the Islamic countries there comes a very profound question with regard to the false universalism of the West, or what I call the imperialism of the universal.[27] France has been the supreme incarnation of this imperialism, which in this very country has given rise to a national populism, associated for me with the name of Herder. If it is true that one form of universalism is no more than a nationalism which invokes the universal (human rights, etc.) in order to impose itself, then it becomes less easy to write off all fundamentalist reaction against it as reactionary. Scientific rationalism—the rationalism of the mathematical models which inspire the policy of the IMF or the World Bank, that of the law firms, great juridical multinationals which impose the traditions of American law on the whole planet, that of rational-action theories, etc.—is both the expression and the justification of a Western arrogance, which leads people to act as if they had the monopoly of reason and could set themselves up as world policemen, in other words as self-appointed holders of the monopoly of legitimate violence, capable of applying the force of arms in the service of universal justice. Terrorist violence, through the irrationalism of the despair which is almost always at its root, refers back to the inert violence of the powers which invoke reason. Economic coercion is often dressed up in juridical reasons. Imperialism drapes itself in the legitimacy of international bodies. And, through the very hypocrisy of the rationalizations intended to mask its double standards, it tends to provoke or justify, among the Arab, South American, or African peoples, a very profound revolt against the reason which cannot be separated from the abuses of power which are armed or justified by reason (economic, scientific, or any other). These "irrationalisms" are partly the product of our rationalism, imperialist, invasive, and conquering or mediocre, narrow, defensive, regressive, and repressive, depending on the place and time. One is still defending reason when one fights those who mask their abuses of power under the appearances of reason or who use the weapons of reason to consolidate or justify an arbitrary empire.

Frankfurt, October 1995

THE TRAIN DRIVER'S REMARK

Text published in *Alternatives Algériennes*, November 1995.

Questioned after the explosion in the second coach of the express metro train he was driving on Tuesday, 17 October, the driver, who according to witnesses had led the evacuation of the passengers with exemplary calm, warned against the temptation to take revenge on the Algerian community. They are, he said simply, "people like us."

This extraordinary remark, a "healthy truth of the people," as Pascal would have said, made a sudden break with the utterances of all the ordinary demagogues who, unconsciously or calculatedly, align themselves with the xenophobia or racism they attribute to the people, while helping to produce them; or who use the supposed expectations of those they sometimes call "simple folk" as an excuse for offering them, as "good enough for them," the simplistic thoughts they attribute to them; or who appeal to the sanctions of the market (and the advertisers), incarnated in audience ratings or opinion polls and cynically identified with the democratic verdict of the largest number, in order to impose their own vulgarity and abject servility on everyone.

This exceptional remark provided the proof that it is possible to resist the violence that is exerted daily, with a clear conscience, on television, on the radio, and in the newspapers, through verbal reflexes, stereotyped images, and conventional words, and the effect of habituation that it produces, imperceptibly raising, throughout the whole population, the threshold of tolerance of racist insults and contempt, reducing critical defences against prelogical thought and verbal confusion (between Islam and Islamicism, between Muslim and Islamicist, or between Islamicist and terrorist, for example), insidiously reinforcing all the habits of thought and behavior inherited from more than a century of colonialism and colonial struggles. Only a detailed analysis of the film of one of the 1,850,000 "identity checks" recently carried out by the police to the great satisfaction of our minister of the interior[28] would give some idea of the multitude of subtle humiliations (condescending use of *tu*, body searches in public, etc.) or flagrant injustices and illegalities (assault, forced entry, violation of privacy) inflicted on a significant proportion of the citizens or guests of this country, once renowned for its openness to foreigners; and also give an idea of the indignation, revolt, or rage that such behavior can arouse. Ministerial pronouncements, visibly designed to reassure, or to satisfy the craving for "law and order," would at once become less reassuring.

That simple remark contained an exhortation by example to combat resolutely all those who, in their desire always to leap to the simplest answer, caricature an ambiguous historical reality in order to reduce it to the reassuring dichotomies of Manichean thought which television, always inclined to confuse a rational dialogue with a wrestling match, has set up as a model. It is infinitely easier to take up a position for or against an idea, a value, a person, an institution, or a situation than to analyze what it truly is, in all its complexity. People are all the quicker to *take sides* on what journalists call a "problem of society"—the question of the Muslim veil,[29] for example—the more incapable they are of analyzing and understanding its meaning, which is often quite contrary to ethnocentric intuition.

Historical realities are always enigmatic and, while appearing to be self-evident, are difficult to decipher; and there is perhaps none which presents these characteristics in a higher degree than Algerian reality. That is why it represents an extraordinary challenge, both for knowledge and for action. This truth-test of all analyses is also and above all a touchstone of all commitments.

In this case more than ever, rigorous analysis of situations and institutions is undoubtedly the best antidote against partial views and against all forms of Manicheism—often associated with the pharisaic indulgences of "communitarian" thought—which, through the representations they engender and the words in which they are expressed, are often fraught with deadly consequences.

Paris, November 1995

AGAINST THE DESTRUCTION
OF A CIVILIZATION

Remarks at the Gare de Lyon, Paris, during the strikes of December 1995. Pierre Bourdieu spoke, in the name of the intellectuals supporting the strikers, alongside representatives of trade unions (in particular, SUD) and associations (AC!, Droits Devant, etc.) with whom he had been associated in previous campaigns, at a mass meeting at the station.

I have come here to express our support to those who have been fighting for the last three weeks against the destruction of a *civilization*, associated with the existence of public service, the civilization of republican equality of rights, rights to education, to health, culture, research, art, and, above all, work.

I have come here to say that we understand this deep-rooted movement, in other words both the despair and the hopes that are expressed in it, and which we too feel, to say that we do not understand (or that we understand only too well) those who do not understand it, like the philosopher[30] who, in the *Journal du Dimanche* of 10 December, discovers with stupefaction the "gulf between the rational understanding of the world," incarnated, according to him, by Prime Minister Juppé—he spells it out for us—and "the deep wishes of the population."

This opposition between the long-term view of the enlightened "elite" and the short-term impulses of the populace or its representatives is typical of reactionary thinking at all times and in all countries; but it now takes a new form, with the state nobility, which derives its conviction of its legitimacy from academic qualifications and from the authority of science, especially economics. For these new governors by divine right, not only reason and modernity but also the movement of change are on the side of the governors—ministers, employers, or "experts"; unreason and archaism, inertia and conservatism are on the side of the people, the trade unions and critical intellectuals.

This technocratic certainty is what Juppé expresses when he declares: "I want France to be a serious country and a happy country." This can be translated as: "I want serious people, in other words the elites, the *énarques*, those who know where the people's happiness lies, to be able to make the people happy, even despite the people, against their will. For the common people, blinded by their desires, as the philosopher said, do not understand their own happiness—and in particular their good fortune in being governed by men who, like Mr. Juppé, understand their happiness better than they do." That is how the technocrats think and that is their notion of democracy. And, not surprisingly, they do not understand it when the people, in whose name they claim to govern, have the supreme ingratitude to go out into the streets and demonstrate against them.

That state nobility, which preaches the withering away of the state and the undivided reign of the market and the consumer, the commercial substitute for the citizen, has kidnapped the state: it has made the public good a private good, has made the "public thing," *res publica*, the Republic, its own thing. What is at stake now is winning back democracy from technocracy. We must put an end to the reign of "experts" in the style of the World Bank or the IMF, who impose without discussion the verdicts of the new Leviathan, the "financial markets," and who do not seek to negotiate but to "explain"; we must break with the new faith in the historical inevitability professed by the theorists of liberalism; we must invent new forms of collective political work capable of taking note of necessities, especially economic ones (that can be the task of the experts), but in order to fight them and, where possible, to neutralize them.

The present crisis is a historical opportunity, for France and no doubt also for all those, ever more numerous, in Europe and throughout the world, who reject this new choice: "liberalism or barbarism." The railway workers, postal workers, teachers, civil servants, students, and so many others, actively or passively engaged in the movement, have, through their demonstrations and declarations, through the countless rethinkings that they have provoked, which the media cannot put the lid on, raised quite fundamental problems, too important to be left to technocrats as self-satisfied as they are unsatisfactory. How do we restore for each of us an enlightened, reasonable definition of the future of the public services, of health, education, transport, and so on, in coordination with those who, in the other countries of Europe, are exposed to the same threats? How do we reinvent the republican school system, rejecting the progressive introduction of a two-track system, symbolized, in higher education, by the split between the faculties and the Grandes Écoles? The same question can be asked about health or transport. How do we struggle against the growing insecurity of employment, threatening all those who work in the public services and leading to all kinds of dependence and submission which are particularly pernicious in cultural activities such as radio, television, or journalism, because of the censorship they entail, or even in education?

In the work of reinventing the public services, intellectuals, writers, artists, scientists, and others have a decisive role to play. They can first help to break the monopoly of technocratic orthodoxy over the means of diffusion. But they can also commit themselves, in an organized and permanent way, and not only in the occasional encounters in a context of crisis, alongside those who are in a position to exert a real influence on the future of society—the associations and unions, in particular—and help to draw up rigorous analyses and inventive proposals about the major questions which the orthodoxy of the media and politics makes it impossible to raise. I am thinking in particular of the question of the unification of the world economy and the economic and social effects of the new international division of labor, or the question of the supposed iron laws of the financial markets in whose name so many political initiatives are sacrificed, the question of the function of education and culture in economies where information has become one of the most decisive productive forces, and so on.

This program may seem purely abstract and theoretical. But it is possible to challenge autocratic technocracy without falling into a populism which has too often been a trap for social movements, and which, once again, serves the interest of the technocrats.

What I wanted to express, in any case, perhaps clumsily—and I apologize to those I may have shocked or bored—is a real solidarity with those who are now fighting to change society. I think that the only effective way of fighting against national and international technocracy is by confronting it on its own preferred terrain, in particular that of economics, and putting forward, in place of the abstract and limited knowledge which it regards as enough, a knowledge more respectful of human beings and of the realities which confront them.

Paris, December 1995

THE MYTH OF "GLOBALIZATION" AND THE EUROPEAN WELFARE STATE

Address to the Greek trade union confederation (GSEE), in Athens, October 1996.

Everywhere we hear it said, all day long—and this is what gives the dominant discourse its strength—that there is nothing to put forward in opposition to the neoliberal view, that it has succeeded in presenting itself as self-evident, that there is no alternative. If it is taken for granted in this way, this is as a result of a whole labor of symbolic inculcation in which journalists and ordinary citizens participate passively and, above all, a certain number of intellectuals participate actively. Against this permanent, insidious imposition, which produces, through impregnation, a real belief, it seems to me that researchers have a role to play. First they can analyze the production and circulation of this discourse. There have been a growing number of studies, in Britain, the United States, and France, which describe very precisely the procedures whereby this worldview is produced, disseminated, and inculcated. Through a whole series of analyses of texts, the journals in which they were published and which have little by little imposed themselves as legitimate, the characteristics of their authors, the seminars in which they meet to produce them, etc., they have shown how, in Britain and France, constant work was done, involving intellectuals, journalists, and businessmen, to impose as self-evident a neoliberal view which, essentially, dresses up the most classic presuppositions of conservative thought of all times and all countries in economic rationalizations. I am thinking of a study of the role of the journal *Preuves*, which was financed by the CIA and had some noted French intellectuals on its editorial board, and which, for twenty or twenty-five years—it takes time for something false to become self-evident—tirelessly, and initially against the current, produced ideas which gradually became taken for granted.[31] The same thing happened in Britain, and Thatcherism was not invented by Mrs. Thatcher. The ground had been prepared over a long period by groups of intellectuals most of whom wrote columns in the leading newspapers.[32] A possible first contribution by researchers could be to make these analyses more generally available, in a form accessible to all.

The work of inculcation, which began a long time ago, continues now. And so we see articles appearing, as if by a miracle, just a few days apart, in all the French papers, with variations linked to the position of each paper in the spectrum of newspapers, commenting on the miraculous economic situation of the United States or Britain. This kind of symbolic drip-feed to which the press and television news contribute very strongly—to a large extent unconsciously, because most of the people who repeat these claims do so in good faith—produces very profound effects. And as a result, neoliberalism comes to be seen as an *inevitability*.

A whole set of presuppositions is being imposed as self-evident: it is taken for granted that maximum growth, and therefore productivity and competitiveness, are the ultimate and sole goal of human actions; or that economic forces cannot be resisted. Or again—a presupposition which is the basis of all the presuppositions of economics—a radical separation is made between the economic and the social, which is left to one side, abandoned to sociologists, as a kind of reject. Another important assumption is the language which invades us: we absorb it as soon as we open a newspaper, as soon as we turn on the radio, and it is largely made up of euphemisms. Unfortunately, I don't have any Greek examples to hand, but I think you would find them easily enough. For example, in France, instead of "the employers [*le patronat*]" they say "the vital forces of the nation [*les forces vives de la nation*]"; a company that fires its workers is "slimming," with a sporting metaphor (an energetic body has to be thin). To announce that a company is sacking 2,000 people, the commentator will refer to "Alcatel's bold social plan." Then there is a whole game with the connotations and associations of words like flexibility, *souplesse*, deregulation, which tends to imply that the neoliberal message is a universalist message of liberation.

Against this *doxa*, one has to try to defend oneself, I believe, by analyzing it and trying to understand the mechanisms through which it is produced and imposed. But that is not enough, although it is important, and there are a certain number of empirical observations that can be brought forward to counter it. In the case of France, the state has started to abandon a number of areas of social policy. The consequence is an enormous amount of suffering of all kinds, not only affecting people afflicted by deep poverty. It can been shown, for example, that the problems seen in the suburban estates of the cities stem from a neoliberal housing policy, implemented in the 1970s (known as "aid to the person"). It led to a social segregation, with on the one hand the subproletariat, made up to a large extent of immigrants, remaining on the large estates, and on the other hand the secure workers with a regular wage and the petite bourgeoisie, leaving to live in small detached houses which they bought with crippling loans. This social separation was brought about by a political measure.[33]

In the United States, the state is splitting into two, with on the one hand a state which provides social guarantees, but only for the privileged, who are sufficiently well-off to provide themselves with insurance, with guarantees, and a repressive, policing state, for the populace. In California, one of the richest states of the United States—once presented by some French sociologists[34] as the paradise of all liberations—and also one of the most conservative, and which has perhaps the most prestigious university in the world, since 1994 the prison budget has been greater than the budget of all the universities together. The blacks in the Chicago ghetto only know the state through the police officer, the judge, the prison warder, and the parole officer. We see there a kind of realization of the dream of the dominant class, a state which, as Loïc Wacquant has shown,[35] is increasingly reduced to its policing function.

What we see happening in America and beginning to emerge in Europe is a process of involution. When one studies the rise of the state in the societies in which it developed earliest, such as France and England, one first sees a concentration of physical force and a concentration of economic force—the two go together, you need money to make war, to police the country and so on, and you need a police force to collect money. Next comes a concentration of cultural capital, and then a concentration of authority. As it develops, this state acquires autonomy, becomes partially independent of the dominant social and economic forces. The state bureaucracy starts to be able to inflect the will of the dominant groups, to interpret them and sometimes to inspire policies.

The process of regression of the state shows that resistance to neoliberal doctrine and policy is that much greater in countries where the state traditions have been strongest. And that is explained by the fact that the state exists in two forms: in objective reality, in the form of a set of institutions such as rules, agencies, offices, etc., and also in people's minds. For example, within the French bureaucracy, when housing finance was being reformed, the welfare ministries fought against the financial ministries to defend the social housing policy. Those civil servants had an interest in defending their ministries and their positions; but they also believed in what they were doing, they were defending their convictions. The state, in every country, is to some extent the trace in reality of social conquests. For example, the Ministry of Labor is a social conquest that has been made a reality, even if, in some circumstances, it can also be an instrument of repression. And the state also exists in the minds of the workers in the form of subjective law ("it's my right," "they can't do that to me"), attachment to "established rights" [les acquis sociaux], etc. For example, one of the great differences between France and Britain is that the Thatcherized British discover that they did not resist as much as they might have, to a large extent because the labor contract is a common law contract and not, as in France, an agreement guaranteed by the state. And now, paradoxically, at the very time when the British model is being held up as an example, British workers look to the Continent and find it offers things that their own labor tradition did not, namely the idea of employment law.

The state is an ambiguous reality. It is not adequate to say that it is an instrument in the hands of the ruling class. The state is certainly not completely neutral, completely independent of the dominant

forces in society, but the older it is and the greater the social advances
it has incorporated, the more autonomous it is. It is a battleground (for
example, between the finance ministries and the spending ministries,
dealing with social problems). To resist the *involution of the state*, in
other words the regression to a penal state concerned with repression
and progressively abandoning its social functions of education, health,
welfare, and so on, the social movement can find support from those
responsible for social policies, who are in charge of organizing aid to
the long-term unemployed, and worried about the breakdown of social
cohesion, unemployment, etc., and opposed to the finance people who
only want to hear about the constraints of "globalization" and the place
of France in the world.

I've used the word "globalization." It is a myth in the strong sense
of the word, a powerful discourse, an *idée force*, an idea which has social force, which obtains belief. It is the main weapon in the battles
against the gains of the welfare state. European workers, we are told,
must compete with the least-favored workers of the rest of the world.
The workers of Europe are thus offered as a model countries which
have no minimum wage, where factory workers work twelve hours
a day for a wage which is between a quarter and a fifth of European
wages, where there are no trade unions, where there is child labor, and
so on. And it is in the name of this model that flexible working, another magic word of neoliberalism, is imposed, meaning night work,
weekend work, irregular working hours, things which have always
been part of the employers' dreams. In a general way, neoliberalism
is a very smart and very modern repackaging of the oldest ideas of the
oldest capitalists. (Magazines in the United States draw up a league
table of these macho bosses, ranked, along with their salary, according to the number of people they have had the courage to sack.) It is
characteristic of *conservative revolutions*, that in Germany in the 1930s,
those of Thatcher, Reagan, and others, that they present restorations
as revolutions. The present conservative revolution takes an unprecedented form: in contrast to earlier ones, it does not invoke an idealized
past, through exaltation of soil and blood, the archaic themes of the
old agrarian mythologies. This new kind of conservative revolution appeals to progress, reason, and science (economics in this case) to justify

the restoration and so tries to write off progressive thought and action as archaic. It sets up as the norm of all practices, and therefore as ideal rules, the real regularities of the economic world abandoned to its own logic, the so-called law of the market. It ratifies and glorifies the reign of what are called the financial markets, in other words the return to a kind of radical capitalism, with no other law than that of maximum profit, an unfettered capitalism without any disguise, but rationalized, pushed to the limit of its economic efficacy by the introduction of modern forms of domination, such as "business administration," and techniques of manipulation, such as market research and advertising.

If this conservative revolution can deceive people, this is because it seems to retain nothing of the old Black Forest pastoral of the conservative revolutionaries of the 1930s; it is dressed up in all the signs of modernity. After all, it comes from Chicago. Galileo said that the natural world is written in the language of mathematics. The neoliberal ideologues want us to believe that the economic and social world is structured by equations. It is by arming itself with mathematics (and power over the media) that neoliberalism has become the supreme form of the conservative sociodicy which started to appear some thirty years ago as "the end of ideology," or more recently, as "the end of history."

To fight against the myth of globalization, which has the function of justifying a restoration, a return to an unrestrained—but rationalized—and cynical capitalism, one has to return to the facts. If we look at the statistics, we see that the competition experienced by European workers is largely intra-European. According to my sources, 70 percent of the trade of European countries is with other European countries. The emphasis placed on the extra-European threat conceals the fact that the main danger comes from the internal competition of other European countries and is sometimes called "social dumping": European countries with less social welfare and lower wages can derive a competitive advantage from this, but in so doing they pull down the others, which are forced to abandon their welfare systems in order to resist. This implies that, in order to break out of this spiral, the workers of the advanced countries have an interest in combining with the workers in less developed countries to protect their social gains and to favor their generalization to all European workers. (This is not easy, because of the differences in national traditions, especially in the weight of the unions with respect to the state and in the means of financing welfare.)

But this is not all. There are also all the effects, visible to everyone, of neoliberal policies. For example, several British studies have shown that Thatcherite policies have resulted in enormous insecurity, a sense of distress, not only among manual workers but also in the middle classes. The same can be seen in the United States, where there is a great rise in the number of insecure, underpaid jobs (which artificially bring down official unemployment rates). The American middle classes, exposed to the threat of suddenly losing their jobs, are feeling a terrible insecurity (which shows that what is important in a job is not only the activity and income it provides, but also the sense of security it gives). In all countries, the proportion of workers with temporary status is growing relative to those with permanent jobs. Increased insecurity and "flexibility" lead to the loss of the modest advantages (often described as the "perks" of the "privileged") which might compensate for low wages, such as long-lasting employment, health insurance, and pension rights. Privatization equally leads to the loss of collective gains. For example, in the case of France, three-quarters of newly recruited workers are taken on on a temporary basis, and only a quarter of those three-quarters will become permanent employees. These new recruits naturally tend to be young people. That is why this insecurity mainly afflicts young people, in France—we observed this in our book *La Misère du monde*—and also in Britain, where the distress of young people has reached very high levels, with consequences such as delinquency and other very costly phenomena.

Added to this, at the present time, is the destruction of the economic and social bases of the most precious cultural gains of humanity. The autonomy of the worlds of cultural production with respect to the market, which had grown steadily through the battles and sacrifices of writers, artists, and scientists, is increasingly threatened. The reign of "commerce" and the "commercial" bears down more strongly every day on literature, particularly through the concentration of publishing, which is more and more subject to the constraints of immediate profit; on literary and artistic criticism, which has been handed over to the most opportunistic servants of the publishers—or of their accomplices, with favor traded for favor; and especially on the cinema (one wonders what will be left in ten years' time of European experimental cinema if nothing is done to provide avant-garde directors with the means of production and perhaps more importantly distribution). Not to mention the social sciences, which are condemned either to subordinate themselves to the directly self-interested sponsorship of corporate or state bureaucracies or wither under the censorship of power (relayed by the opportunists) or money.

While globalization is above all a justificatory myth, there is one case where it is quite real, that of the financial markets. Thanks to the removal of a number of legal restrictions and the development of electronic communications which lead to lower communication costs, we are moving toward a unified financial market—which does not mean a homogeneous market. It is dominated by certain economies, in other words the richest countries, and more especially by the country whose currency is used as an international reserve currency and which therefore enjoys a greater scope within these financial markets. The money market is a field in which the dominant players—in this case the United States—occupy a position such that they can largely define the rules of the game. This unification of the financial markets around a small number of countries holding the dominant position reduces the autonomy of the national financial markets. The French financiers, the Inspectors of Finances, who tell us that we must bow to necessity, forget to tell us that they make themselves the accomplices of that necessity and that, through them, it is the French national state which is abdicating.

In short, globalization is not homogenization; on the contrary, it is the extension of the hold of a small number of dominant nations over the whole set of national financial markets. There follows from this a partial redefinition of the international division of labor, with European workers suffering the consequences, seeing for example the transfer of capital and industries toward low-wage countries. This international capital market tends to reduce the autonomy of the national capital markets, and in particular to prevent nation-states from manipulating exchange rates and interest rates, which are increasingly determined by a power concentrated in the hands of a small number of countries. National authorities are subject to the risk of speculative assaults by agents wielding massive funds, who can provoke a devaluation, with left-wing governments naturally being particularly threatened because they arouse the suspicion of the financial markets (a right-wing government which acts out of line with the ideals of the IMF is in less danger than a left-wing government even if the latter's policy matches the ideals of the IMF). It is the structure of the worldwide field which exerts a structural constraint, and this is what gives the mechanisms an air of inevitability. The policy of a particular state is largely determined by its position in the structure of the distribution of finance capital (which defines the structure of the world economic field).

Faced with these mechanisms, what can one do? The first thing is to reflect on the implicit limits which economic theory accepts. Economic theory, when it assesses the costs of a policy, does not take account of what are called social costs. For example, a housing policy, the one chosen by Giscard d'Estaing when he was finance minister in 1970, implied long-term social costs which do not appear as such: twenty years later, who, apart from sociologists, remembers that measure? Who would link a riot in a suburb of Lyon to a political decision of 1970? Crimes go unpunished because people forget. All the critical forces in society need to insist on the inclusion of the social costs of economic decisions in economic calculations. What will this or that policy cost in the long term in lost jobs, suffering, sickness, suicide, alcoholism, drug addiction, domestic violence, etc., all things which cost a great deal, in money, but also in misery? I think that, even if it may appear very cynical, we need to turn its own weapons against the dominant economy, and point out that, in the logic of enlightened self-interest, a strictly economic policy is not necessarily economical—in terms of the insecurity of persons and property, the consequent policing costs, etc. More precisely, there is a need to radically question the economic view which individualizes everything—production as much as justice or health, costs as well as profits—and which forgets that efficiency, which it defines in narrow, abstract terms, tacitly identifying it with financial profitability, clearly depends on the outcomes by which it is measured, financial profitability for shareholders and investors, as at present, or satisfaction of customers and users, and, more generally, satisfaction and well-being of producers, consumers, and, ultimately, the largest possible number. Against this narrow, short-term economics, we need to put forward an *economics of happiness*, which would take note of all the profits, individual and collective, material and symbolic, associated with activity (such as security), and also all the material and symbolic costs associated with inactivity or precarious employment (for example, consumption of medicines: France holds the world record for use of tranquilizers). You cannot cheat with the *law of the conservation of violence:* all violence is paid for, and, for example, the structural violence exerted by the financial markets, in the form of layoffs, loss of security, etc., is matched sooner or later in the form of suicides, crime and delinquency, drug addiction, alcoholism, a whole host of minor and major everyday acts of violence.

At the present time, the critical efforts of intellectuals, trade unions, or associations should be applied as a matter of priority against the withering away of the state. The national states are undermined from outside by these financial forces, and they are undermined from inside by those who act as the accomplices of these financial forces, in other words, the financiers, bankers, and finance ministry officials. I think that the dominated groups in society have an interest in defending the state, particularly in its social aspect. This defense of the state is not inspired by nationalism. While one can fight against the national state, one has to defend the "universal" functions it fulfils, which can be fulfilled as well, or better, by a supranational state. If we do not want it to be the Bundesbank, which, through interest rates, governs the financial policies of the various states, should we not fight for the creation of a supranational state, relatively autonomous with respect to international political forces and national political forces and capable of developing the social dimension of the European institutions? For example, measures aimed at reducing the working week would take on their full meaning only if they were taken by a European body and were applicable to all the European nations.

Historically, the state has been a force for rationalization, but one which has been put at the service of the dominant forces. To prevent this being the case, it is not sufficient to denounce the technocrats of Brussels. We need to develop a new internationalism, at least at the regional level of Europe, which could offer an alternative to the regression into nationalism which, as a result of the crisis, threatens all the European countries to some degree. This would imply constructing institutions that are capable of standing up to these forces of the financial market, and introducing—the Germans have a wonderful word for this—a *Regressionsverbot*, a ban on backward movement with respect to social gains at the European level. To achieve this, it is absolutely essential that the trade unions operate at this European level, because that is where the forces they are fighting against are in action. It is therefore necessary to try to create the organizational bases for a genuine critical internationalism capable of really combating neoliberalism.

Final point: why are the intellectuals so ambiguous in all this? I will not try to enumerate—it would be too long and too cruel—all the forms of surrender or, worse, collaboration. I will simply allude to the debates of the so-called modern or postmodern philosophers, who, when they are not simply content to let things take their course, occupied as they are in their scholastic games, wrap themselves up in a verbal defense of reason and rational dialogue, or, worse, offer a supposedly postmodern but in fact "radical chic" version of the ideology of the end of ideology, with the condemnation of the great explanatory narratives or the nihilist denunciation of science.

In fact the strength of the neoliberal ideology is that it is based on a kind of social neo-Darwinism: it is "the brightest and the best," as they say at Harvard, who come out on top (Becker, winner of the Nobel Prize for economics, developed the idea that Darwinism is the basis of the aptitude for rational calculation which he ascribes to economic agents). Behind the globalist vision of the International of the dominant groups, there is a philosophy of competence according to which it is the most competent who govern and who have jobs, which implies that those who do not have jobs are not competent. There are the "winners" and the "losers," there is the aristocracy, those I call the state nobility, in other words those people who have all the properties of a

nobility in the medieval sense of the word and who owe their authority to education, or, as they see it, to intelligence, seen as a gift from
Heaven, whereas we know that in reality it is distributed by society
and that inequalities in intelligence are social inequalities. The ideology of competence serves very well to justify an opposition which is
rather like that between masters and slaves. On the one hand there are
full citizens who have very rare and overpaid capacities and activities,
who are able to choose their employer (whereas the others are at best
chosen by their employer), who are able to obtain very high incomes
on the international labor market, who are, both men and women,
overworked (I recently read an excellent British study of these super-
charged executive couples who perpetually jet around the world and
earn more than they could dream of spending in four lifetimes . . .),
and then, on the other side, there is a great mass of people condemned
to borderline jobs or unemployment.

Max Weber said that dominant groups always need a "theodicy of
their own privilege," or more precisely, a sociodicy, in other words a
theoretical justification of the fact that they are privileged. Competence
is nowadays at the heart of that sociodicy, which is accepted, naturally,
by the dominant—it is in their interest—but also by the others.[36] In
the suffering of those excluded from work, in the wretchedness of the
long-term unemployed, there is something more than there was in the
past. The Anglo-American ideology, always somewhat sanctimonious,
distinguished the "underserving poor," who had brought it upon
themselves, from the "deserving poor," who were judged worthy of
charity. Alongside or in place of this ethical justification there is now
an intellectual justification. The poor are not just immoral, alcoholic,
and degenerate, they are stupid, they lack intelligence. A large part of
social suffering stems from the poverty of people's relationship to the
educational system, which not only shapes social destinies but also the
image they have of their destiny (which undoubtedly helps to explain
what is called the passivity of the dominated, the difficulty in mobilizing them etc.). Plato had a view of the social world which resembles
that of our technocrats, with the philosophers, the guardians, and then
the people. This philosophy is inscribed, in implicit form, in the educational system. It is very powerful, and very deeply internalized. Why

have we moved from the committed intellectual to the "uncommitted" intellectual? Partly because intellectuals are holders of cultural capital and, even if they are the dominated among the dominant, they still belong among the dominant. That is one of the foundations of their ambivalence, of their lack of commitment in struggles. They obscurely share this ideology of competence. When they revolt, it is still because, as in Germany in 1933, they think they are not receiving their due in relation to their competence, guaranteed by their qualifications.

Athens, October 1996

THE THOUGHTS OF CHAIRMAN TIETMEYER

Address given at the Rencontres Culturelles Franco-Allemandes on "Social integration as a cultural problem," University of Freiburg, October 1996.

I don't want to be here to put the cultural icing on the cake. The breaking of the bonds of social integration which culture is asked to reconstruct is the direct consequence of a policy, an economic policy. And sociologists are often asked to repair economists' breakages. So, instead of merely offering what, in hospitals, is called palliative treatment, I would like to raise the question of the doctors' contribution to the disease. For it might be that to a large extent the social "diseases" that we deplore are produced by the often brutal medicine given to those who are supposed to be being cured.

To do so, having read in the airplane which took me from Athens to Zurich for an interview with the president of the Bundesbank, who is presented as "the high priest of the deutschmark," neither more nor less, and since I am in a center renowned for its traditions of literary exegesis, I would like to perform a kind of hermeneutic analysis of a text which you will find in full in *Le Monde* of 17 October 1996.

This is what the "high priest of the deutschmark" says: "The crucial issue today is to create the conditions favorable to lasting growth, and the confidence of investors. It is therefore necessary to restrain public spending." In other words—he is more explicit in the following sentences—to bury as quickly as possible the welfare state and its expensive social and cultural policies, so as to reassure investors, who would prefer to take charge of their own cultural investments. I am sure that they all enjoy Romantic music and expressionist paintings and, while I know nothing of the tastes of the president of the Bundesbank, I can well believe that, like the governor of the Banque de France, Mr. Trichet, he reads poetry and sponsors the arts. He goes on: "It is therefore necessary to restrain public spending and reduce taxation to a level that is acceptable in the long term." By which he means: reduce the taxation of investors to a level that is acceptable in the long term to these same investors, lest they be discouraged and driven to take their investments elsewhere. Next: "reform the social welfare system." In other words, bury the welfare state and its policies of social protection, which undermine the confidence of investors and provoke their legitimate distrust, because they are convinced that their economic entitlements—we speak of social entitlements, we could equally speak of economic entitlements—I mean their capital, are not compatible with the social entitlements of the workers, and that these economic entitlements must obviously be safeguarded at all costs, even if this means destroying the meager economic and social benefits of the great majority of the citizens of the Europe to come, those who were frequently described in December 1995 as "feather-bedded" and "privileged."

Mr. Tietmeyer is convinced that the social entitlements of the investors, I mean their economic entitlements, would not survive the perpetuation of a social welfare system. And so this system has to be reformed, and *quickly*, because the economic entitlements of the investors cannot wait any longer. And to prove to you that I am not exaggerating, I read further from the words of Tietmeyer, a high-flying thinker who takes his place in the great lineage of German idealist philosophy: "It is therefore necessary to restrain public spending and reduce taxation to a level that is acceptable in the long term, to reform the social welfare system, dismantle the rigidities in the labor market, since a new phase of growth will only be attained if we make an effort"—the "we make" is magnificent—"toward flexibility in the labor market." There you are: the big words are out of the bag, and Mr. Tietmeyer, in the great tradition of German idealism, gives us a splendid example of the euphemistic rhetoric which prevails in the money markets today. Euphemism is essential in order to maintain the long-term confidence of investors—which, it will have become clear, is the alpha and omega of the whole economic system, the foundation and ultimate goal, the *telos*, of the Europe of the future—without provoking distrust or despair among the workers, who in spite of everything also have to be taken into account if one wants to have the new phase of growth the prospect of which is dangled before them, in order to obtain the required effort from them. For it is indeed from them that this effort is expected, even if Mr. Tietmeyer, who, it can be seen, is a past master of the art of euphemism, does indeed say: "dismantle the rigidities in the labor market, since a new phase of growth will only be attained if *we* make an effort toward flexibility in the labor market." This is splendid rhetorical work and may be translated thus: "Heave ho, workers! All together now, let's make the effort of flexibility that *you* must provide!"

Instead of calmly proceeding to ask a question about the external parity of the euro, its relations with the dollar and the yen, the *Le Monde* journalist, who is equally concerned not to discourage the investors, who read his paper and place large advertisements in it, might have asked Mr. Tietmeyer what he understood by the key words in the language of the investors: "rigidity in the labor market" and "flexibility in the labor market." The workers, if they were to read a paper as indisputably serious as *Le Monde*, would immediately understand what needs to be understood: night work, weekend work, irregular shifts, increased pressure, stress, etc. It can be seen that "in the labor market" functions as a kind of Homeric epithet that can be attached to a certain number of words, and one might be tempted, in order to measure the flexibility of Mr. Tietmeyer's language, to talk for example about flexibility or rigidity in the financial markets. The strangeness of this usage in Mr. Tietmeyer's rigid discourage entitles us to suppose that there would be no question, in his mind, of "dismantling rigidities in the financial markets," or "making an effort toward flexibility on the financial markets." This leads us to think that, contrary to what is suggested by the "we" in Mr. Tietmeyer's "if we make an effort," the workers alone are expected to make this effort and that they are the target of the threat, close to blackmail, contained in the sentence: "since a new phase of growth will only be attained if we make an effort toward flexibility in the labor market." To spell it out: abandon *your* benefits today, so as not to destroy the confidence of the investors, for the sake of the growth that that will bring *us* tomorrow. This logic is well known to the workers concerned, who, to sum up the policy of "participation" offered to them by Gaullism in times gone by, would say "You give me your watch and I'll give you the time of day."

After that commentary, I reread one last time the words of Mr. Tietmeyer: "The crucial issue today is to create the conditions favorable to lasting growth, and the confidence of investors. It is therefore necessary . . ."—note the "therefore"—"to restrain public spending, reduce taxation to a level that is acceptable in the long term, to reform the welfare system, dismantle the rigidities in the labor market, since a new phase of growth will only be attained if we make an effort toward flexibility in the labor market." If such an extraordinary text, so extraordinarily extraordinary, had every chance of passing unnoticed, living the brief life of the ephemeral writings in daily papers, this is because it was perfectly adjusted to the "horizon of expectation" of the great majority of the readers of daily papers that we are. And that invites the question as to who produced and disseminated such a widespread "horizon of expectation" (since the very least that needs to be added to reception theories, in which I am not a great believer, is the question of where that "horizon" comes from). That horizon is the product of social, or rather political, work. If Mr. Tietmeyer's words pass so readily, that is because they are common currency. They are everywhere, in every mouth, they circulate like legal tender, people accept them without hesitation, just as they would with currency, a stable, strong currency of course, as stable and worthy of confidence, belief, credit, as the deutschmark: "lasting growth," "investor confidence," "public spending," "welfare system," "rigidity," "labor market," "flexibility," to which one should add "globalization" (I learned from another newspaper I read in the airplane, showing how widespread the notion has become, that French chefs identify "globalization" as a threat to the national cuisine . . .), "deregulation," "rate cuts"—without even saying which rates—"competitiveness," "productivity," etc.

This economic-sounding discourse would not be able to circulate beyond the circle of its promoters without the collaboration of a host of people—politicians, journalists, and ordinary citizens with a tincture of economic culture sufficient to participate in the generalized circulation of the debased words of an economic vulgate. The questions of the journalist are one indication of the effect produced by media churning. He is so attuned to Mr. Tietmeyer's expectations, so impregnated in advance with the answers, that he could have produced them himself. It is through such passive complicity that a view of the world that is called neoliberal, but is in fact conservative, has progressively taken root, based on an atavistic faith in historical inevitability driven by the primacy of the productive forces unregulated except by the competing wills of the individual producers. And it is perhaps no accident that so many people of my generation have moved from a Marxist fatalism to a neoliberal fatalism: in both cases, economism forbids responsibility and mobilization by cancelling out politics and imposing a whole set of unquestioned ends—maximum growth, competitiveness, productivity. To let oneself be guided by the president of the Bundesbank is to accept such a philosophy. What is surprising is that this fatalistic doctrine gives itself the air of a message of liberation, through a whole series of lexical tricks around the idea of freedom, liberation, deregulation, etc., a whole series of euphemisms or ambiguous uses of words—"reform," for example—designed to present a restoration as a revolution, in a logic which is that of all conservative revolutions.

To conclude, let us come back to the key phrase in Mr. Tietmeyer's discourse, the *confidence of the markets*. It has the virtue of bringing out clearly the historic choice which all those in power have to confront: between the confidence of the markets and the confidence of the people, they must choose. But the policy which aims to keep the confidence of the markets is likely to lose the confidence of the people. According to a recent survey of people's attitude to politicians, two-thirds of those questioned say that politicians are incapable of listening to and taking into account what the French population thinks. This complaint is particularly common among the supporters of the Front National—whose irresistible rise is deplored by political commentators who never think to make the connection between FN and IMF. (This despair at politicians is particularly marked in the age group 18 to 34, among manual and clerical workers and also among supporters of the Communist Party and the Front National. It is relatively high among the supporters of all parties, and rises to 64 percent among supporters of the Socialist Party, a fact which is again not unconnected with the rise of the FN.) If the sacrosanct confidence of the markets is put in the context of the lack of confidence of the citizens, it perhaps becomes clearer where the root of the sickness is. Economics is, with a few exceptions, an abstract science based on the absolutely unjustifiable separation between the economic and the social which defines economism. This separation is the source of the failure of any policy that has no other end than to safeguard "economic order and stability," the new Absolute of which Mr. Tietmeyer has made himself the high priest, a failure to which the political blindness of some is leading us and of which we are all the victims.

Freiburg, October 1996

SOCIAL SCIENTISTS, ECONOMIC SCIENCE, AND THE SOCIAL MOVEMENT

Remarks at the inaugural meeting of the États Généraux du Mouvement Social, Paris, 23–24 November 1996.

The social movement of December 1995 was a movement unprecedented in its scale and above all in its objectives. And if it was seen as extremely important by a large section of the French population and also by many people abroad, this is above all because it introduced some quite new objectives into social struggles. In a rough and confused form it outlined a genuine project for a society, collectively affirmed and capable of being put forward against what is being imposed by the dominant politics, by the revolutionary conservatives who are now in power, both in government and in the media.

Asking myself what social science researchers could offer to an undertaking like the États Généraux, I am convinced of the need for their presence in uncovering the specifically cultural and ideological dimension of this conservative revolution. The movement of last December received strong public support, because it was seen as a defense of the social advances, not of one particular category–even if one category was at the forefront, because it was particularly under attack—but of a whole society, and even of a set of societies. These advances concern work, public education, public transport, everything which is public, and therefore the state, an institution which—contrary to what some people would have us believe—is not necessarily archaic and regressive.

It is no accident that this movement emerged in France; there are historical reasons for that. But what ought to strike observers is that it is continuing, being relayed, in France, in various, unexpected ways—the truck drivers' action: who would have expected it in that form?—and also in Europe: in Spain, right now; in Greece, a few years ago; in Germany, where the movement took inspiration from the French movement and has explicitly declared its affinities with it; in Korea—which is even more important, for symbolic and practical reasons. This kind of rotating struggle is, it seems to me, searching for its theoretical unity and above all its practical unity. The French movement can be seen as the vanguard of a worldwide struggle against neoliberalism and against the new conservative revolution, in which the symbolic dimension is extremely important. One of the weaknesses of all progressive movements lies in the fact that they have underestimated the importance of this dimension and have not always forged appropriate weapons to fight on this front. Social movements are several symbolic revolutions behind their opponents, who use media consultants, public relations consultants, and so on.

The conservative revolution calls itself neoliberal, thereby giving itself a scientific air, and the capacity to act as a theory. One of the theoretical and practical errors of many theories—starting with the Marxist theory—has been the failure to take account of the power of theory. We must no longer make that mistake. We are dealing with opponents who are armed with theories, and I think they need to be fought with intellectual and cultural weapons. In pursuing that struggle, because of the division of labor some are better armed than others, because it is their job. And some of them are ready to set to work. What can they offer? First of all, a certain authority. What name was given to the people who supported the government last December? Experts, although the whole lot of them together did not have the beginnings of the making of an economist. That authority effect has to be fought with an authority effect.

But that is not all. The force of social authority, which is exerted on the social movement and right into the depths of the workers' minds, is very great. It produces a form of demoralization. And one of the reasons for its strength is that it is held by people who all seem to agree with one another—consensus is in general a sign of truth. Another is that it is based on the apparently most powerful instruments now available to thought, in particular mathematics. The role of what is called the dominant ideology is fulfilled nowadays by a certain use of mathematics (I exaggerate, but it is a way of drawing attention to the fact that the work of rationalization—giving reasons to justify things that are often unjustifiable—has now found a very powerful instrument in mathematical economics). This ideology, which dresses up simply conservative thought in the guise of pure reason, has to be fought, with reasons, arguments, refutations, demonstrations; and this implies scientific work.

One of the strengths of neoliberal thought is that it presents itself as a kind of "great chain of Being," as in the old theological metaphor, where at one end there is God and then you work your way down, link by link, to the lowest forms of life. In the neoliberal universe, right at the top, in the place of God, is a mathematician, and at the bottom there is an ideologue of *Esprit*,[37] who doesn't know much about economics but wants to give the impression of knowing something, with the aid of a varnish of technical vocabulary. This very powerful chain has an authority effect. There are doubts, even among activists, which partly result from the essentially social strength of the theory which gives authority to the words of Mr. Trichet or Mr. Tietmeyer, the president of the Bundesbank, or this or that essayist. It is not a sequence of demonstrations, it is a chain of authorities which runs from the mathematician to the banker, from the banker to the philosopher-journalist, from the essayist to the journalist. It is also a channel for the circulation of money and all sorts of economic and social advantages, international invitations, consideration. We sociologists, without denouncing anyone, can undertake to map out these networks and show how the circulation of ideas is subtended by a circulation of power. There are people who exchange ideological services for positions of power. Examples would be needed, but it is sufficient to read the list of signatories of the famous "Petition of experts." What is interesting is that the hidden connections between people who normally work in isolation—even if we often see them appearing in pairs in false debates on television—and between foundations, associations, journals, etc., are then revealed to the light of day.

Collectively, in the mode of consensus, these people utter a fatalistic discourse which consists of transforming economic tendencies into destiny. Now, social laws, economic laws, and so on only take effect to the extent that people let them do so. And if conservatives favor laissez-faire, this is because in general these tendential laws conserve, and they need laissez-faire in order to conserve. Those of the financial markets, in particular, which are we endlessly told about, are laws of conservation, which need laissez-faire in order to operate.

One would need to develop this, argue it, and above all nuance it. I apologize for the somewhat simplifying character of what I have said. As for the social movement, it can be satisfied with existing: it annoys enough people just like that, and no one is going to ask it in addition to produce justifications—whereas intellectuals who associate themselves with the social movement are immediately asked: "But what are you proposing?" We shouldn't fall into the trap of offering a program. There are quite enough parties and apparatuses for that. What we can do is to create, not a counterprogram, but a structure for collective research, interdisciplinary and international, bringing together social scientists, activists, representatives of activists, etc., with the social scientists being placed in a quite definite role: they can participate in a particularly effective way, because it's their job, in working parties and seminars, in association with people who are in the movement.

This rules out from the start a certain number of roles: social scientists are not fellow travellers, in other words hostages and guarantors, figureheads and alibis who sign petitions and who are disposed of as soon as they have been used; nor are they Zhdanovian apparatchiks who come in to exercise apparently intellectual powers within the social movements which they cannot exercise in intellectual life; nor are they experts coming in to give lessons—not even antiexpert experts; nor are they prophets who will provide answers to all questions about the social movement and its future. They are people who can help to define the function of meetings like this one. Or who can point out that the people here are not present as spokespersons, but as citizens who come into a place of discussion and research, with ideas, with arguments, leaving their slogans, platforms, and party habits in the cloakroom. This is not always easy. Among the party habits which threaten to come back are the creation of committees, composite motions often prepared in advance, and so on. Sociology teaches how groups function and how to make use of the laws governing the way they function so as to try to circumvent them.

There is a need to invent new forms of communication between researchers and activists, which means a new division of labor between them. One of the missions which sociologists can fulfill perhaps better than anyone is the fight against saturation by the media. We all hear ready-made phrases all day long. You can't turn on the radio without hearing about the "global village," "globalization," and so on. These are innocent-sounding words, but through them come a whole philosophy and a whole worldview which engender fatalism and submission. We can block this forced feeding by criticizing the words, by helping nonprofessionals to equip themselves with specific weapons of resistance, so as to combat the effects of authority and the grip of television, which plays an absolutely crucial role. It is no longer possible nowadays to conduct social struggles without having a specific program for fighting with and against television. I commend to you Patrick Champagne's book, *Faire l'opinion*, which ought to be a kind of manual for the political campaigner. In that battle, the fight against the media intellectuals is important. Personally, those people do not cause me sleepless nights, and I never think about them when I write, but they have an extremely important role from a political standpoint, and it would be desirable for a proportion of the researchers to agree to devote some of their time and energy, in their activist mode, to countering their effects.

A further objective has to be to invent new forms of symbolic action. On this point, I think that social movements, with a few historic exceptions, have a lot of ground to make up. In his book, Patrick Champagne shows how some big mobilizations may receive less coverage in the newspapers and on television than some minuscule demonstrations that are put on in a way that interests the journalists. It is clearly not a question of fighting against the journalists, who are themselves subject to the constraints of job insecurity, with all the effects of censorship it produces in all the professions of cultural production. But it is essential to realize that an enormous part of what we may say or do will be filtered, in other words often annihilated, by what the journalists will say about it. Including what we are about to do here. And that is a remark that they won't reproduce in their reporting.

To conclude, I will say that one of the problems is to be reflexive—a grand word, but it is not used gratuitously. Our objective is not only to invent responses, but to invent a way of inventing responses, to invent a new form of organization of the work of contestation and of organization of contestation, of the task of activism. Our dream, as social scientists, might be for part of our research to be useful to the social movement, instead of being lost, as is often the case nowadays, because it is intercepted and distorted by journalists or by hostile interpreters, etc. In the framework of groups like Raisons d'Agir, we would like to invent new forms of expression that make it possible to communicate the most advanced findings of research. But that also presupposes a change of language and outlook on the part of the researchers.

To return to the social movement, I think, as I said a moment ago, that we are witnessing successive waves—I could also have mentioned the students' and teachers' strikes in Belgium, the strikes in Italy, etc.—of struggle against neoliberal imperialism, struggles which generally do not recognize each other (and which may take forms which are not always appealing, like some forms of fundamentalism). So at the very least there is a need to unify international information and enable it to circulate. There is a need to reinvent internationalism, which was hijacked by Soviet imperialism, in other words to invent forms of theoretical thought and forms of practical action capable of operating at the level where the fight has to take place. If it is true that most of the dominant economic forces operate at world level, transnationally, it is also true that there is an empty space, that of transnational struggles. It is theoretically empty, because it has not been thought through, and it is practically empty, for lack of genuine international organization of the forces capable of countering the new conservative revolution, at least on a European scale.

Paris, November 1996

FOR A NEW INTERNATIONALISM

Remarks at the third international forum of the Deutscher Gewerkschaftsbund (DGB) of Hesse, Frankfurt, 7 June 1997.

The peoples of Europe are now at a turning point in their history, because the conquests of several centuries of social struggles, of intellectual and political battles for the dignity of workers, are directly threatened. The movements that are seen, first in one place, then in another, throughout Europe, and elsewhere, even in Korea, these movements that follow on from one another, in Germany, France, Greece, Italy, etc., apparently without real coordination, are so many revolts against a policy which takes different forms in different fields and in different countries but which, nevertheless, is always inspired by the same intention, that of removing the social entitlements which are, whatever people say, among the highest achievements of civilization—achievements that ought to be universalized, extended to the whole planet, globalized, instead of using the pretext of "globalization," of the competition from economically and socially less advanced countries, in order to cast doubt on them. Nothing is more natural or more legitimate than the defense of these entitlements, which some people want to present as a form of conservatism or archaism. Would anyone condemn as conservative the defense of the cultural achievements of humanity, Kant or Hegel, Mozart or Beethoven? The social entitlements that I am referring to, the right to work, a health and welfare system, for which men and women have suffered and fought, are achievements which are just as important and precious, and, moreover, they do not only survive in museums, libraries, and academies, but are living and active in people's lives and govern their everyday existence. That is why I cannot help feeling something like a sense of scandal at those who make themselves the allies of the most brutal economic forces and who condemn the people who, in fighting to defend their entitlements, sometimes described as "privileges," defend the rights of all the men and women of Europe and elsewhere. The challenge I made a few months ago to Mr. Tietmeyer has often been misunderstood. It was often taken as an answer to a question which is wrongly posed, precisely because it is posed in terms of the logic of the neoliberal thinking to which Mr. Tietmeyer subscribes. According to that view, monetary integration, symbolized by the creation of the euro, is the obligatory preliminary, the necessary and sufficient condition, for the political integration of Europe. In other words it is assumed that the political integration of Europe will flow necessarily, ineluctably, from economic integration. It follows that anyone who opposes the policy of monetary integration, and opposes its advocates, like Mr. Tietmeyer, will be taken to oppose political integration, in a word, to be "against Europe."

Not at all. What is in question is the role of the state (the currently existing national states, or the European state to be created), particularly as regards the protection of social rights, the role of the social state, which alone can stand up to the implacable mechanisms of the economy relinquished to itself. One can be against a Europe which, like that of Mr. Tietmeyer, would serve as a relay for the financial markets, while being for a Europe which, through a concerted policy, blocks the way of the uncontrolled violence of those markets. But there is no reason to hope for such a policy from the bankers' Europe that is being prepared for us. Monetary integration cannot be expected to secure social integration. On the contrary: for we know that countries that want to maintain their competitiveness within the euro zone relative to their partners will have no option but to reduce wage costs by reducing welfare contributions. "Social dumping" and wage-cutting, the "flexibilization" of the labor market, will be the only devices left to states which can no longer play on exchange rates. Added to these mechanisms will undoubtedly be the pressure of the "monetary authorities," like the Bundesbank and its leaders, who are always eager to preach "wage restraint." Only a European social state would be capable of countering the *disintegratory* effects of monetary economics. But Mr. Tietmeyer and the neoliberals do not want either national states, which they see as simple obstacles to the free functioning of the economy, or, *a fortiori*, the supranational state, which they want to reduce to a bank. And it is clear that, if they want to get rid of the national states (or the Council of Ministers of Community states) by stripping them of their power, this is not in order to create a supranational state which, with enhanced authority, would impose on them the constraints, especially as regards social policy, from which they want at all costs to be freed.

So it is possible to be hostile to the integration of Europe based solely on the single currency, without being in any way hostile to the political integration of Europe; and while calling, on the contrary, for the creation of a European state capable of controlling the European Bank and, more precisely, capable of controlling, by anticipating, the social effects of a union reduced to its purely monetary dimension, in accordance with the neoliberal philosophy which aims to sweep away all the vestiges of the (social) state as so many obstacles to the harmonious functioning of the markets.

It is certain that international (and more especially intra-European) competition is an obstacle to the application *in one country* of what you call the "ban on social regression." That is seen clearly as regards the reduction of the working week or reflation of the economy (despite the fact that a reduced working week is partly self-financing because of the likely increase in productivity and that it is offset by a reduction of the huge amounts spent on unemployment). The British prime minister John Major understood this perfectly well when he said cynically: "You will have the wage costs and we will have the jobs." It has also been understood by the German employers who are starting to relocate some of their production in France, where the destruction of social rights is relatively more "advanced." In fact, however, if it is true that competition is for the most part intra-European and that it is French workers taking jobs away from German workers, and vice versa—as is indeed the case, since *almost three-quarters of the external trade of European countries takes place within the confines of Europe*—it can be seen that the effects of a reduced working week without loss of wages would be very limited if such a measure were decided and applied on a European scale.

The same is true of policies for the revival of demand or for investment in the new technologies: though they may be impossible or ruinous, as the orthodoxy has it, so long as they are carried out in a single country, they become reasonable on the scale of a continent. It is also true, more generally, of any action oriented by the principles of an economics of happiness, which would take account of all the profits and all the costs, material and symbolic, of human behaviors and in particular of activity or inactivity. In short, in place of the monetary Europe that is destroying social gains it is urgent that we put forward a social Europe based on an alliance between the workers of the various European countries, one that is capable of neutralizing attempts to use the workers of each country against the workers of all the others, in particular through "social dumping."

To achieve this, and to move beyond a mere abstract program, it would be necessary to invent a new internationalism, a task which falls, first and foremost, to the trade union organizations. But internationalism, as well as having been discredited, in its traditional form, by its subordination to Soviet imperialism, comes up against great obstacles due to the fact that union structures are national ones (linked to the state and in part produced by the state), separated by different historical traditions. For example, in Germany, there is a strong autonomy of the "social partners," whereas in France there is a tradition of weak trade unions facing a strong state. Equally, the welfare system takes very different forms, from Britain, where it is financed by taxation to Germany and France, where it is paid for by contributions. At the European level, there is almost nothing. What is called "social Europe," which is of little interest to the "guardians of the euro," amounts to a few grand principles, with for example the Community Charter of Fundamental Social Rights defining a set of minimum standards, with implementation being left to the discretion of member states. The social protocol annexed to the Maastricht Treaty provides for the adoption by qualified majority of directives in the areas of working conditions, information to and consultation of workers, and equal treatment of men and women. It also gave the European "social partners" the option to negotiate collective agreements which, when adopted by the Council of Ministers, have the force of law.

All that is well and good, but where is the European social force capable of imposing such agreements on the European employers? The international structures, such as the European Trade Union Confederation, are weak (for example, they exclude a number of unions such as the CGT) in the face of organized employers, and, paradoxically, they almost always leave the initiative to the Community institutions (and the technocrats), even when social rights are at stake. The European works councils could be a powerful recourse, as has been seen in some conflicts within multinational corporations, but they are only consultative bodies and are hindered by the differences of interest which divide them within, or which set them against each other between one country and another. The European coordination of workers' struggles has a lot of ground to make up. The trade union organizations have missed some major opportunities, such as the strike in Germany for the 35-hour week, which was not taken up at the European level, or the great mobilizations which occurred in France in late 1995 and early 1996, against the austerity policy and the dismantling of the public services. The intellectuals—especially in Germany—have remained silent, when they have not simply echoed the dominant discourse.

How are the foundations to be laid for a new internationalism among the trade unions, the intellectuals, and the peoples of Europe? There are two possible forms of action, and they are not mutually exclusive. One is the mobilization of the peoples, which presupposes, in this case, a specific contribution by the intellectuals in as much as demobilization partly results from the demoralization produced by the permanent action of "propaganda" by essayists and journalists, a propaganda which neither the authors nor the recipients perceive as such. The social bases for the success of such a mobilization exist: I will only mention the effects of the transformations of the educational system, with, in particular, the rising levels of education, the devaluation of qualifications and the resulting structural deskilling, and also the blurring of the separation between students and manual workers (there is still a separation between the old and the young, between those in secure jobs and those facing job insecurity or proletarianization, but real connections have been made, through, for example, educated manual workers' children affected by the crisis). But also, and above all, there is the evolution of the social structure, with—contrary to the myth of the enormous middle class, which is so widespread in Germany—the growth in social inequality, the overall income from capital having risen by 60 percent while the income from waged labor has remained stable. This action of international mobilization presupposes that an important role is given to the battle of ideas (breaking with the *ouvriériste* tradition which pervades social movements, especially in France, and which refuses to give intellectual struggles their rightful place in social struggles), and in particular to critique of the representations continuously produced and propagated by the dominant groups and their lackeys in the media: false statistics, myths about full employment in Britain or the United States, and so on.

The second form of intervention in favor of an internationalism capable of promoting a transnational social state is action on and through the national states, which, at the present time, for lack of an overall vision of the future, are incapable of managing the general interest of the Community. We have to act on the national states, first to defend and strengthen the historical advances associated with the national states (which are greatest and most rooted in people's minds where the state has been strongest, as in France); and second to force these states to work for the creation of a European social state combining the greatest social advances of the various national states (more nurseries, schools, and hospitals, fewer soldiers, policemen, and prisons) and to subordinate the creation of the single market to the implementation of the social measures designed to counter the likely social consequences that unbridled competition will have for wage-earners. (We might take example here from Sweden, which has rejected entry into the euro until there is a renegotiation giving priority to the coordination of economic and social policies.) Social cohesion is as important a goal as stable exchange rates and social harmonization is the precondition for the success of a genuine monetary union.

If social harmonization, and the solidarity that it produces and presupposes, are made an absolute precondition, then a number of common objectives must be negotiated immediately, with the same concern for rigor hitherto reserved for economic indicators (such as the sacrosanct 3 percent in the Maastricht Treaty): these include the definition of *minimum wages* (differentiated by zones to take account of regional disparities); bringing in measures *against the corruption and tax fraud* which reduce the contribution of financial activities to public spending, indirectly resulting in excessive taxation of labor, and *against social dumping* between directly competing activities; drawing up a code of *common social rights* which, while accepting a transitional differentiation between zones, would aim to integrate social policies by merging them where they exist and developing them where they do not exist, with for example the definition of a minimum income for persons without paid employment and without other resources, reduction of employees' contributions, development of social rights such as training, the definition of the right to employment and housing, and the invention of an external policy in social matters aimed at spreading and generalizing European social standards; a *common investment policy* corresponding to the general interest—in contrast to the investment strategies resulting from the autonomization of financial activities that are purely speculative and/or directed toward short-term profit, or based on assumptions totally contrary to the general interest, such as the belief that reductions in employment are an index of good management and a guarantee of efficiency, priority would be given to strategies aimed at safeguarding nonrenewable resources and the environment, developing trans-European transport and energy networks, developing public housing and urban regeneration (especially through non-polluting urban transport), investment in research and development in health and the protection of the environment, the financing of new and apparently more risky activities, in forms unknown to the financial world (small businesses, self-employment).[38]

What may look like a simple catalogue of disparate measures is in fact inspired by the will to break out of the fatalism of neoliberal thinking, to "defatalize" by politicizing, by replacing the naturalized economy of neoliberalism with an economy of happiness, based on human initiatives and will, making allowance in its calculations for the costs in suffering and the profits in fulfilment that are ignored by the strictly economistic cult of productivity and profitability.

The future of Europe depends a great deal on the strength of the progressive forces in Germany (trade unions, SPD, Greens) and on their will and capacity to resist the "strong euro" policy advocated by the Bundesbank and the German government. It will also depend on their capacity to stimulate and relay the movement for a reorientation of European policy which is already making itself heard in several countries, in particular in France. In short, against all the prophets of misery who want to convince you that your destiny is in the hands of transcendent, independent, indifferent powers, such as "the financial markets" or the mechanisms of "globalization," I want to declare, with the hope of convincing you, that the future, your future, which is also our future, that of all Europeans, depends a great deal on you, as Germans and as trade unionists.

Frankfurt, June 1997

RETURN TO TELEVISION

Interview of Pierre Bourdieu with P. R. Pires, in *O Globo* (Rio de Janeiro), 4 October 1997, after the publication of the Portugese translation of *On Television*.

Q: *In your book* On Television, *you say that it is necessary to awaken the consciousness of media professionals to the invisible structures of broadcasting. Do you think that the professionals and the public are really still so blind to the mechanisms of the media in a world in which the media are so present? Or is there complicity between them?*

PB: I don't think the professionals are blind. I think they live in a state of dual consciousness: a practical view which leads them to get as much as they can, sometimes cynically, sometimes without realizing it, out of the possibilities offered by the media tool at their disposal (I am talking about the most *powerful* of them); and a theoretical view, moralizing and full of indulgence toward themselves, which leads them to deny publicly what they do, to mask it and even mask it from themselves. Two items of evidence: the reactions to my little book, which the "leading commentators" unanimously and violently condemned as outrageous while proclaiming each more insistently than the other that it contained nothing that was not already known (a truly Freudian logic which I also saw in the reactions to my books on education); and the pontificating, hypocritical commentaries they produced on the role of the journalists in the death of Princess Diana while themselves allowing the journalistic possibilities of this nonevent to be exploited beyond the bounds of decency. This split consciousness—very common among the powerful . . . it was said that the Roman augurs could not look at each other without laughing—means that they can both condemn the objective description of their practice as a scandalous denunciation or a poisonous pamphlet, and say equivalent things out loud when speaking privately or even for the benefit of the sociologist who interviews them (I give examples of this in my book) or indeed even in public statements. Thus Thomas Ferenczi writes in *Le Monde* of 7–8 September, in response to readers' complaints about the paper's treatment of the Princess Diana story, that, yes, "*Le Monde* has changed" and is devoting more and more space to what he discreetly calls "faits de société"—just the truths which he could not bear to see uttered only three months earlier. At a time when the slippage, *imposed by television*, is there for all to see, the paper flaunts it, in the appropriately moralizing tone, as a way of adapting to modernity and "enlarging its curiosity"! (*Added in January 1998*: And the "Ombudsman" [*médiateur*] specially mandated to fob off readers conscious of the ever-growing weight of commercial preoccupations in editorial choices now deploys all his rhetoric to try to prove that one can be the judge in one's own case, while endlessly rehearsing the same tautological arguments. To those who, after the publication of an interview with a fading pop star by an insipid writer,[39] complain that *Le Monde* is "drifting into a kind of demagogy," he can only reply, in the edition dated 18–19 January 1998, that his paper is "committed to openness": "These subjects, and others," he writes, "receive extensive coverage because they shed useful light on the world around us and because, for that very reason, they interest a large section of our readership." To those who, the previous week, condemned the indulgent report by a journalist-intellectual on the situation in Algeria, a betrayal of all the critical ideals of the tradition of the intellectual, he replies, in *Le Monde* dated 25–6 January 1998, that it is not for the journalist to choose between intellectuals. The texts thus produced, week after week, by the defender of the line of the newspaper, no doubt chosen for his extreme prudence, are the greatest imprudence of the paper: the deep unconscious of journalism is progressively revealed, as the readers make their challenges, in a kind of long weekly session of psychoanalysis.) So, split consciousness among the dominant professionals, the nomenklatura of star journalists bound together by common interests and complicities of all kinds.[40] Among "rank-and-file" journalists, the pieceworkers of journalism, the freelancers, all those who earn a precarious living by doing what is most authentically journalistic in journalism, there is, naturally, more lucidity and it is often expressed very directly. It's in part thanks to their testimony that it is possible to learn something about what goes on in the world of television.[41]

Q: *You analyze the formation of what you call the "journalistic field," but your point of view is that of the "sociological field." Do you think there is an incompatibility between those two fields? Does sociology present "truths" and the media present "lies"?*

PB: You are introducing a dichotomy very characteristic of the journalistic vision, which—it's one of its most typical properties—is inclined to be Manichean. It goes without saying that journalists produce some truth and sociologists produce some untruth. In a field, you find everything, by definition! But perhaps in different proportions and with different probabilities . . . Having said that, the first task of the sociologist is to explode that way of formulating questions. And I say in my little book, several times, that sociologists can help lucid and critical journalists (there are a lot of them, but not necessarily in the top jobs in television, radio, and the press) by providing them with instruments of knowledge and understanding, perhaps sometimes of action, that would enable them to work with some effectiveness toward withstanding the economic and social forces that bear on them, particularly by allying with social science researchers, whom they often see as enemies. I'm currently trying (in particular through the magazine *Liber*) to create those kinds of international connections between journalists and researchers and to develop forces of *resistance* against the forces of oppression which weigh on journalism and which journalism brings to bear upon the whole of cultural production and, through that, the whole of society.

Q: *Television is identified as a form of symbolic oppression. What is the democratic potential of television and the media?*

PB: There is an enormous gap between the image that media people have and give of the media and the reality of their action and influence.

The media are, overall, a factor of depoliticization, which naturally acts more strongly on the most depoliticized sections of the public, on women more than men, on the less educated more than the more educated, on the poor more than the rich. It may be a scandalous thing to say this, but it is clearly established from statistical analysis of the probability of formulating an explicit response to a political question or of abstaining (the consequences of this fact, especially in politics, are explored at some length in my recent book *Méditations pascaliennes*). Television (much more than the newspapers) offers an increasingly depoliticized, aseptic, bland view of the world, and it is increasingly dragging down the newspapers in its slide into demagogy and subordination to commercial values. The Princess Diana affair is a perfect example of everything I say in my book, a sort of paroxysm. It is all there at once: a "human interest" story that entertains; the telethon effect, by which I mean the uncontroversial defense of humanitarian causes that are vague, ecumenical, and above all perfectly apolitical. You get the sense that with that event, coming just after the Pope's youth rally in Paris and just before the death of Mother Teresa, the last restraints gave way. (Mother Teresa, who so far as I know was no progressive in relation to abortion and women's liberation, fit perfectly into this world governed by hard-nosed bankers, who have nothing against pious defenders of humanity who come and bandage the wounds which they see as inevitable and which they have helped to inflict.) And so we saw *Le Monde, two weeks after the accident,* devoting its main front-page story to the progress of the inquiry into the crash, while on the TV news the massacres in Algeria and relations between Israel and Palestine were relegated to a few minutes at the end of the program. Incidentally, you were saying a moment ago, lies from journalists, truth from sociologists: I can tell you, as a sociologist who knows Algeria fairly well, that I have great admiration for the newspaper *La Croix*, which has recently published a very precise, rigorous, and courageous dossier on what is really behind the massacres there. The question I ask myself—and so far the answer is negative—is whether the other newspapers, and in particular those which make high claims for their seriousness, will pursue those analyses . . .

Q: *In terms of the famous dichotomy put forward by Umberto Eco in the 1960s, could we say that you are "apocalyptic" as opposed to "integrated"?*

PB: It's a way of putting it. There are certainly a lot of "integrated" people about. And the strength of the new dominant order is that it has found the specific means of "integrating" (in some cases you might say buying, in others seducing) an ever-growing fraction of the intellectuals, all over the world. These "integrated" intellectuals often continue to see themselves as critical (or simply on the left), according to the traditional model. And that helps to give great symbolic efficacy to their work in rallying support for the established order.

Q: *What is your opinion on the role of the media in the Diana affair?*

PB: It's a perfect, almost uncannily extreme illustration of what I was describing in my book. The royal families of Monaco, England, and elsewhere will be kept on as inexhaustible reservoirs of plots for soap operas and *telenovelas*. In any case it is clear that the great media "happening" provoked by the death of Princess Diana fits perfectly into the series of entertainments which enthral the petite bourgeoisie of England and other countries, along with musicals like *Evita* or *Jesus Christ Superstar*, born of the marriage of melodrama and high-tech special effects, mawkish TV serials, sentimental films, airport novels, "music for easy listening," "family entertainments," and all those other products of the cultural industry, poured out all day long by conformist and cynical television and radio channels and combining the lachrymose moralism of the churches with the aesthetic conservatism of bourgeois entertainments.

Q: *What is the possible role of the intellectuals in the "mediated" world?*

PB: It is not certain that they can play the great positive role of the inspired prophet that they sometimes tend to take upon themselves in periods of euphoria. It would be at least something if they could refrain from entering into complicity and collaboration with the forces

which threaten to destroy the very bases of their existence and their
freedom, in other words the forces of the market. It took several centuries, as I showed in my book *The Rules of Art*, for jurists, artists, writers, and scientists to gain their autonomy with respect to the political,
religious, and economic powers, and to be able to impose their own
norms, their specific values, in particular of truth, in their own universe, their microcosm, and sometimes in the social world (Zola in the
Dreyfus affair, Sartre and the 121 in the Algerian war, etc.). These conquests of freedom are sometimes threatened, and not only by colonels,
dictators, and mafias. They are threatened by more insidious forces,
those of the market, but transfigured, reincarnated in models that seduce one group or another: for some, it is the figure of the economist
armed with mathematical formalism, who describes the evolution of
the "globalized" economy as a destiny; for others, the figure of the international star of rock, pop, or rap, presenting a lifestyle that is both
chic and facile (for the first time in history, the seductions of snobbery have become attached to practices and products typical of mass
consumption, such as denim, T-shirts, and Coca-Cola); for others a
"campus radicalism" labeled postmodern and offering the seductive
glamour of seemingly revolutionary celebration of cultural pick-and-
mix, and so on. If there is one area where the "globalization" that is on
the lips of all "integrated" intellectuals is a reality, it is precisely that
of cultural mass production—television (I'm thinking in particular of
the *telenovelas* that have become a Latin American speciality and which
propagate a "Diana" view of the world), popular cinema and magazines, or even, which is much more serious, "social thinking" for the
"quality press," with themes and words that circle the planet, like "the
end of history," "postmodernism," or . . . "globalization." Artists, writers, and researchers (especially sociologists) have the capacity, and the
duty, to combat the most malign of the threats that this global production implies for culture and democracy.

THE GOVERNMENT FINDS
THE PEOPLE IRRESPONSIBLE

Text published in *Les Inrockuptibles*, 8 October 1997, on the bills of ministers Guigou (Justice) and Chevènement (Interior) on French nationality and the residence of foreigners in France.

We have had enough of the slipperiness and prevarication of all the politicians, elected by us, who declare us "irresponsible" when we remind them of the promises they made us. We have had enough of the state racism which they authorize. This very day, a friend of mine, a French citizen of Algerian origin, told me what happened to his daughter when she went to reenroll at the university: at the mere sight of her Arab-looking name, the university employee asked her, as if it were the most natural thing in the world, to show her papers and her passport. To put an end once and for all to all these bullyings and humiliations, which would have been unthinkable a few years ago, we need to make a clear break with hypocritical legislation which is no more than an immense concession to the xenophobia of the Front National. This naturally means repealing the Pasqua and Debré laws, but above all it means putting an end to all the hypocritical language of all the politicians who, at a time when the country is being reminded of the implication of the French authorities in the extermination of the Jews, practically give a free hand to all those in the administration who are in a position to express their most stupidly xenophobic impulses, like the university employee I mentioned a moment ago. There is no point in engaging in subtle legal discussions about the merits of this or that law. What we must do is simply repeal a law which, by its very existence, legitimates the discriminatory practices of civil servants, at every level, by helping to cast a generalized suspicion on foreigners—and not just *any* foreigners, of course. What does it mean to be a citizen if at any moment proof of citizenship has to be produced? (Many French parents of Algerian origin wonder what first names they should give their children to spare them problems later. And the employee who harassed my friend's daughter expressed surprise that she was called Mélanie . . .)

I say that a law is racist when it authorizes any civil servant to cast doubt on the citizenship of a citizen at the mere sight of her face or the sound of her name, as happens now, thousands of times every day. It is regrettable that in the highly controlled government which has been offered to us by Mr. Jospin, there is not a single bearer of one of the stigmata subject to the irreproachable arbitrariness of the functionaries of the French state, a black face or an Arabic-sounding name, to remind Mr. Chevènement that there is a difference between law and behavior and that there are laws which authorize the worst behavior. I offer all this for consideration by all those who are now silent and indifferent and who will come back in thirty years to express their "repentance," [42] at a time when young French citizens of Algerian origin will have the first name Kelkal. [43]

Paris, October 1997

JOB INSECURITY IS EVERYWHERE NOW

Intervention at the Rencontres Européennes contre la Précarité, Grenoble, 12–13 December 1997.

The collective thinking that has gone on here in the last two days is an entirely original undertaking, because it has brought together people who have little opportunity to meet and exchange their views—civil servants and politicians, trade unionists, economists, and sociologists, people in jobs, often insecure ones, and people without jobs. I would like to comment on some of the problems which have been discussed. The first one, which is tacitly excluded from academic meetings, is: what is the final outcome of these debates, or, more brutally, what is the point of all these intellectual discussions? Paradoxically, it is the academics who most worry about this question or whom this question most worries (I am thinking in particular of the economists here present, who are rather unrepresentative of a profession in which very few are concerned with social reality or indeed with reality at all) who have had it put most directly to them (and it is undoubtedly a good thing that this should be so). Both brutal and naive, it reminds the academics of their responsibilities, which may be very great, at least when, by their silence or their complicity, they contribute to the maintenance of the symbolic order which is the condition of the functioning of the economic order.

It has emerged clearly that job insecurity is now everywhere: in the private sector, but also in the public sector, which has greatly increased the number of temporary, part-time, or casual positions; in industry, but also in the institutions of cultural production and diffusion—education, journalism, the media, etc. In all these areas it produces more or less identical effects, which become particularly visible in the extreme case of the unemployed: the destructuring of existence, which is deprived among other things of its temporal structures, and the ensuing deterioration of the whole relationship to the world, time and space. Casualization profoundly affects the person who suffers it: by making the whole future uncertain, it prevents all rational anticipation and, in particular, the basic belief and hope in the future that one needs in order to rebel, especially collectively, against present conditions, even the most intolerable.

Added to these effects of precariousness on those directly touched by it there are the effects on all the others, who are apparently spared. The awareness of it never goes away: it is present at every moment in everyone's mind (except, no doubt, in the minds of the liberal economists, perhaps because, as one of their theoretical opponents has pointed out, they enjoy the protection afforded by tenured positions . . .). It pervades both the conscious and the unconscious mind. The existence of a large reserve army, which, because of the overproduction of graduates, is no longer restricted to the lowest levels of competence and technical qualification, helps to give all those in work the sense that they are in no way irreplaceable and that their work, their jobs, and in some way a privilege, a fragile, threatened privilege (as they are reminded by their employers as soon as they step out of line and by journalists and commentators at the first sign of a strike). Objective insecurity gives rise to a generalized subjective insecurity which is now affecting all workers in our highly developed economy. This kind of "collective mentality" (I use this expression, although I do not much like it, to make myself understood), common to the whole epoch, is the origin of the demoralization and loss of militancy which one can observe (as I did in Algeria in the 1960s) in underdeveloped countries suffering very high rates of unemployment or underemployment and permanently haunted by the specter of joblessness.

The unemployed and the casualized workers, having suffered a blow to their capacity to project themselves into the future, which is the precondition for all so-called rational conducts, starting with economic calculation, or, in a quite different realm, political organization, are scarcely capable of being mobilized. Paradoxically, as I showed in *Travail et travailleurs en Algérie*,[44] my oldest and perhaps most contemporary book, in order to conceive a revolutionary project, in other words a reasoned ambition to transform the present by reference to a projected future, one needs some grasp on the present. The proletarian, unlike the subproletarian, does have this basic minimum of present assurances, security, which is needed in order to conceive the ambition of changing the present with an eye to the future. But, let me say in passing, the worker is also someone who has something to defend, something to lose, a job, even if it is exhausting and badly paid, and a number of the things the worker does, sometimes described as too prudent or even conservative, spring from the fear of falling lower, back into the subproletariat.

When unemployment rises to very high levels, as it has in a number of European countries, and when job insecurity affects a very high proportion of the population—manual workers, clerical workers in commerce and industry, but also journalists, teachers and students, work becomes a rare commodity, desirable at any price, which puts employees at the mercy of employers, who exploit and abuse the power this gives them. Competition for work tends to generate a struggle of all against all, which destroys all the values of solidarity and humanity, and sometimes produces direct violence. Those who deplore the cynicism of the men and women of our time should not omit to relate it to the economic and social conditions which favor or demand it and which reward it.

So insecurity acts directly on those it touches (and whom it renders incapable of mobilizing themselves) and indirectly on all the others, through the fear it arouses, which is methodically exploited by all the *insecurity-inducing strategies,* such as the introduction of the notorious "flexibility"—which, it will have become clear, is inspired as much by political as economic reasons. One thus begins to suspect that insecurity is the product not of an *economic inevitability*, identified with the much-heralded "globalization," but of a *political will*. A "flexible" company in a sense deliberately exploits a situation of insecurity which it helps to reinforce: it seeks to reduce its costs, but also to make this lowering possible by putting the workers in permanent danger of losing their jobs. The whole world of production, material and cultural, public and private, is thus carried along by a process of intensification of insecurity, with, for example, the *deterritorialization* of the company. An industry previously linked to a nation-state or a region (Detroit or Turin for automobiles) tends increasingly to detach itself through what is called the "network corporation," organized on a continental or world scale and linking production segments, technological know-how, communication networks, and training facilities scattered between very distant places.

By facilitating or organizing the mobility of capital and "delocalization" towards the countries with the lowest wages, neoliberal policies have helped to extend competition among workers to a global level. The national (and perhaps nationalized) company, whose field of competition was more or less strictly limited to the national territory, and which went out to win markets abroad, has given way to the multinational corporation which places workers in competition no longer just with their compatriots or even, as the demagogues claim, with the foreigners installed on the national territory, who are in fact clearly the first victims of loss of security, but with workers on the other side of the world, who are forced to accept poverty-line wages.

Casualization of employment is part of a *mode of domination* of a new kind, based on the creation of a generalized and permanent state of insecurity aimed at forcing workers into submission, into the acceptance of exploitation. To characterize this mode of domination, which, although in its effects it closely resembles the wild capitalism of the early days, is entirely unprecedented, a speaker here proposed the very appropriate and expressive concept of *flexploitation*. The word evokes very well this rational management of insecurity which, especially through the concerted manipulation of the space of production, sets up competition between the workers of the countries with the greatest social gains and the best organized union resistance—features that are linked to a national territory and history—and the workers of the socially least advanced countries, and so breaks resistance and obtains obedience and submission, through apparently natural mechanisms which thus serve as their own justification. These submissive dispositions produced by insecurity are the prerequisite for an increasingly "successful" exploitation, based on the division between the growing number who do not work and the diminishing number of those who work, but who work more and more. So it seems to me that what is presented as an economic system governed by the iron laws of a kind of social nature is in reality a *political system* which can only be set up with the active or passive complicity of the officially political powers.

Against this political system, political struggle is possible. In the form of charitable or militant activity, it can first aim to encourage the victims of exploitation, all the present and potential victims of insecurity, to work together against the destructive effects of insecurity (by helping them to live, to "hold on," to save their dignity, to resist destructuring, loss of self-respect, alienation) and above all to mobilize *on an international scale,* that is to say at the same level at which the policy of inducing insecurity exerts its effects, so as to combat this policy and neutralize the competition it seeks to create between the workers of different countries. But it can also try to help workers to break away from the logic of past struggles which, being based on the demand for work and for better pay for work, trap them within work and within the exploitation (or flexploitation) which accompanies it. This implies a redistribution of work (through a significant reduction in the working week throughout Europe), inseparable from a redefinition of the distribution between production time and reproduction time, rest and leisure.

This revolution would have to start with the abandonment of the narrowly calculating and individualistic view which reduces agents to calculators concerned with resolving problems, strictly economic problems in the narrowest sense of the word. In order for the economic system to function, the workers have to bring into it their own conditions of production and reproduction, but also what is needed for the economic system itself to function, starting with their belief in the company, in work, in the necessity of work, and so on. These are all things that the orthodox economists exclude *a priori* from their abstract and partial accountancy, tacitly leaving the responsibility for the production and reproduction of all the hidden economic and social requirements for the economy as they know it to individuals or, paradoxically, to the state, of which they otherwise urge the destruction.

Grenoble, December 1997

THE PROTEST MOVEMENT OF THE UNEMPLOYED, A SOCIAL MIRACLE

Remarks on 17 January 1998, at the time of the occupation of the École Normale Supérieure by the unemployed.

This movement of the unemployed is a unique, extraordinary event. Contrary to what we are told, day in, day out, on television and in the newspapers, this *French exception* is something we can be proud of. All the research on unemployment has shown that it destroys its victims, wiping out their defenses and their subversive dispositions. If that inevitability has been overturned, it is thanks to the tireless work of individuals and associations which have encouraged, supported, and organized the movement. I cannot help finding it extraordinary that left-wing politicians or trade unionists talk of manipulation (in the same terms in which nineteenth-century employers denounced the early trade unions) where they ought to recognize the virtues of the work of activists, without which, it is clear, there would never have been anything resembling a social movement. For my part, I want to express my admiration and gratitude—all the greater because what they were taking on often seemed to me hopeless—for all those, in the unions and associations brought together in the États Généraux du Mouvement Social, who have made possible what is truly a *social miracle*, the virtues and benefits of which will be long-lasting.

The first conquest of this movement is the movement itself, its very existence: it pulls the unemployed, and with them all insecure workers, whose number increases daily, out of invisibility, isolation, silence, in short, out of nonexistence. Reemerging into the light of day, the unemployed give back their existence and some pride in themselves to all the men and women that nonemployment consigns, like them, to oblivion and shame. Above all they remind us that one of the foundations of the present economic and social order is mass unemployment and the threat this implies for all those who still have a job. Far from being wrapped up in an egoistic movement, they are saying that even if no unemployed person is quite like another, the differences between people on welfare-to-work schemes, the unemployed whose benefits have expired or those receiving specific allowances, are not radically different from those between the unemployed and all insecure workers. This is a reality which tends to be masked and forgotten when the emphasis is put on the (so to speak) "sectional" claims of the unemployed, which are liable to separate them from the employed, especially those in the most insecure positions, who may feel forgotten.

Moreover, unemployment and the unemployed haunt work and the worker. Short-term, part-time, and temporary workers of every category, in industry, commerce, education, entertainment, even if there are immense differences between them and the unemployed and also between themselves, all live in fear of unemployment and, very often, under the threat of the blackmail that can be used against them. Instability of employment opens up new strategies of domination and exploitation, based on intimidation through the threat of redundancy, which occurs now at all levels of the hierarchy, in private and even public enterprises and which subjects the whole world of work, especially those in the cultural sector, to a crushing censorship that forbids mobilization and takes away bargaining power. The generalized worsening of working conditions is made possible or even favored by unemployment and it is because they are obscurely aware of this that so many French people feel and express solidarity with the struggle of the unemployed. That is why it is possible to say, without playing with words, that the mobilization of those whose existence is undoubtedly the main factor in a loss of militancy is the most extraordinary encouragement to mobilization, to the rejection of political fatalism.

The movement of the French unemployed is also a call to all the unemployed and all the casualized workers of the whole of Europe: a new subversive idea has appeared on the scene, and it can become an instrument of struggle available to every national movement. The unemployed are reminding all workers that their interests are bound up with those of the unemployed; that the unemployed whose existence weighs so heavily on them and on their working conditions are the product of a policy; that a mobilization capable of overcoming the frontiers that exist, in every country, between workers and nonworkers and the frontiers between all the workers and nonworkers of one country and the workers and nonworkers of every other country could counter the policy which can mean that the nonworkers can force silence and resignation on those who have the dubious "privilege" of a more or less precarious employment.

Paris, January 1998

THE NEGATIVE INTELLECTUAL

This text was written in January 1998; it was published for the first time in the volume *On Television* (1998).

All those who have been there, day after day, year after year, to receive Algerian refugees, to listen to them, help them draw up a curriculum vitae and go through the formalities in the ministries, to accompany them to court, to write letters to the authorities, to go in delegations to see officials, to apply for visas, authorizations and residence permits, who were mobilized, as soon as the first murders started in June 1993, not only to provide help and protection so far as was possible, but to try to inform themselves and inform others, to understand and explain a complex reality, who have fought tirelessly, through public declarations, press conferences and newspaper articles, to rescue the Algerian crisis from one-sided interpretations, all the intellectuals of all countries who have come together to fight indifference or xenophobia, to reinstate respect for the complexity of the world by untangling the confusions that some people deliberately maintain, have suddenly discovered that all their efforts could be undone, swept away, in two strokes, three movements.

Two articles[45] written after a journey planned, mapped out, escorted and watched over by the Algerian authorities or army, and published in the most respected French newspaper, though full of platitudes and errors and entirely oriented towards a simplistic conclusion calculated to give satisfaction to superficial pity and racist hatred, masked as humanist indignation; a unanimist public meeting bringing together the cream of the media intelligentsia and the political class, from the fundamentalist liberal and the opportunist ecologist to the passionaria of the "eradicators";[46] a television program which is entirely one-sided under the appearance of neutrality—and the trick is pulled off. Everything is back to zero. The negative intellectual has done his job: who could want to express solidarity with mass murderers and rapists—especially when they are people who are described, without historical justification, as "madmen of Islam," enveloped under the abominated name of Islamicism, the quintessence of all Oriental fanaticism, designed to give racist contempt the impeccable alibi of ethical and secular legitimacy?

To pose the problem in such terms, you don't need to be a great intellectual. And yet that is how the originator of this crude operation of symbolic policing, which is the absolute antithesis of everything that defines the intellectual—freedom with respect to those in power, the critique of received ideas, the demolition of simplistic either-ors, respect for the complexity of problems—has come to be consecrated by journalists as an intellectual in the full sense of the word.

And yet I know all kinds of people who, though they know all that very well, because they have grappled countless times with those forces, will start again, each in their own way and with their own means, on work that is always liable to be destroyed by a thoughtless, frivolous, or malicious article or to be annexed, if it succeeds, by opportunists and eleventh-hour converts; who will persist in writing corrections, refutations, and rebuttals destined to be overwhelmed by the uninterrupted flow of media chatter, because they are convinced that—as we have seen from the movement of the unemployed, the fruition of obscure efforts, sometimes so desperate that they seem to be the art for art's sake of politics—one can, in the long run, give a push to the rock of Sisyphus without it rolling back.

They do so because, meanwhile, politicians who are skilled in neutralizing the social movements that have brought them to power continue to leave thousands of "unauthorized" immigrants without an answer or to deport them to the country from which they have fled, which could be Algeria.

Paris, January 1998

NEOLIBERALISM, THE UTOPIA (BECOMING A REALITY) OF UNLIMITED EXPLOITATION

Is the economic world really, as the dominant discourse would have us believe, a pure and perfect order, implacably unfolding the logic of its predictable consequences and promptly repressing all deviations from its rules through the sanctions it inflicts, either automatically or, more exceptionally, through its armed agent, the IMF or the OECD and the drastic policies they impose—reduced labor costs, cuts in public spending, and a more "flexible" labor market? What if it were, in reality, only the implementation of a utopia, neoliberalism, thus converted into a *political program*, but a utopia which, with the aid of the economic theory to which it subscribes, manages to see itself as the scientific description of reality?

This tutelary theory is a pure mathematical fiction, based, from the outset, on a gigantic abstraction, which, contrary to what economists who defend their right to inevitable abstraction like to think, cannot be reduced to the effect—constitutive of every scientific project—of object construction as a deliberately selective apprehension of the real. This abstraction, performed in the name of a strict and narrow view of rationality, identified with individual rationality, consists in bracketing off the economic and social conditions of rational dispositions (and in particular those of the calculating disposition applied to economic matters which is the basis of the neoliberal view) and of the economic and social structures which are the condition of their exercise, or, more precisely, of the production and reproduction of those dispositions and those structures. To appreciate the scale of the omission, one only has to think of the educational system, which is never taken into account *as such* at a time when it plays a decisive role both in the production of goods and services and in the production of producers. From this original fault, inscribed in the Walrasian[47] myth of "pure theory," flow all the omissions and shortcomings of the discipline of economics, and the deadly stubbornness with which it clings to the arbitrary opposition it causes to exist, by its very existence, between specifically economic logic—based on competition and promising efficiency—and social logic, subject to the rule of equity.

Having said this, this initially desocialized and dehistoricized "theory" has, now more than ever, the means of *making itself true*, empirically falsifiable. For neoliberal discourse is not a discourse like others. Like psychiatric discourse in the asylum, as described by Erving Goffman,[48] it is a "strong discourse" which is so strong and so hard to fight because it has behind it all the powers of a world of power relations which it helps to make as it is, in particular by orienting the economic choices of those who dominate economic relations and so adding its own—specifically symbolic—force to those power relations. In the name of the scientific program of knowledge, converted into a political program of action, an immense *political operation* is being pursued (denied, because it is apparently purely negative), aimed at creating the conditions for realizing and operating of the "theory"; a *program of methodical destruction of collectives* (neoclassical economics recognizes only individuals, whether it is dealing with companies, trade unions, or families).

The movement, made possible by the policy of financial deregulation, toward the neoliberal utopia of a pure, perfect market takes place through the transforming and, it has to be said, *destructive* action of all the political measures (the most recent being the MAI, the Multilateral Agreement on Investment, intended to protect foreign companies and their investments against national governments) aimed at *putting into question all the collective structures* capable of obstructing the logic of the pure market: the nation-state, whose room for maneuver is steadily shrinking; work groups, with for example the individualization of salaries and careers on the basis of individual performance and the consequent atomization of workers; collectives defending workers' rights—unions, societies, and cooperatives; even the family, which, through the segmentation of the market into age groups, loses some of its control over consumption. Deriving its social force from the political and economic strength of those whose interests it defends—shareholders, financial operators, industrialists, conservative politicians, or social democrats converted to the cozy capitulations of laissez-faire, senior officials of the financial ministries, who are all the more determined to impose a policy implying their own redundancy because, unlike private-sector executives, they run no risk of suffering the consequences—the neoliberal program tends overall to favor the separation between the economy and social realities and so to construct, in reality, an economic system corresponding to the theoretical description, in other words a kind of logical machine, which presents itself as a chain of constraints impelling the economic agents.

The globalization of financial markets, combined with the progress of information technology, ensures an unprecedented mobility of capital and gives investors (or shareholders) concerned about their immediate interests, that is the short-term profitability of their investments, the possibility of continuously comparing the profitability of the largest companies and appropriately sanctioning relative failure. Companies themselves, exposed to this permanent threat, have to adjust ever more rapidly to the demands of the markets, for fear of "losing the confidence of the markets" and with it the support of shareholders who, with their eyes fixed on short-term profitability, are increasingly able to impose their will on the managers, to lay down guidelines for them, through the finance departments, and to shape their policies on recruitment, employment, and wages. This leads to the absolute reign of flexibility, with recruitment on short-term contracts or on a temporary basis and repeated "downsizing," and the creation, within the company itself, of competition between autonomous "profit centers," between teams, forced into providing all their own services, and finally, between individuals, through the individualization of the wage relation. This comes through the setting of individual objectives; individual appraisal interviews; personal increments or bonuses based on individual competence or merit; individualized career paths; strategies of "responsibilization" tending to secure the self-exploitation of some managers who, while remaining wage-earners subject to strong hierarchical authority, are at the same time held responsible for their sales, their products, their branch, their shop, etc., like "independent" proprietors; the demand for "self-appraisal" which extends the "involvement" of employees, in accordance with the techniques of "participatory management," far beyond the executive level—all methods of rational control which, while imposing over investment in work, and not only in posts of responsibility, and work under the pressures of urgency, combine to weaken or destroy collective references and solidarity.[49]

The practical instituting of a Darwinian world in which the springs of commitment to the job and the company are found in insecurity, suffering, and stress[50] would undoubtedly not succeed so completely if it did not benefit from the complicity of the destabilized habitus produced by insecurity and the existence—at all levels of the hierarchy, even the highest, especially among executives—of a reserve army of labor made docile by insecure employment and the permanent threat of unemployment. The ultimate basis of this economic order placed under the banner of individual freedom is indeed the *structural violence* of unemployment, of insecure employment and of the *fear* provoked by the threat of losing employment. The condition of the "harmonious" functioning of the individualist microeconomic model and the principle of individual "motivation" at work lie, in the final analysis, in a mass phenomenon, the existence of the reserve army of the unemployed—though the term "army" is inappropriate, because unemployment isolates, atomizes, individualizes, demobilizes, and strips away solidarity.

This structural violence also bears on what is called the work contract (wilfully rationalized and derealized by the "theory of contracts"). Corporate discourse has never spoken so much about trust, cooperation, loyalty, and corporate culture as now when the worker's unremitting commitment is obtained by sweeping away all temporal guarantees (three-quarters of new hirings are on short-term contracts, the proportion of insecure jobs rises steadily, restrictions on individual redundancies are being removed). This commitment is, moreover, necessarily uncertain and ambiguous, since casualization, fear of redundancy, downsizing can, like unemployment, generate anxiety, demoralization, or conformism (faults which the managerial literature identifies and deplores). In this world without inertia, without an immanent principle of continuity, those at the bottom are like the creatures in a Cartesian universe: they hang on the arbitrary decision of a power responsible for the "continued creation" of their existence—as is shown and confirmed by the threat of plant closure, disinvestment, and relocation.

The particular character of the profound sense of insecurity and uncertainty about themselves and their future which affects all workers exposed to casualization stems from the fact that the principle of the division between those who are thrown back into the reserve army and those who are kept in work lies in *academically guaranteed competence*, which is also the basis of the division, within the "technically advanced" company, between the executives or "technicians" and the production-line workers, the new pariahs of industrial society. The generalization of electronics, IT, and quality standards, which requires all wage-earners to retrain and perpetuates the equivalent of school tests within the enterprise, tends to reinforce the sense of insecurity with a sense of *unworthiness*, deliberately fostered by the hierarchy. The occupational world, and by extension the whole social world, seems based on a ranking by "competence," or, worse, of "intelligence." More, perhaps, than technical manipulations of working relations and the strategies especially designed to obtain the submission and obedience which are the focus of constant attention and permanent reinvention, more than the enormous investment in staff, time, research, and work that is presupposed by the constant reinvention of new forms of "human resource" management, it is the belief in the hierarchy of academically guaranteed competences which underlies order and discipline in private companies and also, increasingly, in the public sector. Manual workers—condemned to job insecurity and threatened with relegation into the indignity of unemployment, forced to define themselves in relation to the great nobility from the top-rank schools, destined for the command posts, and to the lesser nobility of clerks and technicians, who are assigned to tasks of implementation and always on sufferance because they are permanently required to *prove themselves*—can only form a disenchanted image both of themselves and of their group. Once an object of pride, rooted in traditions and sustained by a whole technical and political heritage, manual workers as a group—if indeed it still exists as such—are thrown into demoralization, devaluation, and political disillusionment, which is expressed in the crisis of activism or, worse, in a desperate rallying to the themes of quasifascist extremism.

It can be seen how the neoliberal utopia tends to be embodied in the reality of a kind of infernal machine, its necessity felt even by the dominant themselves—sometimes troubled, like George Soros, or the occasional pension fund manager, by anxiety at the destructive effects of the power they wield and led into compensatory actions inspired by the very logic that they want to neutralize, as with the benefactions of a Bill Gates. Like Marxism in earlier times, with which, in this respect, it has many common features, this utopia generates a potent belief, "free trade faith," not only among those who live from it materially such as financiers, big businessmen, etc., but also those who derive from it their justifications for existing, such as the senior civil servants and politicians who deify the power of the markets in the name of economic efficiency, who demand the lifting of the administrative or political barriers that could hinder the owners of capital in their purely individual pursuit of maximum individual profit instituted as a model of rationality, who want independent central banks, who preach the subordination of the national states to the demands of economic freedom for the masters of the economy, with the suppression of all regulations on all markets, starting with the labor market, the forbidding of deficits and inflation, generalized privatization of public services, and the reduction of public and welfare spending.

Without necessarily sharing the economic and social interests of the true believers, economists have sufficient specific interests in the field of economic science to make a decisive contribution, whatever their emotional responses to the economic and social effects of the utopia that they dress up in mathematical reason, to the production and reproduction of the neoliberal utopia. Cut off by their whole existence and above all by their generally purely abstract and theoretical intellectual training from the real economic and social world, they are, like others in other times in the field of philosophy, particularly inclined to take the things of logic for the logic of things. Trusting in models that they have practically never had the occasion to subject to experimental verification, tending to look down from on high on the conclusions of the other historical sciences, in which they recognize only the purity and crystalline transparency of their mathematical games and whose real necessity and deep complexity they are most often unable to comprehend, they participate and collaborate in an enormous economic and social transformation which, even if some of its consequences horrify them (they may subscribe to the Socialist Party and give considered advice to its representatives in the highest decision-making bodies), cannot entirely displease them, since, with a few "blips," mainly attributable to what they call "speculative fevers," it tends to give reality to the ultraconsistent utopia (like some forms of lunacy) to which they devote their lives.

And yet, the world is there, with the immediately visible effects of the implementation of the great neoliberal utopia: not only the poverty and suffering of a growing proportion of the population of the economically most advanced societies, the extraordinary growth in disparities in incomes, the progressive disappearance of the autonomous worlds of cultural production, cinema, publishing, etc., and therefore, ultimately, of cultural products themselves, because of the growing intrusion of commercial considerations, but also and above all the destruction of all the collective institutions capable of standing up to the effects of the infernal machine—in the forefront of which is the state, the repository of all the universal ideas associated with the idea of the *public*—and the imposition, everywhere, at the highest levels of the economy and the state, or in corporations, of that kind of moral Darwinism which, with the cult of the "winner," establishes the struggle of all against all and *cynicism* as the norm of all practices. And the new moral order, based on the reversal of all sets of values, is displayed in the spectacle, calmly diffused in the media, of all those high representatives of the state who abase the dignity of their position by bowing before the bosses of multinationals, Daewoo or Toyota, or competing to charm Bill Gates with their smiles and gestures of complicity.

Is it reasonable to expect that the extraordinary mass of suffering produced by such a political and economic regime could one day give rise to a movement capable of stopping the rush into the abyss? In fact, we see here an extraordinary paradox: on the one hand, the obstacles encountered on the route to the new order, that of the individual who is solitary, but free, are now seen as attributable to rigidities or archaisms, and any direct or conscious intervention, at least when it comes from the state, through whatever channel, is discredited in advance on the grounds that it is inspired by civil servants pursuing their own interests and oblivious to the interests of the economic agents and it is therefore suggested that that intervention be withdrawn in favor of a pure, anonymous mechanism, the market (which people forget is also the realm of the exercise of interests); yet on the other hand, it is in reality the permanence or the survival of institutions and agents of the old order now being dismantled, and all the work of the different kinds of "social workers," and also all social, familial, and other solidarities, which prevent the social order from collapsing into chaos in spite of the growing volume of the population cast into insecurity. The transition to "liberalism" takes place imperceptibly, like continental drift, concealing its most terrible long-term effects. These effects are thus masked, paradoxically, by the resistances it arouses, even now, from those who defend the old order by drawing on the resources stored up in it, in the legal or practical models of assistance and solidarity that it offered, in the habitus it favored (among nurses, social workers, etc.), in short, in the reserves of social capital which protect a whole block of the present social order from falling into anomie (a capital which, if it is not renewed, reproduced, will inevitably run out, but which is still far from exhaustion).

But these same forces of "conservation," which it is too facile to treat as conservative forces, are also, in another respect, forces of *resistance* to the establishment of the new order, which can become subversive forces—so long as we know how to conduct the symbolic struggle against the incessant work of the neoliberal "thinkers" aimed at discrediting and disqualifying the heritage of words, traditions, and representations associated with the historical conquests of the social movements of the past and the present; on condition, too, that we know how to defend the corresponding institutions, labor law, social welfare, social security, etc., against the endeavor to consign them to the archaism of an outmoded past or, worse, to redefine them perversely as unnecessary and unacceptable privileges. This is not an easy battle and it is not uncommon to have to fight it in the opposite terms. Inspired by a paradoxical intention of *subversion oriented toward conservation or restoration*, the revolutionary conservatives find it easy to define as reactionary resistances the defensive reactions provoked by the conservative actions they describe as revolutionary; and to condemn as the archaic and retrograde defense of "privileges" demands and revolts that appeal to established rights, in other words to a past threatened with deterioration or destruction by their regressive measures—the clearest example being the sacking of trade union representatives or, more radically, of the oldest workers, the trustees of the traditions of the group.

And so if one can retain some reasonable hope, it is that, in state institutions and also in the dispositions of agents (especially those most attached to these institutions, like the minor state nobility), there still exist forces which, under the appearance of simply defending a vanishing order and the corresponding "privileges" (which is what they will be accused of), will in fact, to withstand the pressure, have to work to invent and construct a social order which is not governed solely by the pursuit of selfish interest and individual profit, and which makes room for collectives oriented toward *rational pursuit of collectively defined and approved ends*. Among these collectives—associations, unions, and parties—a special place should surely be made for the state, national or, better still, supranational, in other words a European state (as a stage on the way to a world state), capable of effectively controlling and taxing the profits made on the financial markets; capable also, and above all, of countering the destructive action which these markets exert on the labor market, by organizing, with the aid of the unions, the definition and defense of the *public interest*—which, whether one likes it or not, will never, even by juggling the figures, be produced by the accountant's view of the world (once one would have said "grocer's") which the new belief presents as the supreme form of human achievement.

Paris, January 1998

Part III

Firing Back:
Against the Tyranny of the Market 2

LETTER TO THE AMERICAN READER

I would like my readers on the other side of the Atlantic to know that there are very many of us in Europe and throughout the world, in the countries of Latin America, Africa, and Asia, who are hoping for and awaiting their support in the struggles against what is misleadingly called "globalization" and is merely, as American researchers were the first to demonstrate, the imposition on the entire world of the neoliberal tyranny of the market and the undisputed rule of the economy and of economic powers, within which the United States occupies a dominant position.

I would like them to understand that in the ruthless war being waged not only on the economic ground but also within the realms of culture and, particularly, law through all the agreements typified by the General Agreement on Trade in Services (GATS), through which the World Trade Organization (WTO) seeks to "commodify" education and medicine, and through the great concentration of the means of production and distribution of cultural goods those agreements tend to foster, we cannot carry on the fight without them, and we want to carry it on with them. I would like them to know also that we are ready to provide them with the channels of communication they sometimes lack to bring the results of their work to a world audience, and to grant them the collective support that some national traditions still offer today to nonconformist endeavors and to experiments that break with the dominant vision of the world.

If I stress this point here, it is because I am deeply convinced that the presence of American scholars and activists alongside us would not just make us stronger and more convincing by making us more universal. It would also strip our struggles of the appearance of particularism, even of nationalism, and it would strengthen the critique of and resistance to the neoliberal *doxa* by showing that this critique can strike at, and radiate from, its very nerve center and global hub.

PREFACE

I have brought together here in rough chronological order the texts of several public talks, most of them unpublished, with the intention of contributing to the European social movement that is currently forming. Though I have at times abridged them to avoid repetition, I have attempted to retain the circumstantial features that tie these pieces to a particular time and place.[1] For reasons no doubt relating to my own person and to the state of the world, I have come to believe that those who have the good fortune to be able to devote their lives to the study of the social world cannot stand aside, neutral and indifferent, from the struggles in which the future of that world is at stake. These struggles are, for an essential part, theoretical struggles in which the dominant can count on innumerable complicities (spontaneous or paid), such as the assistance they receive from the tens of thousands of professional lobbyists who, in Brussels, haunt the corridors of the European Commission, the European Council, and the European Parliament. The neoliberal vulgate, an economic and political orthodoxy so universally imposed and unanimously accepted that it seems beyond the reach of discussion and contestation, is not a product of spontaneous generation. It is the result of a prolonged and continual work by an immense intellectual workforce, concentrated and organized in what are effectively enterprises of production, dissemination, and intervention. For example, in the course of 1998 alone, the Association of American Chambers of Commerce, to name but one such organization, published ten books and over sixty reports and took part in some 350 meetings with the European Commission and Parliament. And the list of bodies of this kind, public relations agencies and lobbies for industries or for independent companies, would fill several pages. Against such power, based on the concentration and mobilization of cultural capital, the only efficacious response is a critical force of

contestation backed by a similar mobilization but directed toward entirely other ends.

Today we must renew the tradition that emerged in the nineteenth
century in the scientific field, which refuses to leave the world to the
blind forces of economics and seeks to extend to the entire social world
the values of the scientific universe (no doubt idealized). I am aware
that by calling on researchers to mobilize to defend their autonomy
and to impose the values at the core of their profession, as I do here,
I run the risk of shocking those among them who, opting for the cozy
virtuousness of confinement within their ivory tower, see intervention
outside the academic sphere as a dangerous failing of that famous "axiological neutrality" which is wrongly equated with scientific objectivity. I know I am in danger also of being misunderstood, if not indeed
condemned without even a hearing, in the name of the very academic
virtue that I purport to defend against itself. But I am convinced that
we must at all costs bring the achievements of science and scholarship into public debate, from which they are tragically absent—and, in
passing, call to order the prattling and incompetent essayists who fill
the newspaper columns and the airwaves of radio and television. In so
doing, we will release the critical energy that remains confined within
the walls of the Scientific City, partly as a result of a misconception of
scholarly virtue, which forbids *homo academicus* to engage in the plebe-
ian debates of the journalistic and political world, partly out of habits
of thinking and writing such that specialists find it easier and more
profitable (in terms of specifically academic gains) to reserve the products of their labors for scientific publications read only by their peers.
Many economists who are privately contemptuous of the uses to which
journalists or the governors of central banks put their theories would
no doubt be scandalized if they were reminded that their silence is in
no small measure responsible for the contribution that the science of
economics makes to the justification of policies that are scientifically
unjustifiable and politically unjustified.

We are speaking, then, of taking scholarly knowledge beyond the
walls of the Scientific City or—and this is more difficult—of goading
researchers to intervene in the world of politics. But for what kind of
action, what politics? To fall back on one of the tried and tested models

of intellectual "engagement," that of the intellectual who expresses solidarity and signs petitions, a mere symbolic warrant more or less cynically exploited by the parties; or that of the expert or pedagogical intellectual, sharing his knowledge or providing tailor-made research on demand? We must break out of this inherited alternative to invent a new relationship between researchers and social movements, based on a double rejection of separateness (though without concession to the idea of "fusion") and of a merely instrumental relation (though without yielding to anti-institutional mood and myth). And we must work to design *new forms of organization* capable of bringing together researchers and activists in a collective work of critique and proposition, leading to novel forms of mobilization and action.

But what form are we to give to this political action, and on what scale is it to be conducted—national, European, or global? Have not the traditional targets of struggles and demands become decoys, well designed to deflect attention from the places where the invisible government of the powerful is wielded? Paradoxically, it is *states* that have initiated the economic measures (of deregulation) that have led to their economic disempowerment. And contrary to the claims of both the advocates and the critics of the policy of "globalization," states continue to play a central role by endorsing the very policies that tend to consign them to the sidelines. They fulfill the function of a screen which prevents citizens—if not political leaders themselves—from perceiving their disempowerment and from discovering the loci and stakes of a genuine politics. More precisely, national states operate as *masks*, which, by attracting and attaching attention to straw men, empty figureheads—those names that clamor and clash on the front pages of the national political dailies and in the electoral battles—deflect mobilization, indignation, and protest from their true target.

Politics has been continually moving further and further away from the citizenry. But one has reason to believe that some of the aims of effective political action are located at the European level, insofar as European companies and organizations retain a decisive influence on the evolution of the world. And we may take as a goal to restore politics to Europe or Europe to politics by fighting for the democratic transformation of the profoundly antidemocratic institutions with which it is presently endowed: a central bank freed of any democratic oversight; committees of unelected functionaries working in secrecy and deciding everything under pressure from international business lobbies, outside of any democratic or even bureaucratic control; a Commission that, though it concentrates immense powers, is answerable neither to a sham executive, the council of ministers, nor to a sham legislative body, the Parliament, itself almost entirely helpless in the face of lobbies and devoid of the legitimacy that only election by universal suffrage by the whole population of Europe could give it. These institutions are increasingly subjected to the dictates of international bodies whose aim is to strip the entire world of all obstacles to the exercise of an increasingly concentrated economic power. If they are genuinely to be transformed, it can only be by a vast European social movement, capable of elaborating and imposing an open and coherent vision of a political Europe, rich with all its past cultural and social achievements and armed with a generous and lucid project of social renewal, resolutely open to the entire world.

It seems to me that the most urgent task is to find and mobilize the material, economic, and, above all, *organizational* means to encourage all competent researchers to unite their efforts with those of the responsible activists in order to collectively discuss and elaborate a set of analyses and proposals for progress that today exist only in the virtual state of private and isolated thoughts or circulate in fringe publications, confidential reports, or esoteric journals. It is clear indeed that no compilation made by an archivist, no matter how detailed and exhaustive; no discussion within parties, associations, or trade unions; no synthesis by a theorist can substitute for the product of a confrontation between all those researchers oriented toward action and all the thoughtful and experienced activists of all the European countries. Only the ideal assembly of all those who, be they researchers or activists, have something to contribute to the joint enterprise will be able to build the formidable collective edifice worthy, for once, of the overworked concept of *societal project*.

Paris, November 2000

FOR A SCHOLARSHIP WITH COMMITMENT

Keynote address delivered by videoconference to the Modern Language Association Meetings, Chicago, December 1999, and introduced by MLA president Edward Said.

I would like, first, to thank Edward Said for his invitation to participate in this debate and for his kind words of introduction. I regret that I could not be with you in Chicago on this day due to ill health. Nonetheless, I hope that, thanks to techniques of remote communication, I can be among you in voice and spirit and that we will be able to open a dialogue.

Given that I do not have much time and that I would like my speech to be as effective as possible, I will come directly to the question that I wish to raise before you: Must intellectuals—more precisely, research scholars, or to be more accurate still, social scientists—intervene in the political world, and if so, under what conditions can they interject themselves efficiently? What role can they play in the various social movements active today, at the national level and especially at the international level—that is, at the level where the fate of individuals and societies is increasingly being decided? Can they contribute to inventing a new manner of doing politics fit for the novel dilemmas and threats of our age?

First of all, to avoid misunderstandings, one must posit clearly that a researcher, artist, or writer who intervenes in the political world does not become a politician because of that. According to a model created by Émile Zola on the occasion of the Dreyfus affair, he becomes an intellectual or, as you say in America, a "public intellectual," that is, someone who engages his specific authority and the values associated with the exercise of his or her craft, such as the values of disinterestedness and truth, in a political struggle—in other words, someone who enters the terrain of politics but without forsaking her exigencies and competencies as a researcher.[2] (This is to say, in passing, that the canonical opposition that is made, especially in the Anglo-American tradition, between "scholarship" and "commitment" is devoid of foundation. The intrusions of artists, writers, and scientists—Einstein, Russell, or Sakharov—in the public sphere find their principle and basis in a scientific "community" defined by its commitment to objectivity, probity, and a presumed independence from worldly interests.)

By investing her artistic or scientific competency in civic debates, the scholar risks disappointing (the term is too weak) or, better yet, shocking others. On the one side, she will shock those in her own universe, the academy, who choose the virtuous "way out" by remaining enclosed in their ivory tower and who see in commitment a violation of the famous "axiological neutrality" that is wrongly identified with scientific objectivity when it is in fact a scientifically unimpeachable form of *escapism*. On the other side, she will shock those in the political and journalistic fields who see her as a threat to their monopoly over public speech and, more generally, all those who are disturbed by her intervention in political life. She will risk, in a word, awakening all the forms of anti-intellectualism that were hitherto dormant here and there, among the masters of today's world, bankers, businessmen, and state managers, among journalists and politicians (including those of the "Left"), nearly all of whom are now holders of cultural capital, and of course among intellectuals themselves.

But to indict anti-intellectualism, which is almost always based on *ressentiment*, does not exempt the intellectual from this critique to which every intellectual can and must submit himself or herself or, in another language, from *reflexivity*, which is the absolute prerequisite to any political action by intellectuals. The intellectual world must engage in a permanent critique of all the abuses of power or authority committed in the name of intellectual authority or, if you prefer, in a relentless critique of the use of intellectual authority as a political weapon within the intellectual field. Every scholar must also submit himself or herself to the critique of the *scholastic bias*,[3] whose most perverse form is the propensity to a kind of "paper revolutionism" devoid of genuine target or effect. I believe indeed that the generous but unrealistic impulse that led many European intellectuals of my generation to submit to the dictates of the Communist Party still inspires too often today what I call "campus radicalism," this typically academic propensity to "confuse the things of logic for the logic of things," according to the pitiless formula of Marx, or, closer to our current predicament, to mistake revolutions in the order of words or texts for revolutions in the order of things, verbal sparring at conferences for "interventions" in the affairs of the *polis*.

Having posed these preliminary and apparently negative notions, I can assert that intellectuals (by which I mean artists, writers, and scientists who engage in political action) are indispensable to social struggles, especially nowadays given the quite novel forms that domination assumes. A number of recent historical works have revealed the pivotal role played by "think tanks" in the production and imposition of the neoliberal ideology that rules the world today. To the productions of these reactionary think tanks, which support and broadcast the views of experts appointed by the powerful, we must oppose the productions of critical networks that bring together "specific intellectuals" (in Foucault's sense of the term) into a veritable *collective intellectual* capable of defining by itself the topics and ends of its reflection and action—in short, an autonomous collective intellectual.

This collective intellectual can and must, in the first place, *fulfill negative functions*: it must work to produce and disseminate instruments of defense against symbolic domination that relies increasingly on the authority of science (real or faked). Buttressed by the specific competency and authority of the collective thus formed, it can submit dominant discourse to a merciless logical critique aimed not only at its lexicon ("globalization," "flexibility," "employability," etc.) but also at its mode of reasoning and in particular at the use of metaphors (e.g., the anthropomorphization of the market). It can furthermore subject this discourse to a sociological critique aimed at uncovering the social determinants that bear on the producers of dominant discourse (starting with journalists, especially economic journalists) and on their products. Lastly, it can counter the pseudoscientific authority of authorized experts (chief among them economic experts and advisors) with a genuinely scientific critique of the hidden assumptions and often faulty reasoning that underpin their pronouncements.

But the collective intellectual can also fulfill a *positive function* by contributing to the collective work of political invention. The collapse of Soviet-type regimes and the weakening of communist parties in most European and Latin American countries has freed critical thought. But neoliberal *doxa* has filled the vacuum thus created and critique has retreated into the "small world" of academe, where it enchants itself with itself without ever being in a position to really threaten anyone about anything. The whole edifice of critical thought is in need of reconstruction. And this work of reconstruction cannot be effected, as some have thought in the past, by a single great intellectual, a master thinker endowed with the sole resources of his singular thought, or by the authorized spokesperson for a group or an institution presumed to speak in the name of those without voice.

This is where the collective intellectual can play its unique role, by helping to create the social conditions for the collective production of *realistic utopias*. It can organize or orchestrate joint research on novel forms of political action, on new manners of mobilizing and of making mobilized people work together, on new ways of elaborating projects and bringing them to fruition together. It can play the role of midwife by assisting the dynamics of working groups in their effort to express, and thereby discover, what they are and what they could or should be, and by helping with the reappropriation and accumulation of the immense social stock of knowledge on the social world with which the social world is pregnant. It could thus help the victims of neoliberal policies to discover the differential effects of one and the same cause in apparently radically diverse events and experiences, especially for those who undergo them, associated with the different social universes, that is, in education, medicine, social welfare, criminal justice, etc., within one country or across countries. (This is what we tried to do in the book *The Weight of the World*, which brought to light new forms of social suffering caused by state retrenchment, with the purpose of compelling politicians to address them.)[4]

This task is at once extremely urgent and extremely difficult. For the representations of the social world that must be resisted and countered are issued out of a *conservative revolution*—as was said of the pre-Nazi movements in Weimar Germany. In order to break with the tradition of the welfare state, the "think tanks" from which have emerged the political programs of Reagan and Thatcher and, after them, of Clinton, Blair, Schröder, and Jospin, have had to effect a veritable symbolic counterrevolution and to produce a *paradoxical doxa*. This *doxa* is conservative but presents itself as progressive; it seeks the restoration of the past order in some of its most archaic aspects (especially as regards economic relations), yet it passes regressions, reversals, and surrenders off as forward-looking reforms or revolutions leading to a whole new age of abundance and liberty (as with the language of the so-called new economy and the celebratory discourse around "network firms" and the Internet). All of this can be clearly seen in the efforts to dismantle the welfare state, that is, to destroy the most precious democratic conquests in the areas of labor legislation, health, social protection, and education. To fight such a progressive-retrogressive policy is to risk appearing conservative even as one defends the most progressive achievements of the past. This situation is all the more paradoxical in that one is led to defend programs or institutions that one wishes in any case to change, such as public services and the national state, which no one could rightly want to preserve as is, or unions or even public schooling, which must be continually subjected to the most merciless critique. Thus I am sometimes suspected of conversion or accused of contradiction when I defend a public school system of which I have shown time and again that it fulfills a function of social conservation.

It seems to me that scholars have a decisive role to play in the struggle against the new neoliberal doxa and the purely formal cosmopolitanism of those obsessed with words such as "globalization" or "global competitiveness." This fake universalism serves in reality the interests of the dominant: in the absence of a world state and a world bank financed by taxation of the international circulation of speculative capital, it serves to condemn as a "politically incorrect" regression toward nationalism the recourse to the only force, the national state, presently capable of protecting emergent countries such as South Korea or Malaysia from the stranglehold of multinational corporations. This fake universalism allows one to stigmatize, under demonizing labels such as "Islamism," the efforts of such a Third World country to assert or restore its political autonomy, based on state power. To this verbal universalism, which also plagues relations between the sexes and which leaves citizens isolated and disarmed in the face of the overwhelming power of transnational corporations, committed scholars can oppose a *new internationalism,* capable of tackling with truly international force not only issues such as environmental problems (air pollution, the ozone layer, nonrenewable fuels, or atomic fallout) that are truly "global" because they know no boundaries between nations or between social classes, but also more strictly economic issues such as the foreign debt of emergent countries, or cultural issues such as the question of the hegemony of financial capital in the field of cultural production and diffusion (attested to by the growing concentration of publishing or movie production and distribution). All these can unite intellectuals who are resolutely universal, that is, intent upon universalizing the conditions of access to the universal, beyond the boundaries that separate nations, especially those of the North and South.

To do so, writers, artists, and especially researchers (who, by trade, are already more inclined and more able than any other occupation to overcome national borders) must breach the *sacred boundary* inscribed in their minds—more or less deeply depending on their national tradition—between *scholarship* and *commitment* in order to break out of the academic microcosm and to enter resolutely into sustained exchange with the outside world (that is, especially with unions, grassroots organizations, and issue-oriented activist groups) instead of being content with waging the "political" battles, at once intimate and ultimate, and always a bit unreal, of the scholastic universe. Today's researchers must innovate an improbable but indispensable combination: *scholarship with commitment,* that is, a collective politics of intervention in the political field that follows, as much as possible, the rules that govern the scientific field.

Given the mix of urgency and confusion that usually characterizes the world of political action, this is truly and fully possible only by and for an organization capable of coordinating the collective work of an international network of researchers and artists. In this joint enterprise, scientists are no doubt the ones who have to shoulder the primary role at a time when the powers that be ceaselessly invoke the authority of science—and the science of economics in particular. But writers and above all artists also have their contribution to make (among them, I think in particular of Hans Haacke, who has already invested his talents in critical battles). "True ideas bear no intrinsic force," said Spinoza, and the sociologist is not one to dispute him on this. But she can suggest the unique and irreplaceable role that writers and artists can play in the new division of political labor or, to be more precise, the new manner of doing politics that needs to be invented: to give *symbolic force*, by way of artistic form, to critical ideas and analyses. They can, for instance, give a *visible and sensible* form to the *invisible but scientifically predictable* consequences of political measures inspired by neoliberal ideology.

I would like, by way of conclusion, to recall what happened last month in Seattle. I believe that, without overestimating its importance, we can see in this event a first and exemplary experiment that needs to be analyzed up close in order to uncover the principles of what could be the means and ends of a new form of international political action able to transform the achievements of research into successful political demonstrations; what could be, more generally, the strategies of political struggle of a new nongovernmental organization defined by total commitment to internationalism and full adherence to scholarship.

THE IMPOSITION OF THE AMERICAN
MODEL AND ITS EFFECTS[5]

The economic policies that are now being applied in all European countries and which the major world institutions—the World Bank, the WTO, the IMF—are imposing throughout the world, invoke the authority of economic science. In reality, they are based on a set of ethical and political presuppositions rooted in a particular historical tradition that is embodied today in the United States. (At this point in my presentation, I should say here, in Germany, as a caveat to forestall any misunderstandings so far as I can, that my remarks do not spring from any kind of anti-Americanism, in the sense of an intrinsic hostility or prejudice toward a whole people or any of its representatives. The political critique of the United States is, rather, directed against a relationship of domination and against the policy aimed at perpetuating it or imposing it. That critique can and should mobilize Americans as much as non-Americans, and, indeed, the struggle against the policy of "globalization" has often been pursued by American men and women.)

Between economic theory in its purest—in other words, its most formalized—form, which is never as neutral as economists like to think and try to make others think, and the policies that are implemented in its name or legitimated by reference to it, there intervene agents and institutions imbued with all the presuppositions that come from immersion in a particular economic world, arising from a particular social history. The economy that neoliberal discourse puts forward as a model owes a number of its supposedly universal characteristics to the fact that it is embedded in a particular society—that is to say, rooted in a system of beliefs and values and a moral vision of the world, in short, an *economic common sense*, linked, as such, to the social structures and cognitive structures of a particular social order.

It follows, first, that the model of economic policy that is being implemented throughout the world universalizes the particular case of the American economy, thereby giving it an enormous competitive advantage, both practical and symbolic, since the model justifies it in existing as it does. Second, it follows that one cannot criticize this model without criticizing the United States, which is its prototypical, paradigmatic form, and without falling foul of the a priori condemnation which, especially in Germany, strikes everything that is seen as springing from "anti-Americanism." The model is based on certain premises, which are presented as propositions grounded in theory and validated in reality. The first is that the economy is a separate domain governed by natural, universal laws that governments should not meddle with; the second is that the market is the optimal means of efficiently and equitably organizing production and exchange in democratic societies; the third is that globalization requires the reduction of state spending, especially in the area of unemployment and Social Security entitlements, seen as both costly and dysfunctional.

One only has to break out of the effect of symbolic imposition exerted by the dominant vision to see that this model owes less to the pure principles of economic theory than to the historical features of a particular social tradition, that of the United States, which I would like to sketch quickly.

The first feature is the *weakness of the state*, which, already reduced to a minimum, has been systematically weakened by the ultraliberal conservative revolution (started under Reagan and extended by Clinton, and in particular his "welfare reform," an extraordinary antiphrastic euphemism used to designate the removal of help for the most deprived, such as single mothers), with various consequences characteristic of that paradoxical society, which is very advanced economically and scientifically and very backward socially and politically. I will mention, among other indications, a series of convergent facts: the *monopoly of physical violence* is very imperfectly secured, because of the very widespread private possession of weapons (the existence of a gun lobby, the National Rifle Association, the number of firearm owners—as many as 70 million—or the average annual number of deaths by shooting—30,000—are indications of an instituted tolerance of private violence unparalleled in advanced societies); the state has withdrawn from all economic functions, selling off the enterprises it owned, *converting public goods*, like health, housing, security, education, and culture—books, films, television, and radio—*into commercial goods and users into customers*, subcontracting "public services" to the private sector, renouncing its power to redress inequality (which tends to grow inordinately), and delegating social functions to lower levels (region, town, etc.), all in the name of the old liberal tradition of self-help (inherited from the Calvinist belief that God helps those who help themselves) and the conservative exaltation of individual responsibility—which leads for example to unemployment or economic failure to be blamed on the individuals themselves, rather than on the social order, and which through the equivocal notion of "employability" requires each individual agent, as Franz Schultheis points out, to place him- or herself on the market, becoming a kind of entrepreneurial manager of him or herself as human capital, with the consequence of increasing, with a kind of guilt, the suffering of those who are rejected by the market; "American democracy," contrary to what one might think from the exaltation it enjoys, is marred by serious dysfunctions, such as very high levels of abstaining, party financing, dependence on the media and money, or the excessive role of lobbying.

Second, American society has pushed to its extreme the development and generalization of the "spirit of capitalism"—whose exemplary incarnation Max Weber found in Benjamin Franklin—and the exaltation of the expansion of capital, elevated into a "calling" (*Beruf*). The calculating mentality pervades the whole of life and all areas of practice, without exception, and is embedded in the institutions (for example, in what is called the "academic marketplace") and in everyday exchanges.

Third, the cult of the individual and "individualism," the basis of all neoliberal economic thinking, is one of the pillars of the *doxa* on which, according to Dorothy Ross, the American social sciences have been constructed.[6] Economic science is based on a philosophy of action, methodological individualism, which only recognizes the consciously calculated actions of isolated agents, pursuing individual, selfish aims that are consciously posited. When it comes to collective actions, such as those organized by representative agencies—parties, unions, or associations, and also the state, the agency charged with constituting and imposing the collective consciousness and will and helping to favor the strengthening of solidarity—not only does it find it hard to account for them (with the "free rider" problem), but it tends to reduce them to simple *aggregations of isolated, individual actions* (being unable to recognize them as modes of resolution and working-out of conflicts and as principles of the invention of new forms of social organization). In doing so, it de facto excludes politics, which is reduced to a sum of individual acts which—like the vote, performed in isolation, in the privacy of the polling booth—are the exact equivalent of the solitary act of shopping in a supermarket. The implicit philosophy of the economy and of the relationship between the economic and the political is a political vision which sets up an impermeable boundary between the economic—governed by the fluid, efficient mechanisms of the market—and the social, ruled by the unpredictable arbitrariness of tradition, power, and passions.

Fourth, the other founding topic of the American vulgate, according to Dorothy Ross, the exaltation of the dynamism and mobility of the American social order (the antithesis of the rigidity and fear of risk attributed to European societies), leads its apostles to associate efficiency and productivity with *high flexibility* (as opposed to the constraints induced by a strong social security) and even to *make social insecurity a positive principle of collective organization*, capable of producing economic agents who are more efficient and productive.[7] Labor relations based on institutionalized insecurity (in particular, with the new types of employment contract), and increasingly particularized to suit the firm and the specific demands of the work (length and spacing of working hours, benefits, promotion prospects, forms of appraisal, types of remuneration, retirement, etc.), lead to a desocialization of wage labor and a methodical atomization of the workers.

Fifth and finally, a society that relies on insecurity while exalting individualism and self-help is the embodiment of a *neo-Darwinist vision* (in fact, expressed overtly by some economists like Gary Becker—notably in an article entitled "De Gustibus Non Est Disputandum")[8] that is the absolute opposite of the *social solidarity vision* that the history of the social movement has implanted in the social structures and cognitive structures of European societies.

To understand how this model is capable of universalizing itself, one only has to consider the strength of the economic pressures and constraints imposed by the financial markets, the giant multinational corporations (especially banks), and the international organizations (World Bank, IMF, WTO) and by the monopolistic position it has enjoyed since the collapse of the Soviet Union, identified with communism. One has to bear in mind the specifically symbolic effects that can be produced by think tanks, "experts," and perhaps especially journalists who are subjected to the dominant economic and political forces through the constraints inherent in the structure of the journalistic field. These agents and institutions inculcate new categories of thought with the aid of various mechanisms—mental passivity and laziness, scientism, (paradoxical) snobbery, or, quite simply, conservatism, and do so *with the complicity of the Europeans themselves*, in a logic that has some affinities with that of *colonization*.

Loccum, Germany, October 1999

THE INVISIBLE HAND OF THE POWERFUL

Address to students at Humboldt Universität, Berlin, 10 June 2000.

We have a Europe of banks and bankers, a Europe of corporations and top executives, a Europe of police and police officers, and we shall soon have a Europe of armies and military forces but, though there exists a European Trade Union Confederation, one cannot say that the Europe of trade unions and associations really exists. Similarly, though one loses count of the conferences where Europe is blustered about and of the academic institutions where European problems are spoken of in impeccably academic language, the Europe of artists, writers, and scientists is much less of a reality now than it was in eras past. The paradox is that one cannot criticize this Europe that is being built around and by the powerful, and which is so un-European, without risking being conflated with the archaic resonances put up by reactionary nationalism for a backward-looking reactionary nationalist (and they unfortunately do exist) and hence contributing to making this Europe seem modern, if not progressive.

One must bring (back) into action what is most European in the European tradition, namely, a critical social movement, a movement of social critique capable of *effectively* contesting the process of European construction, that is, with enough intellectual and political forces to produce real effects. The aim of such a critical offensive is not to void the European project, to neutralize it, but on the contrary to *radicalize* it and thereby to bring it *closer* to the citizens, particularly the youngest among them who are often described as depoliticized when they are merely disgusted with the politics that official politicians serve up, disgusted with politics by and for politicians. We must restore meaning to politics and to do this prepare projects for the future capable of giving meaning to an economic and social world that has undergone enormous transformations in recent years.

In the 1930s, Adolf Berle and Gardiner Means described the advent of the rule of "managers" over and at the expense of the "owners," the shareholders.[9] Today we are witnessing the return of the owners, but their comeback is only *apparent*. For owners have no more power than they did in the age of Galbraith's "technostructure." In fact, the masters of the economy are no longer the managers subject to the tyranny of rates of profit, that is, those CEOs now rewarded or dismissed (most often with stupendous severance packages) on the basis of a quarterly evaluation of the "shareholder value" they have achieved, or those executives paid on a short-term basis with a percentage of the business they bring in and who keep a daily eye on the stock market, where the value of their stock options is determined. But the masters of the economy are not the owners either, that is to say, the individual small shareholders depicted in the mythology of the "shareholding democracy."

It is, in fact, the managers of the big institutions, the pension funds, the big insurance companies, and, particularly in the United States, the money market funds or mutual funds who today dominate the field of financial capital, within which financial capital is both stake and weapon (as are certain specific forms of cultural capital that consultants, analysts, and monetary authorities can mobilize with great symbolic efficacy). These managers possess a formidable capacity to pressure both firms and states. They are, in effect, in a position to impose the obligation, which is in turn imposed on them, to obtain from capital what economist Frédéric Lordon calls, in an ironic reference to minimum income legislation, a *minimum guaranteed shareholder income*. Present everywhere on the boards of companies ("corporate governance"), they are compelled by the logic of the system they dominate to improve the pursuit of ever higher profits (returns of 12, 15, and even 18 percent on capital invested), which firms can yield only through mass layoffs. They thus transfer the imperative of short-term profit—which, in complete disregard of ecological and, above all, human consequences, becomes the practical purpose of the entire system—onto the company managers, who in turn transfer that risk to the wage earners, notably through "downsizing." In short, because the dominant in this game are dominated by the rules of the game they dominate (the rule of profit), this field functions as a kind of infernal machine without subject, which imposes its will on both states and firms.

Within companies, too, the pursuit of short-term profit governs all decisions, particularly the recruitment policy (subjected to the imperatives of flexibility and mobility as with hires on short-term contracts or on a temporary basis), the individualization of the wage relation, and the absence of long-term planning particularly as regards the workforce. With "downsizing" a constant threat, the whole life of wage earners is placed under the sign of insecurity and uncertainty. The previous system provided security of employment and a relatively high level of remuneration by fueling demand which sustained growth and profits. By contrast, the new mode of production maximizes profit by reducing payroll through layoffs and the compression of wages, the shareholder being concerned only with stock market value, on which his nominal income depends, and with price stability, necessary to keep his real income as close as possible to the nominal. Thus has come into being an economic regime that is inseparable from a political regime, a mode of production that entails a mode of domination based on the *institution of insecurity*, domination through precariousness: a deregulated financial market fosters a deregulated labor market and thereby the casualization of labor that cows workers into submission.

We are dealing, within companies, with a rational management utilizing the weapon of insecurity (among others) to put workers in a state of risk, stress, and tension. Unlike "traditional" casual labor in the service sector and the construction industry, *institutionalized precariousness* inside the firms of the future becomes a principle of work organization and a style of life. As Gilles Balbastre has shown, some telesales or telemarketing companies, whose employees have to telephone potential clients at home in order to generate sales, have put in place a work regime that in terms of productivity, control and supervision, working hours, and the absence of career prospects amounts to a veritable service-sector Taylorism. By contrast with the unskilled workers of factory Taylorism, the employees are often highly qualified.

But the prototype of the unskilled worker of the "new economy" is the supermarket checkout girl whom bar-coding and computerization have converted into a genuine assembly-line worker, her cadence timed, clocked, and controlled across a schedule determined by variations in the flow of customers: she has neither the life nor the lifestyle of a factory worker, but she occupies an equivalent position in the new structure.

These companies, which offer no security to their employees and contribute to instituting a consumerist vision of the world, herald an economic reality akin to the social philosophy inherent in neoclassical theory. It is as if the instantaneist, individualistic, ultrasubjectivist philosophy of neoclassical economics had found in neoliberal policy the means of its own realization, had created the conditions for its own verification. This *chronically unstable system* is structurally exposed to risk (and not just because crisis, linked to speculative bubbles, hovers over it constantly like the sword of Damocles). One sees in passing that when Ulrich Beck and Anthony Giddens extol the advent of the "risk society" and make the myth of the transformation of all wage earners into dynamic small entrepreneurs their own, they are merely instituting as societal norms those rules imposed on the dominated by the needs of the economy (from which the dominant are careful to exempt themselves).

However, the main consequence of this new mode of production is the establishment of a *dual economy* (which, paradoxically, has many features in common with the dualistic economy I observed in Algeria in the 1960s, with, on the one hand, an enormous industrial reserve army, made up of a subproletariat with no employment prospects, no future, no plans, either individual or collective, and hence condemned to millenarian dreaming rather than revolutionary ambitions, and, on the other, a small privileged minority of secure workers with a regular wage). The duality of income and status is growing continually. There are more and more low-level service jobs that are underpaid and low-productivity, unskilled or underskilled (based on hasty on-the-job training), with no career prospects—in short, the *throwaway jobs* of what André Gorz calls a "society of servants." According to economist Jean Gadrey, quoting an American study, of the thirty jobs that will grow fastest in the next decade, seventeen require no skills and only eight require higher education and qualification. At the other end of social space, the *dominated dominant*, that is, the managers, are experiencing a new form of alienation. They occupy an ambiguous position, equivalent to that of the petty bourgeois at another historical stage in the structure, which leads to forms of organized self-exploitation (average annual working hours are increasing in the United States, with a correlative decline in leisure time: executives earn a lot of money but do not have the time to spend it). Overworked, stressed, and threatened with dismissal, they are nonetheless chained to the company.

Whatever the prophets of the "new economy" may say, this dualism is nowhere so apparent as in the *social uses of computing*. The advocates of the "new economy" and of the Silicon Valley vision tend to regard current economic and social changes as an inevitable effect of technology, whereas they are the product of the economically and socially conditioned social uses made of that technology. Contrary to the illusion of unprecedented novelty, the structural constraints built into the social order—such as the logic of the transmission of cultural and academic capital, which is the precondition for the true mastery of the new tools, both technological and financial—continue to bear on the present and to shape what is novel and innovative. Statistical analysis of the use and users of information technology shows that there exists a pronounced divide between the "interactors" and the "interacted," based on the unequal distribution of cultural capital and hence, ultimately, on the school system and the familial transmission of capital. The modal information technology user is a thirty-five-year-old highly educated English-speaking urban male with a high income. And the virtuosi capable of writing their own programs have little or nothing in common with the new workers of the informatics production line such as the telephone operators who work in shifts round the clock to staff the hotline for twenty-four-hour access providers, or the "Net surfers" building up directories, or the "integrators" doing copying and pasting—atomized, isolated occupations shorn of any form of union representation and fated to rapid turnover. Similarly, in terms of economic and financial use, there is an opposition between those with Internet connections, who have computers and software that enable them to trade and do their banking online from home, and those lacking that access. And the facts clearly give lie to the myth that the Internet would change relations between North and South: in 1997, the richest 20 percent of the world's population represented 93.3 percent of Internet users, while the poorest 20 percent made up 0.2 percent. Whether at the level of individuals or nations, the "immaterial" rests on very real structures, such as education systems and laboratories, not to mention banks and firms.

In the richest societies, this dualism is based for the most part on the unequal distribution of cultural capital, which, apart from continuing to determine the division of labor to a large extent, constitutes a very powerful instrument of *sociodicy*. The ruling class no doubt owes its extraordinary *arrogance* to the fact that, being endowed with very high cultural capital (most obviously of academic origin, but also non-academic), it feels perfectly justified in existing as it currently exists, the living paradigm of the new conquering bourgeois being Bill Gates. The educational diploma is not merely a mark of academic distinction; it is perceived as a warrant of natural intelligence, of giftedness. Thus the "new economy" has all the characteristics required to appear as the "brave new world" (in Huxley's sense). It is global and those who dominate it are often international, polyglot, and polycultural (by opposition to the locals, the "national" or "parochial"). It is immaterial or "weightless": it produces and circulates weightless objects such as information and cultural products. As a consequence, it can appear as an *economy of intelligence*, reserved for "intelligent" people (which earns it the sympathy of "hip" journalists and executives). Sociodicy here takes the form of a *racism of intelligence*: today's poor are not poor, as they were thought to be in the nineteenth century, because they are improvident, spendthrift, intemperate, etc.—by opposition to the "deserving poor"—but because they are dumb, intellectually incapable, idiotic. In short, in academic terms "they got their just deserts" (one thinks here of the phantasm of *The Bell Curve*). Some economists such as Gary Becker may find an incontrovertible justification for the rule of the "best and the brightest" in a neo-Darwinism that makes the rationality postulated by economic theory the product of the natural selection of the most capable. And the circle is completed when economics calls on mathematics (which has itself become one of the major instruments of social selection) to provide the most incontestable *epistemocratic* justification for the established order. The victims of such a powerful mode of domination, which can appeal to a principle of domination and legitimation as universal as rationality (upheld by the education system), are very deeply damaged in their self-image. And it is no doubt through this mediation that a relationship—most often unnoticed or misunderstood—can be traced between neoliberal politics and certain fascistoid forms of revolt among those who, feeling excluded from access to intelligence and modernity, are driven to take refuge in the national and nationalism.

(If it is difficult to combat the neoliberal vision effectively, this is because, though conservative, it presents itself as progressive. As a result, it is able to deflect all critiques, especially those that point to the destruction of the social conquests of the past, by dubbing them conservative or even backward-looking. Thus governments that claim to embody social democracy can dismiss under the label "red-brown," as "extremists" of the far left and the far right both those who criticize them for renouncing their socialist program and the victims of that renunciation who reproach them for what they believe to be their socialism.)

Neoliberalism aims to destroy the social state, the "left hand" of the state, which, as can easily be shown, safeguards the interests of the dominated, the culturally and economically dispossessed, women, stigmatized ethnic groups, etc.[10] The most exemplary case is that of health, which neoliberal policy attacks from two directions, by contributing to an increase in the incidence of illness and the number of sick people (through the correlation between poverty and pathology: alcoholism, drugs, delinquency, industrial accidents, etc.) and by reducing medical resources and the provision of care (take the example of Britain and Russia, where life expectancy has fallen by ten years in ten years!).

In some European countries, such as France, we are witnessing the emergence of a new form of multipurpose social work *accompanying the collective shift toward neoliberalism*: on the one hand, this provides work, in the manner of the *Ateliers nationaux* in an earlier era, for people with devalued academic qualifications (many of them whole-hearted, committed people) by setting them to supervise others in a homologous position; on the other hand, it keeps the academic rejects out of mischief by offering them make-work, making them wage earners without wages, entrepreneurs without an enterprise, continuing students with no hope of qualifications or degrees. All these programs of social supervision, which foster a kind of collective self-mystification by, among other things, blurring the boundary between work and non-work, between study and work, etc., and a belief in a sham universe whose symbol is the idea of the "project," rest on a "charitable" social philosophy and a "soft" sociology that regards itself as based on "understanding" and which, purporting to adopt the standpoint of the "subjects" it wishes to set in action ("action sociology"), ends up endorsing the mystified and mystifying vision of social work (by contrast with a rigorous sociology which, from that standpoint, is doomed to appear deterministic and pessimistic because it takes account of structures and their effects).

In the face of such a complex and refined mode of domination, in which symbolic power has such an important place, one must invent new forms of struggle. Given the particular role of "ideas" in this scheme, researchers have a key part to play. They have to provide political action with new ends—the demolition of the dominant beliefs—and new means—technical weapons—based on research and a command of scientific knowledge, and symbolic weapons, capable of undermining common beliefs by putting research findings into an accessible form.

The European social movement that needs to be created has for objective a utopia, namely, a Europe in which all the critical social forces, currently very diverse and dispersed, would be sufficiently integrated and organized to be a force of critical movement. And there is something utopian about such a movement itself, so great are the linguistic, economic, and technical obstacles to such a gathering. The multiplicity and diversity of movements that pursue some or all of the aims we propose for ourselves are, in fact, the first and foremost justification for a collective undertaking aimed at unifying and integrating them, without monopolizing them or taking them over, by working to help the individuals and organizations committed on this front to overcome the effects of competition. The first task, then, is to offer a *coherent set of alternative propositions, developed jointly by researchers and activists* (while avoiding any form of instrumentalization of one by the other), capable of unifying the social movement by overcoming the divisions between national traditions and, within each nation, between occupational categories and social categories (especially that between workers and the unemployed), the sexes, the generations, and those of different ethnic origins (immigrants and nationals). Only the enormous collective work required to coordinate the critical activities, both theoretical and practical, of all the social movements born of the desire to fill the gap left by the depoliticizing political action of social democratic governments will enable us to invent the structures of inquiry, discussion, and mobilization at many levels (international, national, and local) that will gradually inscribe in minds and in things a new manner of doing politics.

AGAINST THE POLICY OF DEPOLITICIZATION

Everything contained in the descriptive and normative term "globalization" is the effect not of economic inevitability but of a conscious and deliberate policy, if a policy more often than not unaware of its consequences. That policy is quite paradoxical in that it is a *policy of depoliticization*. Drawing shamelessly on the lexicon of liberty, liberalism, and deregulation, it aims to grant economic determinisms a fatal stranglehold by *liberating* them from all controls, and to obtain the submission of citizens and governments to the economic and social forces thus "liberated." Incubated in the meetings of great international institutions such as the World Trade Organization and the European Commission, or within the "networks" of multinational corporations, this policy has imposed itself through the most varied means, especially juridical, on the liberal—or even social democratic—governments of a set of economically advanced countries, leading them gradually to divest themselves of the power to control economic forces.

Against this policy of depoliticization, our aim must be to *restore politics*, that is, political thinking and action, and to find the correct point of application for that action, which now lies beyond the borders of the nation-state, as well as the appropriate means, which can no longer be reduced to political and trade union struggles within national states. We must admit that the task is extremely difficult for many reasons. First, the political agencies to be combated are very remote, not just in geographical terms, and they are not at all like the institutions that traditional social struggles used to confront, either in their methods or the agents concerned. Second, the power of the agents and mechanisms that dominate the economic and social world today rests on an extraordinary concentration of all the species of capital—economic, political, military, cultural, scientific, and technological—as the foundation of a symbolic domination without precedent, wielded in particular via the stranglehold of the media, themselves manipulated, most often unbeknownst to themselves, by the major international communications companies and by the logic of competition that sets them against one another.

It remains that some of the objectives of an efficacious political action are located at the European level, insofar at least as European firms and organizations form a decisive element among the dominant forces at the global level. It follows that the construction of a unified, Europe-wide social movement, capable of gathering together the various movements that are presently divided, both nationally and internationally, presents itself as a reasoned objective for all those who intend to effectively resist the dominant forces.

AN OPEN-ENDED COORDINATION

No matter how diverse they are in their origins, aims, and objectives, contemporary social movements all have a set of *common features* that creates a family resemblance among them. First, because they often originate in a refusal of traditional forms of political mobilization—especially those forms that perpetuate the tradition of Soviet-type parties—they are inclined to exclude any kind of monopolization by minorities and to promote instead the direct participation of all concerned (thanks in part to the emergence of leaders of a new type, endowed with a political culture superior to that of traditional officials and capable of perceiving and expressing new kinds of social aspirations). They are close to the libertarian tradition in that they are attached to forms of organization inspired by theories of self-management, characterized by a reduced role for the apparatus and enabling agents to recapture their role as active subjects—particularly from the political parties whose monopoly over civic intervention they contest.

A second common feature is that they invent, or reinvent, forms of action that are original in both ends and means and have a high symbolic content. They orient themselves toward precise, concrete objectives that are important in social life, such as housing, employment, health, legal status for illegal immigrants, etc., and strive for direct and practical solutions. And they ensure that both their proposals and their refusals are concretized in exemplary actions, directly linked to the particular problem concerned and requiring a high level of personal commitment on the part of activists and leaders, most of whom have mastered the art of creating events, of dramatizing a condition so as to focus media attention—and, consequently, political attention—on them, thanks to a firm grasp of the functioning of the journalistic world. This does not mean that these movements are mere artifacts, created from scratch by a small minority with the support of the media. In fact, the realistic use of the media has been combined with activist work that, carried on over a long period on the fringes of the "traditional" movements (parties and trade unions), and sometimes with the collaboration and support of a fraction, itself marginal and minor, of these movements, has found in various conjunctures the opportunity to become more visible and thus to expand its social base, at least temporarily. The most remarkable fact about these new movements is that they have immediately assumed an international form, partly by virtue of their exemplary character and partly because new forms of action have been invented simultaneously in different countries (as in the case of campaigns over housing).

(The specificity of these new forms of struggle lies nonetheless in the fact that they feed on the publicity given to them, sometimes reluctantly, by the media and that the number of people involved in a protest is now less important than the amount of media coverage and political impact achieved by a demonstration or action. But media visibility is by definition partial as well as hardly impartial and, above all, ephemeral. The spokespersons are interviewed, a few emotion-laden reports are broadcast, but the demands of the movements are seldom taken seriously in public debate, as a consequence of the media's limited understanding. This is why it is essential to sustain activist work and an effort at theoretical elaboration *over the long term*, irrespective of opportunities for media exposure.)

A third characteristic typical of these movements is that they reject neoliberal policies aimed at imposing the will of the big institutional investors and multinationals. A fourth feature is that they are, to varying degrees, international and internationalist. This is particularly visible in the case of the movement of the unemployed or the movement led by José Bové's Confédération paysanne, where there is both a concern and a resolve to defend not only small farmers in France but also the landless peasants of South America and other parts of the world. All these movements are both particularistic and internationalist: they do not defend an insular, isolated Europe, but through Europe they defend a certain type of social management of the economy that clearly must be achieved by establishing a liaison with other countries—with Korea, for example, where many have great expectations of what can be achieved by transcontinental solidarity. As a final distinctive, shared characteristic, these movements extol solidarity, which is the tacit principle of most of their struggles, and they strive to implement it in their action (including all the have-nots within their ambit: the jobless, the homeless, the immigrants without papers, etc.) and in the encompassing form of organization they adopt.

Such a kinship of ends and means among these political struggles demands that we seek, if not to unify all the scattered movements, as is often clamored for by activists, especially the youngest among them who are struck by the degree of overlap and convergence, then at least to establish *a coordination of demands and actions while excluding attempts of any kind to take these movements over*. Such coordination should take the form of a *network* capable of bringing individuals and groups together under conditions such that no one can dominate or cut down the others and such that the resources linked to the diversity of experience, standpoints, and programs is preserved. The main function of such a network would be to prevent the actions of social movements from becoming fragmented and dispersed—being absorbed by the particularism of local initiatives—and to enable them to overcome the sporadic character of their action or an alternation between moments of intense mobilization and periods of latency. This must be done, moreover, without leading to a concentration of power in bureaucratic structures.

There are currently many connections between movements and many shared undertakings, but these remain extremely dispersed within each country and even more so *between* countries. For example, there exist a great many critical newspapers, weeklies, or magazines in each country, not to mention Internet sites, that are full of analyses, suggestions, and proposals for the future of Europe and the world, but all this work is fragmented and no one reads it all. Those who produce these works are often in competition with one another; they criticize each other when their contributions are complementary and can be cumulated. The dominant in our society travel; they have money; they are polyglot; and they are linked together by affinities of culture and lifestyle. Ranged against them are people who are dispersed geographically and separated by linguistic or social barriers. Bringing all these people together is at once very necessary and very difficult. There are numerous obstacles, for many progressive forces and structures of resistance, starting with the trade unions, are linked to the national state. And this is true not just of institutional structures but of mental structures. People are used to thinking and waging struggles at the national level. The question is whether the new structures of transnational mobilization will succeed in bringing the traditional structures, which are national, along with them. What is certain is that this new social movement will have to rely on the state while changing the state, to rely on the trade unions while changing the trade unions, and this entails massive work, much of it intellectual. One of the functions of researchers could (ideally) be to play the role of organizational advisors to the social movements by helping the various groups to overcome their disagreements.

This coordination, flexible and permanent, should set itself two distinct objectives: on the one hand, to organize campaigns of short-term action with precise objectives, through one-time ad hoc meetings; on the other, to submit issues of general interest for discussion and to work on elaborating longer-term research programs by periodically bringing together representatives of all the groups concerned. The aim would in effect be to discover and work out general objectives to which all can subscribe, at the point where the concerns of all the different groups intersect, and on which all can collaborate by contributing their own skills and methods. It is not too much to hope that democratic confrontation among individuals and groups with shared assumptions may gradually produce a set of coherent and meaningful responses to basic problems for which neither trade unions nor parties can provide any overall solution.

A RENEWED TRADE UNIONISM

A European social movement is inconceivable without the participation of renewed trade unions, capable of surmounting the external and internal obstacles, on a European scale, to unification and reinforcement. It is only an apparent paradox to regard the decline of trade unionism as an indirect and delayed effect of its triumph: many of the demands that motivated trade union battles in the past are now inscribed in institutions that, being henceforth the foundation of obligations and rights pertaining to social protection, have become stakes of struggles between the unions themselves. Transformed into parastate bodies, often subsidized by the state, the trade union bureaucrats partake in the redistribution of wealth and safeguard the social compromise by avoiding ruptures and clashes. And when trade union officials become converted into administrators, removed from the preoccupations of those whom they represent, they can be led by competition between or within trade union "machines" to defend their own interests rather than the interests of those whom they are supposed to be safeguarding. This cannot but have contributed in part to distancing wage earners from the trade unions and to deterring trade union members themselves from active participation in the organization.

But these internal causes alone cannot explain why trade union members are ever less numerous and active. Neoliberal policy also contributes to the weakening of the unions. The flexibility and, above all, casualization of an increasing number of wage earners and the ensuing transformation of working conditions and labor standards help to make any united action difficult. Even the work of keeping wage earners informed is made difficult as the remnants of public aid continue to protect a fraction of wage earners. This shows how essential and difficult it is to renovate trade union action, which would require rotation of positions and calling into question the model of unconditional delegation, as well as the invention of new techniques needed to mobilize fragmented, casualized workers.

This organization of an entirely new type that has to be created must be capable of overcoming the fragmentation on grounds of goals and nations, as well as the division into movements and trade unions, by escaping both the hazards of monopolization (or, more precisely, the temptation and attempts at appropriation that haunt all social movements) and the immobilism often generated by the quasineurotic fear of such hazards. The existence of a stable and efficacious international network of trade unions and movements, energized by mutual confrontation within forums for negotiation and discussion, such as the *Estates General of the European social movement*, should make it possible to develop an international campaign that would be altogether different from the activities of the official bodies in which some trade unions are represented (such as the European Trade Union Confederation). It would also consolidate the actions of all the movements constantly grappling with specific and hence limited situations.

BRINGING TOGETHER RESEARCHERS AND ACTIVISTS

The work required to overcome the divisions between social movements and thereby to bring together all the available forces arrayed against the dominant forces, themselves consciously and methodically coordinated, must also be directed against another, equally fateful division: that between researchers and activists. Given an economic and political balance of forces in which the economic powers that be are in a position to enlist unprecedented scientific, technical, and cultural resources at their behest, the work of academic researchers is indispensable to disclose and dismantle the strategies incubated and implemented by the big multinationals and international bodies, such as the World Trade Organization, which produce and impose putatively universal regulations capable of gradually turning the neoliberal utopia of generalized deregulation into reality. The social obstacles to such rapprochement are no less great than those that stand between the different movements, or between the movements and the trade unions. Though they are different in their training and social trajectories, researchers engaged in activist work and activists interested in research must learn to work together, overcoming all the prejudices they may harbor about one another. They must endeavor to cast off the routines and presuppositions associated with membership in universes governed by different laws and logics by establishing modes of communication and discussion of a new type. This is one of the preconditions for the collective invention, in and through the critical confrontation of experiences and competencies, of a set of responses that will draw their political force from being both systematic and rooted in common aspirations and convictions.

Only a European social movement, strong with all the forces accumulated in the different organizations of the different countries and with the instruments of information and critique elaborated in common forums of discussion such as the Estates General, will be capable of resisting the forces, at once economic and intellectual, of the large international corporations and of their armies of consultants, experts, and lawyers in their public relations agencies, think tanks, and lobbying agencies. Such a movement will be able also to replace the aims cynically imposed by bodies guided by the pursuit of maximum, short-term profit with the economically and politically democratic objectives of a European social state equipped with the political, juridical, and financial instruments required to curb the brute and brutal force of narrowly economic interests. The call for an Estates General of the European social movement is in line with such a vision (see the Web site www.samizdat.net/mse). It does not in any way aim to represent the whole of the European social movement, still less to monopolize it in the tradition of "democratic centralism" dear to the erstwhile servants of Sovietism, but intends to contribute practically to making it happen by working ceaselessly for a gathering of all the forces of social resistance, on a par with the economic and cultural forces currently mobilized in the service of the policy of "globalization."

AMBIGUOUS EUROPE: REASONS TO ACT AT THE EUROPEAN LEVEL

Europe is fundamentally ambiguous but that ambiguity tends to dissipate when one views it in a dynamic perspective. There is, on the one hand, a Europe autonomous from the dominant economic and political forces and capable, as such, of playing a political role on a world scale. On the other, there is the Europe bound by a kind of customs union to the United States and condemned, as a result, to a fate similar to that of Canada, that is to say, to be gradually dispossessed of any economic and cultural independence from the dominant power. In fact, truly European Europe functions as a decoy, concealing the Euro-American Europe that is on the horizon and which it fosters by winning over the support of those who expect of Europe the very opposite of what it is doing and of what it is becoming.

Everything leads one to believe that, barring a thoroughly improbable rupture, the tendencies leading Europe to submit to transatlantic powers, symbolized and materialized by the Transatlantic Business Dialogue, an umbrella organization of the 150 largest European firms that is working to abolish barriers to world trade and investment, will triumph. Due to the fact that it concentrates at the highest level all the species of capital, the United States is in a position to dominate the global field of the economy. And it can do so thanks to such juridical-political mechanisms as the General Agreement on Trade in Services, a set of evolving regulations aimed at limiting obstacles to "free movement," and stipulated provisions, drafted in the greatest secrecy and functioning with lagged effects, in the manner of computer viruses, by destroying judicial defense systems, that pave the way for the advent of a sort of *invisible world government* in the service of the dominant economic powers, which is the exact opposite of the Kantian idea of the universal state.

Contrary to the widespread idea that the policy of "globalization" tends to foster the withering away of states, in fact states continue to play a crucial role in the service of the politics that weakens them. It is remarkable that the policies aimed at disarming states to the benefit of the financial markets have been decreed by states—and, moreover, states governed by socialists. This means that states, particularly those led by social democrats, are contributing to the triumph of neoliberalism, not only by working for the destruction of the social state (most notably, the destruction of workers' and women's rights, which depend directly on the "left hand" of the state) but also by concealing the powers they relay. And they also function as decoys: they draw the attention of citizens to fictitious targets (strictly national debates, whose prototype is everything having to do in France with "cohabitation") kept alive by a whole range of factors, such as the absence of a European public space and the strictly national character of political, trade union, and media structures. One would need here to demonstrate how the desire to boost circulation inclines newspapers to confine themselves ever more to national politics, if not national politicking, which remains profoundly rooted in national institutional structures, such as families, churches, schools, and trade unions.

All this means that politics is continually moving farther away from ordinary citizens, shifting from the national (or local) to the international level, from an immediate concrete reality to a distant abstraction, from the visible to the invisible. It also means that individual or, to use Sartre's term, "serial" actions (invoked by those who never stop talking of democracy and "citizen control") count for little in the face of the ruling economic powers and the lobbies they hire at their service. It follows that one of the most important and difficult questions is to know at what level to carry on political action—local, national, European, or world. In fact, scientific imperatives are in agreement with political necessities here and require that we travel along the chain of causality back to the most general cause, that is, to the locus, now most often global, where the fundamental determinants of the phenomenon concerned reside, which is the appropriate point of application for action aimed at effecting genuine change. Thus if we take immigration, for instance, it is clear that at the national level we only grasp factors such as the policy of the national state which, aside from fluctuating to meet the interests of the dominant social forces, leave untouched the root of the matter, namely, the effects of neoliberal policies or, to be more precise, the effects of so-called structural adjustment policies and especially of privatization. In many countries these policies lead to economic collapse, followed by massive layoffs that foster a mass movement of forced emigration and the formation of a *global reserve army of labor*, which bears with all its weight on the national workforce and on its collective claims. This is happening at a time when ruling bodies are expressing openly, most notably in the texts of the WTO, their nostalgia for old-style emigration, that is, an emigration composed of disposable, temporary, single workers with no families and no social protection (like the French *sans papiers*) ideally suited to providing the overworked executives of the dominant economy with the cheap and largely feminine services they need. One could make a similar argument in relation to women and the gender inequalities visited upon them insofar as women's fate is inextricably linked to the "left hand" of the state, both for work (they are particularly represented in the health, education, and cultural sectors) and for the services they need in the present state of the sexual division of labor (child care, hospitals, social services, etc.); they are the prime victims of the dismantling of the social state. The same could also be said of dominated ethnic groups, such as blacks in the United States, who, as Loïc Wacquant has pointed out, suffer directly from downsizing of public employment insofar as the Afro-American bourgeoisie, which grew after the civil rights movement, rests essentially on government jobs at the local, state, and federal levels. As for political action, if it wishes to avoid going after decoys and deluding itself with inefficient intervention, it too must track back to the actual causes. Having said this, those actions that, like those deployed in Seattle, are targeted at the highest level, i.e., against the bodies that make up the invisible world government, are the most difficult to organize and also the most ephemeral—all the more so as they are mainly the product of an aggregation of autonomous forces, even if they base themselves on networks and organizations.

This is why it seems to me, first, that it is at the European level that actions purporting to produce effects can and must be targeted. Second, if they are to go beyond mere "happenings," symbolically efficacious but temporary and discontinuous, these actions must be based on a *concentration of already concentrated social forces*, that is, on a confluence of social movements that already exist throughout Europe. Informed by theoretical work aimed at formulating realistic political and social objectives for a genuine social Europe (such as the replacement of the European Commission by a genuine executive responsible to a parliament elected by universal suffrage), these collective actions, carried out through the coordination of a collective, must work to constitute a credible counterpower. They must, that is, work to create a "unified" or "coordinated" European social movement (thus the singular), capable, by its mere existence, of bringing into existence a European political space that currently does not exist.

Paris, July 2000–January 2001

FOR A EUROPEAN SOCIAL MOVEMENT

This article first appeared in *Le Monde diplomatique*, June 1999.

It is no easy matter when speaking of Europe merely to make yourself heard. The journalistic field, which filters, intercepts, and interprets all public statements in terms of its most typical logic, that of "all or nothing," strives to force everyone into the mindless choice imposed on all those who remain trapped within that logic: you are either "for" Europe, that is to say, progressive, open, modern, liberal, or "not for" Europe—in which case you condemn yourself to being thought of as archaic, outdated, reactionary, and nationalist, if not pro–Le Pen and even anti-Semitic. As if there were no other legitimate option but the unconditional endorsement of Europe *as it is*, a Europe reduced to a central bank and a single currency, and subjected to the rule of unfettered competition. But it would be a mistake to think that one really escapes this crude alternative as soon as one speaks of a "social Europe." Discourses on "social Europe" have so far failed to be translated in any significant way into concrete norms governing the daily life of citizens in matters of work, health, housing, retirement, etc. Meanwhile the directives on competition are overturning daily the supply of goods and services and are rapidly undoing national public services—not even to mention how the European central bank can conduct its policy outside of any democratic debate. One can draw up a "social" charter and at the same time combine wage austerity, the reduction of social rights, the repression of protest movements, and the like. *European construction currently amounts to social destruction.* Those who put up these rhetorical smoke screens, such as the French socialists, are merely raising to a higher degree of ambiguity the strategies of political equivocation of British-style "social liberalism," that barely made-over Thatcherism that relies, to sell itself, on the opportunistic exploitation of the symbolics of socialism recycled for mere media consumption. This way, the social democrats currently in power in Europe are able to collaborate, in the name of monetary stability and budgetary rigor, to the sacking of the most admirable conquests of the social struggles of the past two centuries—universalism, egalitarianism (by making Jesuitical distinctions between equality and equity), and internationalism—and to the destruction of the very essence of the socialist idea or ideal, that is to say, broadly put, the ambition to protect or reconstruct through collective and organized action the *solidarities* threatened by the play of economic forces.

The almost simultaneous accession of social democrats to the leadership of several European countries has opened up a real opportunity for them to conceive and carry out a genuine social policy together. Is it not sadly significant that, at this very moment, it does not even occur to them to explore the paths of specifically political actions that are thus open to them in matters of taxation but also in the areas of employment, trade, labor law, training, or social housing? Is it not amazing and revealing that they do not even try to give themselves the means to effectively thwart the already well-advanced process of dismantlement of social rights embodied by the welfare state, for example by establishing within the European zone common social standards with regard to the minimum wage (rationally modulated across countries), working hours, or vocational training for young people? Is it not shocking that they hurry on the contrary to gather and foster the freewheeling operation of the "financial markets," rather than control them by measures such as the institution of an international taxation of capital, particularly of short-term, speculative movements of capital (only included yesterday in their electoral platforms), or the reconstruction of a monetary system capable of ensuring stable relations between economies? And is it not surprising that the power to veto social policies, which is granted, outside of all democratic control, to the "guardians of the Euro" (tacitly identified with Europe), forbids the funding of a major public program of economic and social development based on the proactive establishment of a coherent set of European framework laws, especially in the fields of education, health, and social protection? This would lead to the creation of transnational institutions that would gradually substitute, in part at least, for the national or regional bureaucracies that the logic of a strictly monetary and commercial unification condemns to enter into perverse competition with each other. Given the preponderant part played by intra-European trade in the foreign exchanges of the different countries of Europe, the governments of these countries could implement a common policy aimed at least at limiting the effects of intra-European competition and at mounting collective resistance to the non-European nations—particularly to American injunctions, which often do not conform to the rules of pure and perfect competition they are supposed to safeguard. They could do this instead of invoking the specter of "globalization" to put through (in the name of international competition) the regressive social program that big business has unremittingly promoted, by word and deed, since the mid-1970s: less state intervention, more mobility and "flexibility" of labor (with the pluralization and casualization of employment, the curtailing of union rights, and greater freedom to fire), public aid for private investment through tax policy, the lowering of employers' Social Security contributions, etc. In short, by doing just about nothing to actualize the policy they profess, even as all the conditions for implementing it are present, these governments clearly betray the fact that they do not really want such a policy.

Social history teaches that there is no social policy without a social movement capable of imposing it and that it was not the market, as some would have us believe today, but the labor movement that "civilized" the market economy while greatly contributing to its effectiveness. Consequently, for all those who genuinely wish to oppose a social Europe to the Europe of the banks and money—flanked by a police and penitentiary Europe (which is already far advanced) and a military Europe (a probable consequence of intervention in Kosovo)— the question is how to mobilize the forces capable of achieving that end and which bodies to call on to carry out this work of mobilization. The European Trade Union Confederation comes to mind. But no one can contradict the specialists, such as Corinne Gobin, who have shown how that body behaves first and foremost as a "partner," desirous of playing its part, with dignity and propriety, in the management of European affairs by carrying out well-tempered lobbying in the spirit of "dialogue" so dear to Jacques Delors. And one cannot deny that it has done little to give itself the means to effectively countervail the desiderata of employers (themselves grouped into UNICE, the Union of Industrial and Employers' Confederations of Europe, and endowed with a powerful lobbying organization capable of dictating its will in Brussels) and to impose genuine collective agreements on a European scale through the use of the normal weapons of social struggle (strikes, demonstrations, etc.).

Since we cannot, at least in the short term, wait for the European Trade Union Confederation to espouse a resolutely militant unionism, we must turn, first and provisionally, to the national trade unions. At the same time we must not overlook the formidable obstacles to the veritable *conversion* that they would have to effect in order to avoid technocratic-diplomatic temptations at the European level, and at the national level the routines and forms of thinking that tend to enclose them within the boundaries of a single country. And this at a moment when, under the impact of, among other things, neoliberal policies and economic forces left to run free (with the privatization of many large state enterprises and the proliferation of casual jobs, most often in the service sector and hence temporary and part-time), the very foundations of trade union activism are under threat, as attested to not merely by the decline in unionization but also by the low rate of participation of young people and especially of youth from immigrant families, who elicit so much concern but whom no one seriously thinks of mobilizing on this front.

European trade unionism, which could be the engine of a social Europe, thus remains to be invented, and it will be invented only at the cost of a whole series of more or less radical breaks. We need to break first with the national if not nationalistic particularisms of trade union traditions, that are always confined within the limits of the states from which they expect a large proportion of the resources essential to their existence and that circumscribe the terrain and define the stakes of their claims and actions. Next we need to break with an attitude of conciliation, which tends to discredit critical thought and action and to valorize social consensus to the point of encouraging trade unions to share responsibility for a policy aimed at making the dominated

accept their subordination. We must forsake also the economic fatalism fostered not only by the reigning political-journalistic discourse
on the inescapable necessities of "globalization" and the rule of the
financial markets (behind which political leaders like to conceal their
freedom of choice) but also by the very conduct of social democratic
governments, which, by extending or adapting the policy of conservative governments, make this policy appear as the only possible one,
and which attempt to give deregulation measures complicit with business demands the appearance of invaluable achievements of a genuine
social policy. We must break, finally, with a neoliberalism skilled in
presenting the inflexible demands of one-sided employment contracts
under the trappings of "flexibility" (as, for example, with negotiations
on the reduction of working hours and the French law on the thirty-
five-hour week, which exploit all the objective ambiguities of a balance
of forces made increasingly unequal by the generalization of job precariousness and by the inertia of a state that is more inclined to ratify
that imbalance than help remedy it).

This renewed trade unionism would call for mobilizing agents
animated by a profoundly internationalist spirit and capable of overcoming the obstacles linked to national juridical and administrative
traditions, as well as the social barriers internal to each country—those
that separate the different occupational sectors and categories, but also
divisions of gender, age, and ethnic origin. It is paradoxical indeed that
young people, particularly from immigrant families, who are so obses-
sively present in the collective phantasms of social fear engendered
and sustained by the dialectic of political competition for xenophobic
votes and the media competition for audience ratings, occupy in the
concerns of progressive parties and trade unions a place inversely
proportional to the place they are granted throughout Europe in the
discourse of "law and order" and the policies it promotes. We should
look to, or hope for, the formation of a veritable International of "immigrants" from all countries—Turks, Kabyles, Moroccans, Surinam-
ese, and others—to engage in transnational action, in association with
the native workers of the different European countries, against the
dominant economic forces that, through various mediations, are also
responsible for their emigration. These youth, whom we stubbornly

insist on calling "immigrants," currently have no way out other than resigned submission (sometimes preached to them under the label of "integration"), petty delinquency or criminal careers, or that modern form of peasant revolt that are the riots that periodically rock the social housing estates of the urban periphery. European societies would in fact have much to gain if these youths ceased to be the passive objects of "law and order" measures and became active agents of an innovative and constructive social movement. The reintegration of "immigrants" into the social movement should be the first step toward a transnational politics.

But we must also ponder a whole range of measures (no doubt scattered and disparate) to develop in each citizen the internationalist dispositions that now are the precondition for all effective strategies of resistance. Among them are the creation of a European trade union college; the bolstering within every trade union organization of departments specifically set up to deal with organizations in other nations and responsible in particular for gathering and disseminating international information; the progressive establishment of rules for coordinating trade union action on wages, working conditions, and terms of employment (in order to fight the temptation to accept agreements on moderating wage demands or, as in some British companies, to give up the right to strike); the creation of coordinating committees between the trade unions of different industries, on the pattern of those that already exist in transport (rail and road); the strengthening, within multinational firms, of international works committees capable of resisting the fragmenting pressures from central management; the promotion of policies of recruitment and mobilization among immigrants so as to transform them from pawns in the strategies of parties into agents of resistance and change, so that they would no longer be used within progressive organizations themselves to sow division and incite regression toward nationalistic or even racist thinking. Measures could also be introduced to recognize and institutionalize new forms of mobilization and action, such as grassroots "coordinations" (which have played a major role in recent social upheavals in France) and the establishment of links of active cooperation between unions in the private and public sectors, which have very different weights from one country to another. Further measures could be adopted to effect that "conversion of minds" (inside and outside unions) necessary to break with the narrow definition of "the social," reduced to the world of wage work closed unto itself, to link claims about work to demands in matters of health, housing, transport, training, leisure, and gender relations, and to launch drives to unionize sectors traditionally bereft of mechanisms of collective protection (services, temporary work).

But an objective as visibly utopian as the *construction of a unified European trade union confederation* remains indispensable. Such a project is no doubt essential to inspire and guide the collective search for the innumerable transformations in collective institutions and the thousands of conversions of individual dispositions that will be required to "make" the European social movement. There is indeed no requirement for the construction of such a movement more essential than the repudiation of all our habitual ways of conceiving trade unionism, social movements, and national differences in these areas. There is no task more urgent than the invention of novel ways of thinking and acting forced upon us by the casualization of employment. Generalized precariousness, which is the basis of a new form of social discipline generated by job insecurity and the fear of unemployment, which now affect even the best-placed workers, can be the basis for solidarities of a new kind, both in scope and in principle. This can be the case particularly in the event of those crises seen as especially scandalous when they take the form of mass layoffs by profitable firms which impose them in order to generate yet higher returns for their shareholders. The new trade unionism will have to learn to rely on new solidarities among the victims of the policy of job insecurity, who today are found almost as often among occupations requiring a high level of cultural capital, such as teaching, the health care professions, and communications (as with journalists), as among clerks and blue-collar workers. But it will first have to work to produce and disseminate as widely as possible a critical analysis of all the strategies, often very subtle, in which certain actions of social democratic governments collaborate, sometimes unwittingly. The fact that these ambiguous strategies of the new mode of domination are themselves very often implemented, at all levels of the social hierarchy, by victims of similar strategies makes this analysis all the more difficult to conduct and, particularly, to convey to all those whom it wishes to arm so that they may gain a clear view of their condition. One thinks for example of precariously employed teachers, overburdened with marginalized high school or university students who are themselves destined for casual work; or of social workers with no stable status, entrusted to guide and assist populations whose social condition is not far removed from their own, all of whom are inclined to embrace and spread shared illusions.

Only a rational utopia such as that which would offer the hope of a true social Europe could provide the trade unions with the mass base of grassroots activists they currently lack and could encourage or force them to jettison the short-term corporatist interests that arise in the competition for the best position in the existing market of trade union services and benefits. Only the universalistic voluntarism of a social movement capable of transcending the limits of the traditional organizations, in particular by fully integrating the movement of the unemployed, would be able effectively to fight and thwart economic and financial powers at the international level at which they now exert their rule. Recent international movements, of which the European Marches Against Unemployment are only the most exemplary, are no doubt the first, as yet fleeting, sign of the collective discovery, within the social movement and beyond, of the vital need for internationalism or, more precisely, for the internationalization of modes of thinking and forms of action.

GRAINS OF SAND

This piece first appeared in the French TV listings magazine *Télérama*, 4 October 2000.

If I say that culture is in danger today, if I say that it is threatened by the rule of money and commerce and by a mercenary spirit that takes many forms—audience ratings, market research, pressure from advertisers, sales figures, the bestseller list—it will be said that I am exaggerating.

If I say that politicians, who sign international agreements consigning cultural works to the common fate of interchangeable commodities subject to the same laws that apply to corn, bananas, or citrus fruit, are contributing (without always knowing it) to the abasement of culture and minds, it will be said that I am exaggerating.

If I say that publishers, film producers, critics, distributors, and heads of TV and radio stations, who rush to submit to the law of commercial circulation, that of the pursuit of bestsellers, media stars, and of the production and glorification of success in the short term and at all costs, but also to the law of the circular exchange of worldly favors and concessions—if I say that all of them are collaborating with the imbecile forces of the market and participating in their triumph, it will be said that I am exaggerating.

And yet . . .

If I recall now that the possibility of stopping this infernal machine in its tracks lies with all those who, having some power over cultural, artistic, and literary matters, can, each in their own place and their own fashion, and to however small an extent, throw their grain of sand into the well-oiled machinery of resigned complicities; and if, lastly, I add that those who have the good fortune to work for

Télérama (not necessarily in the most eminent or most visible positions) would, by conviction and tradition, be among the best placed to do this, it will be said perhaps, for once, that I am being desperately optimistic.

And yet . . .

CULTURE IS IN DANGER

Keynote address to the International Forum on Literature, Doeson Foundation, Seoul, Korea, 26–29 September 2000.

I have often warned against the prophetic temptation and the pretension of social scientists to announce, so as to denounce them, present and future ills. But I find myself led by the logic of my work to exceed the limits I had set for myself in the name of a conception of objectivity that has gradually appeared to me as a form of censorship. So, today, in the face of the impending threats to culture that are overlooked by most, including writers, artists, and scientists themselves, even as they are the ones primarily concerned, I believe that it is necessary to make known as widely as possible what seems to me to be the standpoint of the most advanced research on the effects that so-called globalization processes may have on matters cultural.

AUTONOMY THREATENED

I have described and analyzed (in my book *The Rules of Art*, in particular) the long process of autonomization at the end of which, in a number of Western countries, were constituted those social microcosms that I call "fields": the literary field, the scientific field, and the artistic field.[11] I have shown that these universes obey laws that are proper to them (the etymological meaning of the word "autonomy") and at variance with the laws of the surrounding social world, particularly at the economic level. The literary and artistic worlds, for example, are very largely emancipated, at least in their most autonomous sectors, from the rule of money and interest. I have always stressed the fact that this process is not in any sense a linear and teleological development of the

Hegelian type and that progress toward autonomy could be suddenly interrupted, as we have seen whenever dictatorial regimes, capable of divesting the artistic worlds of their past achievements, have been established. But what is currently happening to the universes of artistic production throughout the developed world is entirely novel and truly without precedent: the hard-won independence of cultural production and circulation from the necessities of the economy is being threatened, in its very principle, by the intrusion of commercial logic at every stage of the production and circulation of cultural goods.

The prophets of the new neoliberal gospel profess that, in cultural matters as elsewhere, the logic of the market can bring nothing but boons. Recusing the specificity of cultural goods either tacitly or explicitly (as with regard to the book trade, for which they reject any kind of protection), they assert, for example, that technological novelties and the economic innovations introduced to exploit them can only increase the quantity and quality of cultural goods on offer, and hence the satisfaction of consumers. This is on the condition, naturally, that everything the new technology and economically integrated communications groups put into circulation—that is to say, televised messages as well as books, films, or games, all generally subsumed under the term of "information"—be conceived as a mere commodity, and consequently treated as any other product and subjected to the law of profit. Thus the profusion that the increase in the number of themed digital television channels is to bring about should lead to an "explosion of media choice," such that all demands, all tastes are satisfied. In this realm as in others, competition should, by its sole logic and especially by its association with technological progress, foster creativity. The law of profit would, here as elsewhere, be democratic since it sanctions those products with greatest popular appeal. I could back up each of these assertions with dozens of references and citations, but these would be somewhat redundant. Instead, let me offer a single quotation, from Jean-Marie Messier, the head of Vivendi-Universal, which condenses almost everything I have just said: "Millions of jobs have been created in the United States thanks to the complete deregulation of the telecommunications industry and technologies. Let us wish that France will follow suit! The competitiveness of our economy and the employment of our children are at stake. We must shed our fears and open wide the doors of competition and creativity."

How valid are these arguments? To the mythology of the extraordinary differentiation and diversification of products one can counterpose the trend toward uniform supply at both the national and international levels. Far from promoting diversity, competition breeds homogeneity. The pursuit of audience ratings leads producers to look for omnibus products that can be consumed by *audiences of all backgrounds in all countries* because they are weakly differentiated and differentiating: Hollywood films, *telenovelas*, TV serials, soap operas, police series, commercial music, boulevard or Broadway theater, all-purpose magazines, and bestsellers produced directly for the world market. Furthermore, competition regresses continually with the concentration of the apparatus of production and, more important, of distribution: the multiple communications networks tend increasingly to broadcast, often at the same time, the same type of products, born of the pursuit of maximum profit for minimum outlay. As is shown by the most recent merger between Viacom and CBS, that is, between a group oriented toward the production of content and a group oriented toward its distribution, the extraordinary concentration of communications corporations leads to *vertical integration such that distribution governs production*, imposing a veritable censorship by money. The integration of production, distribution, and screening leads to abuses of dominant market position such that a group's own films receive preferential treatment: 80 percent of new film releases on the Parisian market are screened in Gaumont, Pathé, and UGC cinemas or in cinemas within their groups. One would need to mention also the proliferation of multiplex cinemas, which are thoroughly subordinated to the demands of the distributors and compete unfairly with small independent cinemas, often forcing them to close.

The key point, however, is that commercial concerns, the pursuit of maximum *short-term* profit and the "aesthetic" that derives from that pursuit, are being ever more intensely and widely imposed on cultural production. The consequences of such a policy are exactly the same in the field of publishing, where very high concentration of ownership is also found: in the United States at least, apart from two independent publishers, W.W. Norton and Houghton Mifflin, a few university presses that are themselves increasingly subjected to commercial constraints, and a handful of combative small publishers, the book trade is in the hands of eight giant media corporations. The great majority of publishers must assume an unequivocally commercial orientation and this has led, among other things, to an invasion of their lists by media stars and to censorship by money. This is particularly the case when, being integrated within multimedia conglomerates, publishers must achieve very high rates of profit. (Here I could quote Mr. Thomas Middlehoff, CEO of Bertelsmann, who, according to *La Tribune*, has given its 350 profit centers two years to ensure a return on investment of at least 10 percent.) How could one not see that the logic of profit, particularly short-term profit, is the very negation of culture, which presupposes investment for no financial return or for uncertain and often posthumous returns?

What is at stake here is the perpetuation of a cultural production that is not oriented toward exclusively commercial ends and is not subject to the verdicts of those who dominate mass media production, especially by way of the hold they exert over major channels of distribution. Indeed, one of the difficulties of the battle that must be fought on this front is that it may assume antidemocratic appearances insofar as the mass productions of the culture industry do in a sense have the backing of the general public, and particularly of young people the world over, both because they are more accessible (the consumption of these products requires less cultural capital) and because they are the object of a kind of *inverted snobbery*. Indeed, it is the first time in history that the cheapest products of a popular culture (of a society which is economically and politically dominant) are imposing themselves as chic. The adolescents of all countries who wear baggy pants with the crotch down at knee level do not know that the fashion they regard as both ultrachic and ultramodern finds its origin in U.S. jails, as did a certain taste for tattoos! This is to say that the "civilization" of jeans, Coca-Cola, and McDonald's has not only economic power on its side but also the symbolic power exerted through a seduction to which the victims themselves contribute. By taking as their chief targets children and adolescents, particularly those most shorn of specific immune defenses, with the support of advertising and the media which are both constrained and complicit, the big cultural production and distribution companies gain an extraordinary, unprecedented hold over all contemporary societies—societies that, as a result, find themselves virtually infantilized.

When, as Ernst Gombrich pointed out, the "ecological conditions of art" are destroyed, art soon dies. Culture is threatened because the economic and social conditions in which it can develop are profoundly affected by the logic of profit in the advanced countries where there is already substantial accumulated capital (the precondition for autonomy) and a fortiori in other countries. The relatively autonomous microcosms within which culture is produced must, along with the education system, ensure the production of both producers and consumers. It took painters nearly five centuries to achieve the social conditions that made a Picasso possible. We know from reading their contracts that they had to struggle against their patrons to stop their work from being treated as a mere product whose worth is determined by the surface painted and the cost of the colors used. They had to struggle to win the right to sign their works, that is to say, the right to be treated as authors. They had to fight for the right to choose the colors they used, the manner in which those colors are used, and even, at the very end—particularly with abstract art—the subject itself, on which the power of patronage bore especially strongly. Others, writers or musicians, have had to fight for what only recently have begun to be called "droits d'auteurs," copyright and royalties; they have had to struggle for scarcity, uniqueness, and quality, and only with the collaboration of critics, biographers, professors of art history, and others have they been able to assert themselves as artists, as "creators."

Similarly, it would take forever to enumerate the conditions that have to be fulfilled for experimental works of cinema to emerge, along with an audience to appreciate them. To list but a few: special journals and critics to sustain them, small "art-house" cinemas frequented by students, film clubs run by enthusiasts, filmmakers prepared to sacrifice everything to make films that do not achieve instant success, informed critics, producers who are sufficiently aware and cultured to finance them—in short, that whole social microcosm in which avant-garde cinema is recognized and valued, and which is presently threatened by the irruption of commercial cinema and, above all, by the domination of the big distributors, with whom producers (when they are not themselves distributors) must reckon. Now, all of that is under threat today by the reduction of works of art to products and commodities. The current struggles of filmmakers over the "final cut" and against the pretension of producers to ultimate rights over the work are the exact equivalent of the struggles of the painters of the Quattrocentro.[12]

These autonomous universes, which are the outcome of a protracted process of *emergence*, of evolution, have today started upon a process of *involution*: they are the locus of a backward turn, a regression from work to product, from author to engineers or technicians deploying technical resources they have not invented themselves (such as the vaunted "special effects") or to the famous stars celebrated in the mass-market magazines and liable to pull in large audiences ill-equipped to appreciate specific, particularly formal, experimentation. And, above all, they must put these extremely costly resources to purely commercial ends, that is to say, organize them, in a quasicynical manner, so as to seduce the largest possible number of viewers by playing to their basic drives which other technicians, the marketing specialists, attempt to predict. So we are also seeing the emergence, in all the cultural universes, of imitation cultural productions (one could find instances of them in the realm of the novel as well as in cinema, and even in poetry with what Jacques Roubaud calls "muesli poetry"). These may go so far as to mimic the experimentation of the avant-garde while exploiting the most traditional mechanisms of commercial productions. And, given their ambiguity, they may, thanks to an effect of *allodoxia*, deceive critics and consumers with modernist pretensions.

It will be clear that the choice is not one between "globalization" understood as submission to the laws of commerce and hence to the reign of "commercialism," which is always and everywhere the opposite of what we understand by culture, and the defense of national cultures or this or that particular form of cultural nationalism. The kitsch products of commercial "globalization"—of blockbuster and "special effects" movies, or of "world fiction," whose authors can be indifferently Italian, Indian, or English, as well as American—are in every respect opposed to the products of the *literary, artistic, and cinematic International*, that chosen circle whose center is everywhere and nowhere, even if it was for a long time located in Paris. As Pascale Casanova showed in *La République mondiale des lettres*, the "denationalized International of creators," the Joyces, Faulkners, Kafkas, Becketts, or Gombrowiczes, pure products of Ireland, the United States, Czechoslovakia, or Poland, but who were made in Paris; or the Kaurismakis, Manoel de Oliveiras, Satyajit Rays, Kieslowskis, or Kiarostamis, and so many other contemporary filmmakers of all countries, haughtily ignored by the Hollywood aesthetic, could never have existed and subsisted without an international tradition of artistic internationalism or, more precisely, without the microcosm of producers, critics, and informed audiences required for its survival and which, having been constituted long ago, has managed to survive in precious few places spared by the commercial invasion.

FOR A NEW INTERNATIONALISM

Despite appearances, this tradition of specific internationalism, proper to the realm of culture, stands radically opposed to what is called "globalization." That term, which operates both as a password and as a watchword, is in effect the justificatory mask sported by a policy aimed at universalizing the particular interests and the particular tradition of the economically and politically dominant powers (principally the United States). It seeks to extend to the whole world the economic and cultural model most favorable to those powers, by presenting that model as a norm, an imperative, an inevitable development, and a universal destiny, so as to obtain universal allegiance—or at least universal resignation—to it. That is to say, in matters cultural it strives to universalize, by imposing them on the whole universe, the particularities of a cultural tradition within which commercial logic has been developed to the full. (Actually, but it would take too long to demonstrate this, the force of commercial logic is nothing other than the effect of a radical form of laissez-faire, characteristic of a social order that has given itself over to the logic of interest and immediate gratification, transformed into sources of profit, even as it presents itself under the trappings of progressive modernity. The fields of cultural production, which were instituted only very gradually through enormous sacrifices, are extremely vulnerable to the combined forces of technology and economics. Indeed, those who, in each of the cultural fields, can content themselves simply to bend with the dictates of market demand and to reap the economic or symbolic profit, such as today's "media intellectuals" and other producers of bestsellers, are always, as if by definition, more numerous and more influential in worldly terms than those who work without the slightest concession to any form of demand, that is, for a market that does not exist.)

Those who remain wedded to this tradition of cultural internationalism—be they artists, writers, scholars, but also publishers, gallery directors, or critics—in every country must now mobilize at a time when the forces of the economy, which tend by their own logic to subject cultural production and distribution to the law of immediate profit, are being powerfully bolstered by the so-called liberalization policies that the economically and culturally dominant powers aim to impose universally under cover of "globalization." I must speak here, somewhat unwillingly, of trivial realities that normally have no place in a gathering of writers. And I must do so, moreover, knowing that I will no doubt seem to be exaggerating, that I will appear as a prophet of doom, so great are the threats that neoliberal measures pose to culture. I am thinking of the General Agreement on Trade in Services (GATS), to which various states have subscribed when they joined the World Trade Organization and whose implementation is currently being negotiated. As a number of analysts (notably Lori Wallach, Agnès Bertrand, and Raoul Jennar) have shown, the aim of that agreement is to force the 136 member states to open up all services to the laws of free exchange and hence to make it possible to turn all service activities into commodities and sources of profit, including those responding to such fundamental rights as education and culture. Clearly, this would put an end to the notion of public service and to crucial social achievements such as universal access to free education and culture in the broad sense of the term (the measure is also supposed to apply, following a recasting of current classifications, to such services as audiovisual services, libraries, archives and museums, botanical gardens and zoos, and all the services linked to entertainment, arts, theater, radio and television, sport, etc.). It is self-evident that such a program, which purports to treat as "restraints of trade" national policies aimed at safeguarding national cultural particularities—and hence constituting obstacles to the transnational cultural industries—cannot but deny most countries (particularly those least endowed with economic and cultural resources) any hope of a development adapted to national and local particularities and respectful of diversity, in cultural matters as in all other realms. This is effected particularly by urging them to submit all national measures, domestic regulations, subsidies to establishments or institutions, licenses, etc., to the dictates of an organization that seeks to confer upon the demands of the transnational economic powers the appearance of a universal norm.

The extraordinary perversity of this policy resides in two cumulative effects: first, it is protected from criticism and opposition by the secrecy in which those who produce it have shrouded themselves; second, it is fraught with consequences, some of them intentional, that pass unnoticed at the moment of implementation by those whom they affect and which will appear only after a more or less extended time lag, thus preventing its victims from denouncing them at the outset (it is the case, for example, with all cost-minimization policies in the realm of health).

Such a policy, which puts the intellectual resources that money can mobilize in the service of economic interests (as with the "think tanks" where hired thinkers and mercenary researchers are brought together with journalists and public relations experts), should elicit unanimous rejection by all the artists, writers, and scientists most committed to autonomous research, who are its prime victims. However, apart from the fact that they are not always equipped to achieve knowledge and awareness of the mechanisms and actions that concur to destroy the world with which their very existence is bound up, they are ill-prepared—by dint of their supremely justified, visceral attachment to autonomy (particularly from politics)—to commit themselves on the terrain of politics, be that to defend their autonomy. Ready to mobilize for a universal cause, of which the paradigm will forever be Émile Zola's intervention on behalf of Dreyfus, they are less inclined to engage in actions that have for main purpose the defense of their own specific interests and which therefore seem to them tainted with a kind of corporatist selfishness. This is to forget that by defending the interests most directly linked to their very existence (through actions of the type mounted by French filmmakers against the Multilateral Agreement on Investment), they are contributing to the defense of the most universal values, which are, through them, very directly under threat.

Actions of this type are rare and difficult: political mobilization for causes that extend beyond the corporate interests of a particular social category—truck drivers, nurses, bank clerks, or filmmakers—has always required a great deal of effort and time, and sometimes a great deal of heroism. Today the "targets" of political mobilization are extremely abstract and far removed from the daily experience of citizens, even highly educated ones: the big multinational firms and their international boards, the great international institutions, the WTO, the IMF, and the World Bank, with their many subsidiary bodies, designated by complicated and often unpronounceable acronyms, and all the corresponding commissions and committees of unelected technocrats little known to the wider public constitute a veritable *invisible world government*, unnoticed by most people, which wields its power upon national governments themselves. This sort of "Big Brother," endowed with interconnected databases on all economic and cultural institutions, is already there, in action, efficiently going about its business, deciding what we shall eat or not eat, read or not read, see or not see on television or at the movies, and so on. Meanwhile some of the most enlightened thinkers cling to the belief that what we are dealing with here is of the order of the scholastic speculations on the project of a universal state in the manner of eighteenth-century philosophers.

Through the almost absolute power they hold over the major communications companies, that is to say, over the totality of the instruments of production and distribution of cultural goods, the new masters of the world tend to concentrate the different forms of power (economic, cultural, and symbolic) that in most societies remained distinct from, if not opposed to, one another. As a result, they are in a position to impose very broadly a worldview suited to their interests. Though they are not, properly speaking, its direct producers, and though the ways they express it in the public statements of their leaders are neither among the most original nor among the most subtle, the major communications companies play a decisive role in the quasiuniversal circulation of the pervasive and rampant *doxa* of neoliberalism, whose *rhetoric* calls for detailed analysis.

There are the logical monstrosities, such as *normative observations* (e.g., "The economy is becoming global, we must globalize our economy," "Things are changing very quickly, we have to change"); preemptory and fallacious "deductions" ("If capitalism is winning everywhere, this is because it reflects humanity's deepest nature"); nonfalsifiable theses ("It is by creating wealth that you create employment," "Too much taxation kills off taxation," this latter formula being backed up for the more highly educated by the famous Laffer curve, which another economist and professor at the Collège de France, Roger Guesnerie, demonstrated to be undemonstrable—but who is aware of this?); commonplaces that seem so far beyond question that the fact of questioning them itself seems questionable ("The welfare state and security of employment are things of the past," and "How can you still defend the principle of public service?"); teratological paralogisms (of the type "More market means more equality" or "Egalitarianism condemns thousands of people to poverty"); technocratic euphemisms ("restructuring companies" rather than firing workers); and a welter of semantically indeterminate ready-made notions or locutions, routinized by automatic usage, that function as magic formulas, endlessly repeated for their incantatory value ("deregulation," "voluntary redundancy," "free trade," "the free flow of capital," "competitiveness," "creativity," "technological revolution," "economic growth," "fighting inflation," "reducing the national debt," "lowering labor costs," "reducing welfare expenditures").

Because it assails us constantly from all sides, this *doxa* comes in the end to acquire the quiet force of the taken-for-granted. Those who undertake to fight it can count, within the fields of cultural production themselves, neither on the support of journalism, which (with few exceptions) is structurally bound to the productions and producers most directly oriented toward the direct gratification of the widest audience, nor on that of "media intellectuals," who, concerned above all with worldly success, owe their existence to this submission to market demands and who, in some extreme but also particularly revealing cases, can sell in the commercial sphere imitations or simulations of the avant-garde that has constructed itself against the market. This is to say that the position of the most autonomous cultural producers, who are gradually being stripped of their means of production and especially of distribution, has never been so threatened and so weak. But it has also never been so rare, useful, and precious.

Oddly, the "purest," most disinterested, most "formal" producers of culture thus find themselves, often unwittingly, at the forefront of the struggle for the defense of the highest values of humanity. By defending their singularity, they are defending the most universal values of all.

UNITE AND RULE

Public lecture delivered at Keisen University, Tokyo, Japan, 3 October 2000.

Historically, the economic field has been constructed within the framework of the national state, with which it is intrinsically linked. Indeed, the state contributes in many respects to unifying the economic space (which contributes in return to the emergence of the state). As Karl Polanyi shows in *The Great Transformation*, the emergence of national markets in Europe was not the mechanical product of the gradual extension of economic exchanges, but the product of a deliberately mercantilist state policy aimed at increasing domestic and foreign trade (especially by fostering the commercialization of land, money, and labor).[13] But, far from leading to a process of homogenization, as one might believe, unification and integration are accompanied by a concentration of power, which can go all the way to monopolization and, at the same time, by the dispossession of part of the population thus integrated. This is to say that integration into the state and the territory it controls is in fact the precondition for domination (as can be readily seen in all situations of colonization). As I was able to observe in Algeria, unification of the economic field tends, in particular through monetary unification and the generalization of monetary exchanges that ensue, to pitch all social agents into an economic game for which they are not equally prepared and equipped, culturally and economically.[14] It tends, by the same token, to subject them to the norm objectively imposed by competition from more efficient productive forces and modes of production, as can clearly be seen with small producers from the countryside, who are increasingly wrenched from a state of autarky. In short, *unification benefits the dominant*, whose difference is turned into capital by the mere fact of their being brought into relation. (To take a recent example, in the 1930s Franklin D. Roosevelt had to establish common social rules in matters of employment such as the minimum wage, the limitation of working hours, old-age pensions, etc. to avoid the deterioration in wages and working conditions attendant upon the integration of unequally developed regions into a single national entity.)

But in other respects, the process of unification and concentration remained confined within national borders; it was limited by all the barriers, especially juridical ones, to the free movement of goods and persons (customs duties, exchange controls, etc.). And it was limited also by the fact that production and particularly the circulation of goods remained closely bound to geographical place (owing in part to transport costs). It is these limits on the extension of economic fields that tend today to weaken or disappear under the impact of various factors: on the one hand, purely technical factors, such as the development of new means of communication (air transport and the Internet); on the other, more properly political or juridical-political factors, such as policies of liberalization and deregulation. Together they foster the formation of *a global economic field*, particularly in the financial realm (where computerized means of communication tend to eliminate the time gaps that traditionally separated the various national markets).

THE DOUBLE MEANING OF "GLOBALIZATION"

We must return here to the word "globalization." We have seen that, in a rigorous sense, it could refer to the unification of the global economic field or to the expansion of that field to the entire world. But it is also made to mean something quite different, in a surreptitious slide from the descriptive meaning of the concept, such as I just formulated, to a normative or, better yet, *performative* meaning. In this second sense, "globalization" refers to an *economic policy* aimed at unifying the economic field by means of a whole set of juridical-political measures designed to tear down all the obstacles to that unification—obstacles that are mostly linked to the nation-state. And this very precisely defines the neoliberal policy inseparable from the veritable economic propaganda that lends it part of its symbolic force by playing on the ambiguity of the notion.

Economic globalization is not a mechanical effect of the laws of technology or the economy but the product of a policy implemented by a set of agents and institutions, and the result of the application of rules deliberately created for specific ends, namely, trade liberalization (that is, the elimination of all national regulations restricting companies and their investments). In other words, the "global market" is *a political creation*, just as the national market had been, the product of a more or less consciously concerted policy. And, as was the case with the policy that led to the emergence of national markets, this policy has as an effect (and perhaps also as an end, at least among the most lucid and the most cynical of the advocates of neoliberalism) the creation of the conditions for domination by brutally confronting agents and firms hitherto confined within national boundaries with competition from more efficient and more powerful forces and modes of production. Thus in the emerging economies the disappearance of protection spells ruin for national enterprises. In countries such as South Korea, Thailand, Indonesia, or Brazil, the elimination of all obstacles to foreign investment leads to the collapse of local enterprises, which are then bought up, often at ridiculously low prices, by the multinationals. For these countries, public procurement contracts remain one of the only methods that enable local companies to compete with the big Northern concerns. Whereas they are presented as necessary for the creation of a "global field of action," the directives of the World Trade Organization on competition and public procurement policies would, by establishing competition "on an equal footing" between the big multinationals and small national producers, cause the mass destruction of the latter. For we know that, as a general rule, formal equality in a situation of real inequality favors the dominant.

The word "globalization" is, as we can see, a *pseudoconcept, at once descriptive and prescriptive*, that has supplanted the term "modernization," long ago used by American social scientists in a euphemistic manner to impose a naively ethnocentric evolutionary model according to which the different societies of the world are classified in terms of their distance from the most economically advanced society, that is, U.S. society, instituted as the endpoint and end goal of all human history. (This is the case, for instance, when the criterion used to measure the degree of evolution is one of the distinctive, but apparently neutral and undisputable, properties of that society, such as energy consumption per capita as criticized by Claude Lévi-Strauss in *Race and History*).[15] This word embodies the most accomplished form of the *imperialism of the universal*, which consists, in universalizing for a society, its own particularity by tacitly instituting it as a universal yardstick (as French society did for a long time when, as the supposed historical incarnation of human rights and of the legacy of the French Revolution, it was posited—especially by the Marxist tradition—as the model of all possible revolutions).

Through this word, then, it is the process of unification of the global economic and financial field, that is, the integration of hitherto compartmentalized national economic universes, that is now organized along the lines of an economy rooted in the historical particularities of a particular social tradition, that of American society, which is instituted both as inevitable destiny and as political project of universal liberation, as the endpoint of a *natural evolution* and as the civic and ethical ideal that promises political emancipation for the peoples of all countries, in the name of a postulated connection between democracy and the market. The most fully accomplished form of this *utopian capitalism* is no doubt the myth of the "stockholders' democracy," that is, a universe of wage earners who, being paid in the form of shares, would collectively become "owners of their companies," thereby bringing about the perfect association between capital and labor. And the triumphant ethnocentrism of "modernization" theories reaches sublime heights with the most inspired prophets of the new economic religion who see the United States as the new homeland of "realized socialism" (we see here in passing that a certain scientistic madness triumphant today in Chicago concedes nothing to the most exalted ravings about "scientific socialism" that flourished in another age and place, with consequences that are well known).

We would need to pause here to demonstrate, firstly, that what is universally proposed and imposed as the norm of all rational economic practice is in reality the universalization of the particular characteristics of an economy embedded in a particular history and social structure, that of the United States; and that by the same token the United States

is, by definition, the fully realized form of a political and economic
ideal that for the most part is the product of the idealization of its own
economic and social organization, characterized among other things
by the weakness of the social state. But we would also have to demonstrate, secondly, that the United States occupies a dominant position
in the global economic field which it owes to the fact that it cumulates
a set of exceptional competitive advantages: *financial advantages*, including the exceptional position of the dollar, which enables Washing-
ton to drain off from all over the world (that is, from countries with a
strong savings rate, such as Japan, but also from the ruling oligarchies
of poor countries and from global networks of trafficking and money
laundering) the capital it needs to finance its enormous public and
trade deficits and to compensate for an exceedingly low rate of savings,
and which enables it to implement the monetary policy of its choice
without worrying about its repercussions for other countries, especially the poorest of them, which are objectively chained to American
economic decisions and which have contributed to American growth
not only by virtue of the low costs in dollars of their labor and products
(particularly raw materials) but also with the levies they have paid into
the coffers of American banks; *economic advantage*, with the strength
and competitiveness of the sector of capital goods and investment and,
in particular, of industrial microelectronics, or the role of banking in
the private financing of innovation; *political and military advantages*, its
diplomatic weight allowing the United States to impose economic and
commercial norms favorable to its interests; *cultural and linguistic advantages*, with the exceptional quality of the public and private system
of scientific research (as measured by the number of Nobel laureates),
the power of lawyers and of the big law firms, not to forget the practical universality of English, which dominates telecommunications and
the whole of commercial cultural production; *symbolic advantage*, with
the imposition of a lifestyle quasiuniversally recognized, at least by
adolescents, especially through the production and diffusion of representations of the world (as in movies) to which an image of modernity
is attached. (We see in passing that the superiority of the American
economy, which in reality is moving further and further away from the
model of pure and perfect competition in the name of which it is being

thrust onto the rest of the world, *is due to effects of structure and not to the particular efficacy of a given economic policy,* even as it has benefited from the intensification of work and the unprecedented lengthening of hours worked combined with very low wages for the least skilled, and also from the emergence of new economic sectors driven by science and information technology.)

One of the most unquestionable expressions of the relations of force being established within the global economic field is the asymmetry and "double standard" that allows, for example, the dominant powers and particularly the United States to resort to the very protectionist measures and public subsidies they deny to developing countries (which are prohibited from limiting imports of a product inflicting serious damage on their industry or from regulating flows of foreign investment). And it takes a great deal of goodwill to believe that concern for social standards and economic rights in the countries of the South (as with the prevention of child labor) is shorn of protectionist designs when we see that concern coming from countries, such as the United States, engaged in the wholesale deregulation of their own labor market and in sharply curtailing trade union rights. The policy of "globalization" is no doubt in itself the best illustration of this asymmetry since it aims at extending to the entire world, but *without reciprocity,* on a one-way basis (that is, in combination with redoubled isolationism and particularism), the organization most favorable to the dominant.

The unification of the global economic field through the imposition of the absolute rule of free exchange, the free movement of capital, and export-led growth is marked by the same ambiguity as integration into the national economic field was in another age. While featuring all the outward signs of a boundless universalism, a kind of ecumenism justified by the universal diffusion of the "cheap" lifestyle of the "civilization" of McDonald's, jeans, and Coca-Cola, or by "juridical harmonization," often regarded as an indicator of positive "globalization," this "societal project" serves the dominant, that is, the big investors who, while standing above states, can count on the major states and in particular on the most powerful of them politically and militarily, the United States, and on the major international institutions—the

World Bank, the International Monetary Fund, and the World Trade Organization—which those states control, to ensure conditions favorable to the conduct of their economic activities. *The effect of domination linked to integration within inequality* can be clearly seen in the fate of Canada (which could well be the fate of Europe if the latter moves toward a kind of customs union with the United States): due to the lowering of its traditional protective barriers, which has left it defenseless particularly in matters of culture, this country is undergoing virtual economic and cultural integration into the American empire.

Like the old national states, the dominant economic forces are in effect capable of making (international) law and the great international organizations, which are exposed to the influence of lobbyists, operate to their advantage. The lobbies work to clothe the economic interests of powerful firms or nations with juridical justifications (for example, by guaranteeing industrial investors maximum rights and prerogatives); and they devote a very substantial part of their intellectual energies to dismantling national laws, such as legislation and regulations that ensure the protection of consumers. Without fulfilling all the functions ordinarily assigned to national states (such as those pertaining to social welfare), the international institutions invisibly govern the national governments which, seeing their role increasingly reduced to managing secondary matters, form a political smoke screen that effectively masks the true sites of decision making. They reinforce at the symbolic level the quasimechanical action of economic competition which compels national states to vie with each other in terms of both taxation (by lowering rates and granting special breaks) and competitive advantage (by providing free infrastructures).

THE STATE OF THE GLOBAL ECONOMIC FIELD

The global economic field presents itself as a set of global subfields, each of which corresponds to an "industry," understood as a set of firms competing to produce and commercialize a homogeneous category of products. The almost always oligopolistic structure of each of these subfields corresponds to the structure of the distribution of capital (in its different forms) between the different firms capable of acquiring and maintaining the status of efficient competitor at the global level, the position of a firm in each country being dependent on the position occupied by that firm in all the other countries. The global field is highly polarized. Owing to their mere weight within the structure (which functions as a barrier to entry), the dominant national economies tend to concentrate the assets of companies and to appropriate the profits they produce, as well as to orient the tendencies immanent in the functioning of the field. The position of each firm in the national and international field depends not only on its own specific assets but also on the economic, political, cultural, and linguistic resources that flow from its membership in a particular nation, with this kind of "national capital" exerting a positive or negative multiplier effect on the structural competitiveness of the different firms.

Today these different fields are structurally subordinated to the global financial field. That field was abruptly released (through measures such as the French financial deregulation law of 1985–86) from all the regulations that had been imposed on it for almost two centuries and which had been strengthened after the great string of banking collapses of the 1930s. Having thus achieved almost complete autonomy and integration, the global field of finance has become one among many sites within which to generate returns on capital. The large concentrations of money effected by the big investors (pension funds, insurance companies, investment funds) have become an autonomous force, controlled solely by bankers who increasingly favor speculation, financial operations with no end other than financial, at the cost of productive investment. The international economy of speculation thereby finds itself freed from the control of the national institutions, such as central banks, which used to regulate financial operations, and long-term interest rates tend henceforth to be determined not by national bodies but by a small number of international operators who set the trends on the financial markets.

The concentration of finance capital in the pension funds and mutual funds that attract and manage collective savings enables the transstate managers of those savings to impose onto firms, in the name of shareholder interests, demands for financial profitability that gradually divert and direct their strategies. This is effected in particular

by restricting their opportunities for diversification and by requiring
them to engage in "downsizing" or in mergers and acquisitions in
which all the risks are borne by the employees (who are sometimes
fictitiously associated with profits, at least the higher-ranking among
them, through remuneration in the form of shares). The increased
freedom to invest and, perhaps more crucially, to divest capital so as
to obtain the highest financial profitability promotes the mobility of
capital and the generalized delocalization of industrial or banking enterprises. Direct investment abroad makes it possible to exploit the
differences between nations or regions in terms of capital and labor
costs and to move closer to the most favorable markets. Just as nascent
nations transformed autonomous fiefs into provinces subordinated to
the central power, "network firms" find in a market that is both internal and international the means for "internalizing" transactions, as Oliver Williamson puts it, that is, for organizing them within production
units that incorporate the firms absorbed and thereby reduces them to
the status of "subsidiary" of a "parent company," while others look to
outsourcing as another way of establishing relations of subordination
within relative independence.[16]

Integration into the global economic field thus tends to weaken all
regional or national powers. By discrediting the other paths of development, and particularly national models condemned from the outset as
nationalistic, the formal cosmopolitanism in which that integration is
draped leaves citizens powerless in the face of the transnational economic and financial powers. The so-called policies of structural adjustment aim at ensuring the incorporation through subordination of the
dominated economies by reducing the role of all the so-called artificial
or arbitrary mechanisms of political regulation of the economy associated with the social welfare state (the only body capable of opposing
the transnational firms and the international financial institutions)
in favor of the so-called free market through a series of converging
measures of deregulation and privatization, such as abolishing all
protection for the domestic market and relaxing controls on foreign
investment, in the name of the Darwinian tenet that exposure to competition will make firms more efficient. In so doing, they tend to grant
concentrated capital almost total freedom and allow free rein to the big

multinationals that more or less directly inspire these policies. (Conversely, they contribute to neutralizing the attempts of the so-called emerging nations, that is to say, those nations capable of mounting effective competition, to rely on the national state in order to construct an economic infrastructure and to create a national market by protecting national production and fostering the development of a real demand linked to the access of peasants and workers to consumption by way of increased purchasing power, itself promoted by state policies such as agrarian reform or the introduction of progressive income taxation.)

The relations of force of which these policies are a thinly euphemized expression, and which tend more and more to reduce the most dispossessed nations to an economy relying almost exclusively on the extensive or intensive exploitation of natural resources, are also manifested in the asymmetrical treatment granted by the global institutions to various nations depending on the position they occupy within the structure of the distribution of capital. The most striking example of this is no doubt the fact that requests by the International Monetary Fund that the United States reduce its persistent public deficit have long fallen on deaf ears, whereas the same body has forced many an African economy, already greatly at risk, to reduce its deficit at the cost of increasing levels of unemployment and poverty. And we know also that the same countries that preach the opening of borders and the dismantling of the welfare state to the whole world can practice more or less subtle forms of protectionism through import quotas, voluntary export restrictions, the imposition of quality or safety standards, and enforced currency revaluations, not to mention certain self-righteous calls for the universal enforcement of labor rights, or yet through state assistance via what are called "mixed oligopolies" (based on state intervention aimed at dividing up markets through VRAs, voluntary restraint agreements), or through production quotas for foreign subsidiaries.

Unlike the unification that took place in centuries past at the national state level in Europe, present-day unification at the global level is carried out without the state—counter to the wish of John Maynard Keynes to see the creation of a world central bank issuing a neutral reserve currency liable to guarantee trade on an equal footing between all countries—and at the exclusive service of the interests of the dominant, who, contrary to the jurists who presided over the origins of the European states, do not really need to wrap the policies that suit their interests in the trappings of universalism. It is the naked logic of the field and the intrinsic force of concentrated capital that impose relations of force favorable to the interests of the dominant. The latter have the means to transform these relations of force into apparently universal rules of the game through the falsely neutral interventions of the great international bodies (IMF, WTO) they dominate, or under cover of the representations of the economy and politics that they are able to inspire and disseminate. These representations have found their most thorough formulation in the draft Multilateral Agreement on Investment (MAI). This quasiutopia of a world freed of all state restraints and turned over to the arbitrary whim of investors alone allows us to gain a realistic idea of the truly "globalized" world that the conservative International of heads and executives of the industrial and financial multinationals of all nations intends to impose by relying on the political, diplomatic, and military power of an imperial state gradually reduced to its function of law enforcement in domestic and foreign theaters.[17] It is therefore vain to hope that this unification produced by the "harmonization" of national legal provisions will, by its own logic, lead to a genuine universalization, embodied by a universal state. But it is not unreasonable to expect that the effects of the policy of a small oligarchy looking only after its own short-term economic interest will foster the gradual emergence of political forces, themselves also global, capable of demanding the creation of transnational bodies entrusted with controlling the dominant economic forces so as to subordinate them to truly universal ends.

Part IV

Interviews and
New Acts of Resistance

FOR A REAL MOBILIZATION
OF ORGANIZED FORCES

Video message broadcast in Zurich on 27 January 2001 on the occasion of the Davos countersummit.

I want first of all to thank the organizers of this demonstration for giving me the opportunity to rank myself among the spoilsports gathered here and trying to bait the great media-political show of the "masters of the world," who, under police protection and surrounded by their court of journalists, are going to tell us how they see the world.

This world that appears to them as involved in an inevitable process of globalization, is in reality, and this is the worst of it, the product of a systematic, organized, and orchestrated policy. This policy began in the late 1970s in the United States—to be precise, in 1979, with the measures taken to raise interest rates—and was then extended by a whole series of measures aiming to deregulate financial markets in the big industrialized countries. Its purpose was to stimulate the rates of profit on capital and restore the position of owners in relation to managers.

This series of measures had the effect of favoring an ever greater autonomy of the world financial field, the world of finance, which was put to functioning according to its own inherent logic, that of pure profit, and independently in every way from the development of industry. Finance, indeed, is relatively little involved in the industrial field; we know for example that the contribution of the stock market to investment is extremely weak.

In order to produce this independent financial field, which in a certain sense spins around in thin air, its only recognized purpose being the constant increase of profit—in order to produce this world, it was necessary to invent and establish a whole series of financial institutions designed to promote free financial movement. And it is these institutions that have to be brought under control. It seems to me, however, that we need more than a simple measure of regulation, as those lobbying for the introduction of a Tobin tax seem to think, even though I do of course support this. As I see it, we cannot be satisfied with this kind of measure, and the question I want to raise today is that of the means to establish genuine and permanent control over these processes. The question, therefore, of a genuine political action, based on genuine political mobilization, and aiming at the imposition of such controls.

However necessary it may be, such a mobilization is also very difficult. In fact, the policy of globalization, which has nothing inevitable about it, is accompanied by a policy of depoliticization. The appearance of inevitability that I referred to, and that is normally associated with the idea of globalization, is the product of an incessant propaganda action (no other word is possible), involving the collaboration of a whole series of social agents, from the think tanks that produce official representations of the world through to the journalists who reproduce and circulate these. We must try therefore to conceive of a political action able to struggle against this depoliticization and at the same time against the policy of globalization that draws support from such depoliticization in order to impose itself.

How will it be possible to establish and exercise genuine and effective controls over monetary mechanisms and great concentrations of capital such as pension funds? As I see it, this could be done by the intermediary of central banks; in particular, since we are in Europe, by the European Central Bank. But to succeed in taking control of these financial bodies, the first requirement is to regain control of political bodies. This can only be done by a broad social movement that can enter into the system of controlling instances of economic forces and impose the establishment of international bodies rooted in a genuine popular movement.

I have spoken of a popular movement. It is true that we are currently in a period in which the dominated are demoralized and demobilized, particularly by the policy of depoliticization that I mentioned earlier. But there is also the fact that for the most deprived, those whom official discourse refers to as "excluded," very subtle policies of social control have been put in place in every developed country, which in fact are nothing more than the brutal and rather simplistic control, based more or less on policing, of an earlier era. These policies could even be seen as a deliberate project: it all takes place as if a certain number of agents—educators, organizers, social workers—had the function of teaching the most deprived—and particularly those who have been rejected by the education system and thrown out of the labor market—something like a parody of the capitalist spirit, the spirit of capitalist enterprise. A kind of self-help has been organized which is quite in conformity with the Anglo-Saxon political ideal. In order to establish and effectively exercise democratic control, regulations are not enough, nor are polished writings and polite approaches to political bodies. We need to invent a new kind of transnational action. Why do I see it as important to locate this action at the European level, at least initially? Because this is where a whole set of very varied movements, trade unions, community groups, etc., are to be found, which despite their disparate aspect—which is doubtless very well illustrated in this hall—despite their appearance of disorder and dispersion, their disagreements and divergence, their competition and even conflict, have a great deal in common. They have in common a vision of the social world that could be called libertarian, a desire to find a new way of doing politics. They also have in common a very deep internationalism, of which Third Worldism is simply a particular form. By transcending this diversity we shall be able to mobilize a broad movement capable of exerting constant pressure on national and international governmental bodies; and, to achieve a kind of provisional unification, we must overcome the hegemonic temptations that many social movements have inherited from a former era. It is imperative to exorcise authoritarian temptations, if we are to invent the collective forms of organization that will enable us to build up political forces without letting these cancel each other out in internal quarrels and divisions.

This assembling in a broad and united European movement, bringing together trade unions, community organizations, and scholars, could be the social force that, by giving itself flexible forms of organization, as little centralized as possible, will be able to build up

European critical traditions in liaison with progressive forces across the world; able to resist the dominant economic forces and propose a new progressive utopia. It would have to take back control of economic forces at a level at which they offer a lever (which is why I referred to European bodies and the European Central Bank), at the same time as putting its utopia into practice.

I think that the European social movement as I conceive it, free from any kind of Eurocentrism and strong in its progressive tradition of anti-imperialism and internationalist solidarity, should be established in liaison with the countries of the Third World, Latin America, Africa, and Asia, in such a way as to bring together all the forces needed so that those who are today having their celebrations in Davos are subject at each moment to the kind of sword of Damocles that a social movement present at all times and places, not just for the occasional heroic "happening," would provide. The point is to constitute a force that would be constantly there, representing a permanent mobilization of people already mobilized and organs of mobilization. No matter how restive we are—and God knows that I am very restive—it is impossible to do without organizations, organizers, and professional activists. Calling the organizers of resistance to band together, to unite in a great European confederation, would—in my view—contribute to creating a force of resistance and control at the scale of the economic and political forces gathered in Davos.

FOR A PERMANENT ORGANIZATION OF RESISTANCE TO THE NEW WORLD ORDER

A declaration transmitted by video to the demonstrators at the people's summit in Québec, 4 April 2001.

Very many of you here are disturbed, indignant, revolted by the world as it is today, the world that is being made for us by economic and political powers. Those powers that, long embodied by the deceptive figures of B-movie stars, have today taken the blinkered and mulish face of George W. Bush.

Very many of you here in Québec, but also in Berlin, Tokyo, Rio, Paris, and across the world, are rebelling against the policy of "globalization" of which the "summit of the Americas" is a new stage, after Seattle, Seoul, and Prague. Because, just as this meeting that aims to establish free exchange on an all-American scale shows very well, the "globalization" that is presented to us as a *fatality*, the inevitable destiny of advanced societies, is actually a *policy*, a policy that aims to impose those conditions that are most favorable to economic forces.

What actually is this "free exchange" that they tell us about? It is enough to read the General Agreement on Trade in Services, of which the Montréal agreement is certainly just a variant, to be enlightened and edified. But, let us say in passing, who will have the courage to read these thousands of pages that are deliberately confusing, drawn up by experts in the pay of the big international lobbies? You need only read these pages to understand that what is on the agenda above all is the destruction of all the *defense systems* that protect the most precious social and cultural conquests of the advanced societies; to understand that the point is to transform into commodities and sources of profit all service activities, including those that meet such fundamental needs as education, culture, and health. The measures that the WTO is concocting are supposed to be applied to such services as libraries, audio-visual media, archives, and museums, and all the services bound up with entertainment, performance, sport, theatre, radio, and television, etc. I could, to make clear the effects of the unmitigated reign of money, take the example of theatre or cinema—increasingly abandoned to blockbuster films with special effects that brutalize and stun the whole world—but I shall stick to the terrain of sport, where the logic of profit (bound up in particular with televised broadcasts of sporting events) has led to the disappearance of everything that was connected with a form of amateurism (starting with the beauty of performance) and introduced corruption, doping, the concentration of sporting resources in the hands of a few big clubs with the ability to pay exorbitant transfer fees—I am thinking here of football.

I have spoken of the destruction of *immune defense systems*, and this is precisely what is involved. Is it not readily apparent that a program like that of the WTO, which treats as "obstacles to trade" policies aimed at preserving national cultural particularities, and by that fact constituting barriers to the transnational culture industries, can only have the effect of depriving the majority of countries—and in particular those less well endowed with economic and cultural resources—of any hope of a development adapted to cultural particularities and respectful of diversities, in cultural matters as well as in other fields? This is particularly by compelling them to submit all national measures, domestic regulations, subsidies to establishments or institutions, licenses, etc., to the verdict of an organization that seeks to confer the appearance of a universal norm on the requirements of transnational economic powers.

The myth of free exchange between equal partners masks, beneath the polite façade of legally guaranteed international agreements, the brutal logic of relations of force that is asserted in fact in the dissymmetry of the double standard, two weights and two measures: this logic means that the dominant, and in particular the United States, can resort to protectionism and subsidies that they forbid countries in the course of development (forbidden for example to restrict the import of products that cause serious damage to their own industries, or to regulate foreign investments). Foreign laws by which the dominant place themselves above the law. The Kabyle people have a name for this kind of contract, which gives the dominated the right to be eaten by the dominant; they speak of a contract between a lion and a donkey.

You are particularly well placed here, in Canada, to observe the effects of free-exchange agreements between unequal powers, and to analyze the effect of domination that integration into inequality involves. As a result of an abolition of protective measures that has left it defenseless, particularly in matters of culture, Canada is in the process of experiencing a regular economic and cultural integration by its southern neighbor. The customs union has had the effect of dispossessing the dominated society of all economic and cultural independence from the dominant power, with the brain drain, the concentration of press and publishing, etc., to the benefit of the United States. It would be useful to have a detailed analysis of the particular part that the French-speaking province of Québec plays in resistance to this process; the language barrier can be a protection (a further example would be the comparison between Britain and France). I see an indication of this in the contribution of the Québécois to the struggle against globalization—for example, the role of Québécoise women in drawing up the magnificent World Charter of Women.

Thus, everything that is described by the term "globalization"—a term that is both descriptive and prescriptive—is the effect not of economic fatality but of a conscious policy. This policy is quite paradoxical, in that it is actually a policy of depoliticization: shamelessly drawing on the lexicon of liberty, liberalism, liberalization, deregulation, yet aiming to confer a fatal grip of economic determinism by liberating this from all control, and obtaining the submission of governments and citizens to the economic and social forces that are "liberated" in this way. Against this policy of deregulation, we need to reestablish politics, i.e., political thinking and action, and find the correct application point of this action, which is today beyond the borders of the national state, and its specific means, which cannot be reduced to political and trade-union struggles within national states. We must oppose the agreement of the governments of North and South America with a social movement of the two continents, bringing together Americans from North and South—a project that is not so unrealistic as it might appear, if you bear in mind that it is often the United States itself that has provided—with people like Ralph Nader, Susan George, and Lori Wallach—the first movements to challenge the policy of globalization. This movement will find a natural ally in the European social movement, which brings together trade unions, community organizations, and critical scholars from all European countries, and is currently in the process of construction.

And one could conceive, therefore, in connection with other international movements such as the World March of Women, the establishment of a permanent organization of resistance, able to oppose its slogans (of boycott, for example), its demonstrations, its critical analyses, and symbolic productions (artistic ones in particular) to the faceless violence of economic forces, and to the symbolic powers that bend themselves to the service of these, particularly in the press, television, and radio.

THE INTELLECTUAL IS NOT
ETHICALLY NEUTRAL

Interview of Pierre Bourdieu with Thanassis Yalketsis for *Eleftherotypia*, Athens, October 1996.

Thanassis Yalketsis: *For the Greek public, you are the author of books on sociology. Could you briefly outline what led you to sociology?*

Pierre Bourdieu: I started with ethnological research in Kabylia, where cultural traditions common to all the societies around the Mediterranean still live on. In the 1960s I took part in two symposia where specialists on various Mediterranean societies—Greece, Spain, Egypt, Kabylia, Turkey—including my friend John Peristiany, the founder of the Athens Social Research Centre, presented analyses, in particular on honor and shame, that brought out some astonishing similarities. I recently returned to the area of study in which I started for an article on "Masculine Domination." Kabyle society presents an enlarged, and intact, image of the phallocentric mythology that haunts the unconscious of the men and women of Western societies. I carried out my initial research during the Algerian war of liberation, and, to understand the revolutionary movement then sweeping across the country, I undertook research that can be called sociological (I have never understood or accepted the distinction between ethnology and sociology) on questions of work and unemployment. While continuing to analyze the material I had collected in Algeria, again in order to better understand what I was doing, I started statistical work on students in France, whose dissatisfaction had made an impression on me. This was not long before May 1968. The book, *The Inheritors*, which resulted from that research, was discussed at length by students before and during the student revolt. It showed, among other things, the unequal chances of entering higher education and of succeeding in it depending on one's social status (this stands in opposition to the illusion of "school as a liberatory force," which is very strong in France, especially on the Left), and it tried to determine the factors explaining these inequalities: external factors, such as the cultural capital inherited from the family, and factors internal to the educational system, such as implicit pedagogy, which favors those already favored. From there, I moved on to a whole series of research projects on cultural practices: photography, art gallery and museum attendance in Europe (the survey was carried out in five countries, including Greece), and, more generally, the whole range of consumptions, cultural or not . . . But I'll stop there, it would take too long . . .

TY: *Mr. Bourdieu, you are a professor, a sociologist, a thinker—according to many people, one of the major thinkers of our time. What I would like to know is how, exactly, does one arrive at knowledge? Is there a specific route?*

PB: The answer is simple: by doing a lot of work both to acquire the knowledge already established and to break with the knowledge that has been reduced to a routine by academic transmission. I think that professors and elite schools are one of the greatest obstacles to the progress of truly innovative research.

TY: *To your dual experience—the initial and decisive experience of an ethnologist and that of a sociologist—you have also brought the training of a philosopher and what you derive from a profound knowledge of the various intellectual traditions and a great range of cultural productions. Your project is to contribute to an entire social science, to manage to apprehend "the fundamental unity of human practice." How would you now define the field of your work?*

PB: I could say that it is a general anthropology, or an economics of practices, both economic and noneconomic practices. But labels don't mean much. What I do think is that, given the stage that the social sciences have reached, one needs to be deeply distrustful of all divisions in disciplines. Now, as in the past, the most interesting problems and research are almost always situated at the intersections between disciplines, which are often abandoned territory.

TY: *Sociological thought risks becoming an academic reflection, and political practice is in danger of falling into an empiricism devoid of theoretical foundations. If you accept that political action is necessary, what should be the foundation of political engagement, once we have given up the eschatological, millenarian conception of one strand of Marxism? What are the possibilities for grounding viable political action in a theoretical conception that explains reality scientifically?*

PB: You present the problem very well: I think that the mythology of the "ethical neutrality" of the scientist or philosopher as an "impartial spectator," which means that all the burning questions are left at the door of the laboratory, is as pernicious as the subordination of research to political ends. As researchers in the social sciences, we always need to be on our guard against the intrusion of problems that are part of fashionable discussion; but this vigilance can blind us to important questions. To give you an idea of the efforts we make to avoid that dilemma, I will cite the example of the work we are doing in the framework of an international association called *Raisons d'agir* ("reasons to act," a phrase that well expresses our intention): on the one hand we are making a systematic analysis of the social demand for research—in other words, the research programs financed by national and international organizations, so as to create some freedom for ourselves with respect to those commissions; on the other hand, we are working to produce research on objects that are left aside by the governmental agencies. It seems to us that, if one is not to fall into an irresponsible utopianism, and to avoid incurring failures and unintended consequences, political action must be based on the knowledge established by the social sciences, which—although they cannot enable one to say what *must* be done (first because it is not the role of science to define ends)—do supply the means, in most cases, of saying what *should not* be done if one is not to produce negative effects, or no effect at all. In the area of education, for example (the area that I know best), intelligent and effective action would have to proceed through a multitude of prudent, coordinated small measures, taking into account both the general laws of functioning of the system and the interests and dispositions that the different categories of agents owe to their positions in the system and, consequently, the proposals and suggestions—appropriately scrutinized—that they may make, on the basis of their knowledge of their particular situations. This may seem very abstract, but it could be translated not into great reforming laws but into a complex organization capable of mobilizing and channeling energies on the basis of a global vision of the logics of functioning. But to reply briefly to your question, I would say that it seems to me quite inconceivable that one can aspire to govern nowadays without reference to the knowledge established by the social sciences, by which I do not just mean economics, especially in the truncated definition that people often have of it.

TY: *You say, "What I defend above all is the possibility and the necessity of the critical intellectual. There can be no effective democracy without a real intellectual countervailing power." How would you define the role of the critical intellectual at the present time?*

PB: The intellectual can no longer be just a voice of critical conscience, seeking to assert within the political world the truths and values that prevail in his or her universe. He or she must also bring a genuine specific competence into the service of the causes he or she wants to defend.

TY: *We are living in a time of disillusionment with politics. Intellectuals have steadily withdrawn from the realm of political action into that of culture. How can one react against this tendency toward depoliticization?*

PB: From a survey on the intellectuals that we published in two recent issues of the journal *Liber* (one of the instruments for mobilizing a collective intellectual that I was referring to), it does indeed become clear that the "committed" intellectual has almost everywhere surrendered the ground to that disenchanted figure attracted more by success in the media and material or symbolic gratifications than by critical battles. But there is no cause for despair in the situation, and we are also witnessing the emergence of new forms of action, less spectacular but perhaps more effective and radical, in the feminist and gay movements, in associations for solidarity with the most deprived, and so on. These movements and campaigns have not yet found their expression in the illusory discourse produced by those journalist-intellectuals who are destroying the figure of the intellectual through the caricature or parody that they present of it while at the same time proclaiming the demise of the intellectuals.

TY: *In contrast to the classic figure of the "committed" and "universal" intellectual (Sartre) there arose that of the "dissident" and "specific" intellectual (Foucault). What is your view of the role of the intellectual in relation to that dichotomy?*

PB: Indeed, one has to give up the ambition of the total intellectual as embodied by Sartre. But to give reality to the figure of the specific intellectual as Michel Foucault conceived it, I think one has to abandon the romantic myth of the solitary creator and conceive a collective individual, capable of placing multiple and varied competences in the service of the critical ends that are implied in any literary, scientific, or artistic enterprise worthy of the name. I have applied a lot of effort in the last few years to creating the practical conditions for the functioning of such a collective intellectual. I am thinking, for example, of the journal *Liber*, published in a dozen countries and languages, or the various networks of writers (the International Parliament) or researchers (*Raisons d'agir*) that have been created to facilitate generous but also effective and competent interventions by intellectuals of all countries.

TY: *Many people see you as the person capable of telling them the real truth about society and the world. How do you experience that responsibility? As an intellectual, do you feel a responsibility toward that function of shaping mentalities? How do you feel about that?*

PB: I think that intellectuals overestimate their power, or rather that they overestimate the power, especially the critical power, that they can exercise individually, while they underestimate the power they can exert collectively, especially when they relax their vigilance and, through their withdrawals or their compromises with the temporal powers of whatever kind, they reinforce the tendencies of the economic and social world. That is what is happening now with the attraction of intellectuals to the delights of neoliberalism or the nihilistic pseudosubversions of postmodernism.

TY: *Why did you decide to come to Greece? Could you say a few words about your relationship to the country?*

PB: For a whole set of reasons that it is hard to set out in detail: first, to express my gratitude to my translator, Nicos Panayatopoulos, who has devoted himself with the greatest generosity and the greatest intelligence to translating my work into Greek; and to my publishers, who took the risk of publishing a difficult author, little known in Greece; and to the editor of the journal *Synchrona Themata*, Mr. Pesmazoglou, with whom we jointly publish our journal *Liber*; and also to the many friends—teachers and researchers—I have in this country, in particular Professor Lambiri-Dimaki, who instigated the honor bestowed on me by the University of Athens. But I also have a longstanding and very intense attachment to Greece, its language, and its culture. I can't tell you the emotion I felt when I first saw a text of mine printed in Greek . . . I would fear to appear self-indulgent if I told you of everything that attaches me to the Greece of the past and the present—its philosophy, of course, which I regularly read (in the original), and its literature, but also its monuments and landscapes, through all the happy times I have spent, in various visits, to Athens, Delphi, or Mythymna on the island of Lesbos. And also I think that, for all kinds of reasons—in particular their tradition of international openness (which I very much hope nothing will change)—the Greeks can play a decisive role in the undertakings of the collective intellectual that I am working to bring about.

A SOCIOLOGIST IN THE WORLD

Interview with Pierre Bourdieu (in *Revue d'études palestiniennes* 22, winter 2000). Questions by Catherine Lévy, Farouk Mardam-Bey, and Elias Sanbar.

Revue d'études palestiniennes (REP):   *To say the least, your trilogy* Les Héritiers, Un Art moyen, *and* L'Amour de l'art, *followed by* La Reproduction *shortly after May 1968, strongly marked the sociology of culture. When you look back at those books now, what do you think of your approach and what you achieved, in terms of changes in the educational system and cultural institutions, but also in relation to present-day debates and your own development? Would you still say that your critics on the Left, and specifically the Marxists, were speaking from a "useless" thinking, whose economism prevents it from grasping the relations of domination?*

Pierre Bourdieu: Yes, the times have changed, as the phrase goes, especially in the intellectual world, and to get an idea of the change one has only to think of all those former "revolutionary" leaders of May 1968 who now strut the corridors of power or preach the new gospel of neoliberalism in the media. But the realities and mechanisms that we were describing then have not changed much. The theoretical and empirical knowledge gained about the contribution that the educational system makes to the reproduction of the structure of the social space (it's not an elegant expression, but it's rigorous) is endlessly confirmed in reality, both in France and in all contemporary societies—the United States or Japan, Mali or Chile. Every researcher worthy of the name has to start out from that knowledge, every politician concerned about efficacy has to take note of the mechanisms brought to light, especially if he or she aspires to act in the direction of democratization.

That's not to say that nothing has changed in the functioning of

schools and universities since the early 1970s. And I have continued
to observe those changes in order to try to understand and explain
them. I'd have to mention the whole series of books and articles that
I've published or that have been published in *Actes de la recherche en sciences sociales*, which aim to specify, refine, or systematize analyses that
are not reducible to a "thesis" (the so-called "thesis of reproduction,"
which is often presented in caricature). I'm thinking, for example, of
The State Nobility, which builds on twenty years of research. Published
in 1989, at a time when the socialist *énarques* were triumphantly cele-
brating the bicentenary of the Revolution of 1789, it described in detail
how the contemporary nobility is produced and reproduced, endowed
with all the social properties of the nobility of the ancien régime, with,
in addition, the certainty that it owes its elect status only to its merit
and its intelligence. Another example would be the description in *The
Weight of the World* of the different forms taken over the course of time
by the relationship between children from the lower classes and the
educational system. Whereas until quite recently (roughly the 1960s)
they were excluded very early from the educational system (at the age
of twelve or fourteen), these children began to enter secondary education in massive numbers—discovering the status of adolescent that
was previously reserved for children of bourgeois families—and found
themselves very rapidly condemned to the state of "excluded insiders,"
at once present and absent in an educational institution ill-equipped
to receive them. All these analyses, which were often difficult because
they were based on complex statistical data and methods, obviously
had some political implications that were as shocking, if not more so,
for people on the Left (who clung to the myth of "schooling as a liberatory force") as for those on the Right.

As for the second part of your question, it is certain that, as you
suggest, what aroused most resistance on the Left was the effort I
made to produce a materialist theory of symbolic goods (or forms),
breaking with the economism still dominant in the "progressive" tradition, which prevents one from rigorously analyzing (and therefore
effectively combating) the effect of symbolic domination and, more
generally, from understanding the specifically symbolic dimension

of social relations (I'm thinking, for example, of national conflicts with a linguistic or religious dimension). Only a genuine economy of symbolic goods—in other words, of the quite real, though immaterial, costs and profits associated with the loss or recovery of one's language, religion, or quite simply one's identity and name (and the right to call oneself Irish, or Catalan, or Palestinian)—makes it possible to understand past or present wars of religion, or national liberation struggles, which are not the simple explosions of passion or irrational belief that they are generally thought to be. They have a form of rationality, but it is not that of the economy or politics in the ordinary sense.

It is clear that in proposing such a materialist economy of immaterial realities, I was inevitably exposing myself to the criticisms of the materialists, who found me idealist, especially as regards the economy, and the spiritualists, who found me too materialist, especially as regards art and literature.

REP: *You developed that critique in depth in* Distinction, *in which you perhaps most extensively set out your conception of social classes, then in* Homo Academicus, *which is an analysis of the university system, and finally in* The State Nobility, *which reveals among other things, starting from the case of the Grandes Écoles, what is hidden behind the word "competence." But your approach has sometimes been denounced as a theorization of fatalism, and therefore as an invitation to immobility. In your view, is the reform of the education system an impossible task, which would contradict your endorsement, in the late 1980s, of the education policies of the socialist government?*

PB: I never, as you put it, endorsed the education policies of the socialist government; I only chaired the discussions of the professors of the Collège de France, in 1986, when the president of the Republic invited them to put forward their vision for the future of the French education system. The fundamental principle of the whole project was not to suggest anything that was not achievable within the limits of the education system. This amounted, in practice, to excluding any

attempt to "democratize" access to the system, which, it has to be acknowledged, is not very well placed to fulfill that function. One could
say, in broad terms, that all that can be expected of this system is that
it should not intensify the effects of the social mechanisms which tend
to ensure the transmission of cultural capital and which thereby contribute even more to the reproduction of inequalities.

Having said that, I have always had, and still have, the conviction
that the school and university system can and should be reformed.
But I have always also thought that, because they do not fully understand this institution and those who run it, politicians have always
underestimated the forces of inertia, which are enormous, and the factors of change, which are also considerable, so that they have always
ended up reinforcing the conservative forces, which they provoke with
clumsy and often arrogant measures, and discouraging those prepared
to work for change, whom they need to know and respect in order
to be able to mobilize them. (The education system, like the hospital
system and many other public services, is full of people disposed to
offer their dedication and enthusiasm, which has the effect of limiting, even nowadays, the force of the measures aimed at bringing
into it the logic of calculation of costs and profits and therefore the
often destructive impact of preoccupations with performance and efficiency, which are more or less definable and generally misplaced.).
A policy aimed at fairly radically transforming the system would succeed only if—renouncing the very idea of reform as it is usually understood, i.e., as a set of comprehensive measures, preferably spectacular
ones (to impress the media and the public, which generally leads to
demagogy)—it sought to put in place (very progressively and therefore very discreetly in strategic places in the system) agents and institutional mechanisms generating positive changes, and in parallel,
to take equally discreet and invisible measures capable of weakening
the mechanisms and institutions responsible for the dysfunctions of
the system. Such an approach would have to combine a systematic,
global vision, the only one capable of giving meaning to local, specific
interventions, with attention to the details—the infinitely small things
in the daily life of institutions that do not interest ignorant, arrogant,
and hasty reformers.

Within the framework of an association dedicated to thinking about change in higher education and research, the ARESER (*Association de réflexion sur les enseignements supérieurs et la recherche*) that I set up with some colleagues—sociologists, historians of education, and economists very familiar with various aspects of the educational system—tried to put forward "Some diagnoses and urgent remedies for a university system in danger" (*Quelques diagnostics et remèdes urgents pour une université en peril*, the title of the collective work we published in the *Raisons d'agir* series), an attempt to set out, if not a systematic action program, at least the guiding principles for effective, modest change in education. One example of a mechanism tending to generate positive innovations was the "Parliament of the Universities" that we proposed, which would enable teachers, students, and administrative staff to debate publicly on the ends and means of education. Naturally, we invited the minister of education to discuss these proposals, which had arisen from a democratic debate among competent academics with varied affiliations and statuses. He preferred to rely on commissions of experts appointed by him (on account of their supposed docility or their visibility in the media more than their competence, which he is anyway not in a position to judge) whom he asked primarily to give a gloss of legitimacy to his autocratic decisions.

REP: *Your first book, or certainly one of the first, was on the sociology of Algeria. And since that time you have never ceased to refer back to your Algerian fieldwork right up to* Masculine Domination, *where the Kabyle tradition is treated as a "paradigmatic realization of the Mediterranean tradition." How has Algeria fed into your work as a sociologist here in France? And what has been your subsequent relationship with Arab and Islamic studies in general?*

PB: Algeria was for me like a scientific and also personal "first love." The encounter with Arabo-Berber societies made a deep impression on me and has left unforgettable memories. That was where I learned my craft, in the difficult (and dangerous) conditions of the war of liberation; it was probably also where I "learned about life," as people sometimes say, through contact with simple and admirable men and women in all kinds of social positions. My first work as a sociologist, published under the title *Sociologie de l'Algérie,*[1] aimed to acquaint the French, and especially the intellectuals, with societies of which they knew almost nothing, even if they readily backed their causes, and my first strictly ethnological research had inseparably scientific and political goals: the aim was to make sense of the mysteries of a fascinating and enigmatic "culture" (the agrarian rites, the matrimonial traditions, the economy of honor) and, thereby, to rehabilitate the bearers of that culture, who were subject to racist stigmatization. It was also then that I encountered Islam, which all the "specialists," in particular the economists (with, as ever, some notable exceptions), already treated as a *diabolus ex machina,* the ultimate explanatory factor of all time lags and archaisms. So I confronted the Orientalist tradition with all the weapons then at my disposal, and I was delighted to observe, much later, in the writings of Edward Said, much of what I had experienced in my battles with some of my (to say the least) ultraconservative colleagues at the Faculty of Algiers. (While there I learned, among other things, that intellectual rivalries could, when the occasion presented itself, take the most violent forms, and I had had to go into hiding, around May 13, 1958,[2] because I had been put—no doubt at the instigation of some of my colleagues—on the "red list" of individuals to be "neutralized.") I think that many of the problems that I have been led to address, such as that of the logic of practice, and the very concepts I had to develop to resolve them sprang from my effort to understand men and women who found themselves thrown into an alien economic cosmos imported by colonization, with mental schemes and dispositions, especially economic ones, acquired in a precapitalist universe.

REP: *In your book on Heidegger, and then in* Pascalian Meditations, *you explicitly reconnect with philosophy, but you do so in order to conduct a "critique of scholastic reason." From that point of view, how do you analyze the French philosophical field, from Sartre to the present day?*

PB: I won't, of course, even try to sketch here a description of the French philosophical field and its evolution, from Sartre to the present day. All I can say is that I only recently discovered the root of the malaise I had always felt toward (or in) that field, which I set out in *Pascalian Meditations*—namely, what I call the "scholastic point of view," or the viewpoint of the spectator who, unaware that he is a spectator, unconsciously universalizes himself, imposing himself in place of the viewpoint of the agents engaged in practice. It was probably because I had had to "objectify" this point of view to be able to understand the practices (especially the rituals) that I was trying to objectify—and trying to adopt (in thought) the practical viewpoint of the agents engaged in the action—that I was able to develop the theory of the theoretical posture that separates us from the logic of practice, and from our own practice; at the same time I also recovered my own primary experience of the social world, which had always kept me removed from comfortable immersion in the scholastic illusion.

REP: *Few social science journals have had so wide a readership and so much influence as* Actes de la recherche en sciences sociales, *the journal you founded in 1975. Twenty-five years on, how do you assess the experience of that publication, and, more particularly, how has it changed the craft of sociology?*

PB: I am glad that you mention *Actes de la recherche en sciences sociales*, because it is, I think, of all my undertakings (perhaps together with the *Sens Commun* series that I edited for many years at Éditions de Minuit and which continues now at Seuil under the title *Liber*) the one that gives the clearest idea of the scientific collective that I have tried to foster. Those who know only my books, or even, like most journalists, only the slimmest and most exoteric of them, *On Television* (which they often amalgamate with Serge Halimi's book, *Les Nouveaux Chiens de garde*, published in the same series), will not have an accurate idea of the collective enterprise, and the collective contribution, that a whole cohort of researchers, both old and young, French and foreign, known and unknown (at least at the time of their first publication) have made to the conception and implementation of a new definition of sociology that has progressively imposed itself on the whole scientific field. (Our adversaries often describe it as "dominant," without adding that the principle of this "domination" is neither academic power—which, as I can only regret, and contrary to what some people would sometimes like others to believe, is almost nonexistent—nor economic power.) Although it gives copious thanks to prestigious university institutions—the Collège de France, the Écoles des hautes études, the Maison des sciences de l'homme, the Centre national de la recherche scientifique—until very recently it has been resourced only from its sales (even for the purchase of "compocards" in their day, then computers) and the dedication of a small number of people administratively attached to the institutions that I have mentioned, in particular the Maison des sciences de l'homme, which, from the time of Fernand Braudel and Clemens Heller, never wavered in its moral support. It introduced many innovations (many of them subsequently much imitated) into the rhetoric of scientific discourse in the social sciences: facsimiles of original documents, boxes of illustrative text, photographs, etc. But the most important thing is that it imposed as self-evident a choice of scientific objects that systematically ignored the social hierarchy of objects (in particular, the distinction between noble and ignoble subjects) and above all a way of handling them based on a refusal of the break between the theoretical and the empirical (or, as the Anglo-Americans and others who let their vision be forced on them say, between "theory" and "methodology"). Or, more precisely, its explicit principle of selection is the pursuit of work raising important theoretical problems in relation to empirical objects that are very precisely characterized and sometimes socially or politically insignificant (one article that posed the question of "fetishism"—sacrosanct at a time when *armchair Marxism*[3] was triumphant—was based on analysis of the haute-couture market). Except for some didactic clarifications on some instruments in common use within the group, such as the concepts of cultural capital or social capital, the journal never indulged in the academic complacencies of theoretical discourse in itself and for itself (and that was probably one of the reasons for the success of its sales). In short, as François Furet put it at a time when he had more sympathy for the enterprise than in recent years, *Actes* is the product of a "workshop" in which the participants acquire, in practice, schemes of perception and appreciation, instruments for object construction, technical skills and methods of analysis. (We are preparing an issue specially devoted to the arsenal of methods that we have devised or refined, from techniques for statistical analysis of data such as multiple correspondence analysis or regression analysis to techniques of sociographic description and analysis, exemplified in the journal by authors such as Yvette Delsaut, Abdelmalek Sayad, or Michel Pialoux, or new ways of conducting and presenting interviews, with, once again, the intention or the hope of breaking the—always hierarchical—divisions between so-called quantitative techniques, which are classified on the side of the serious, the *hard*,[4] the masculine, and so-called qualitative or descriptive techniques.) In this way, *Actes* has been able to play a key role as an instrument for teaching research. Articles that we may consider excellent in other respects (for example, on the theory of the state in Hegel and Durkheim) have tended to be excluded from *Actes*, not, as is sometimes thought, in the name of some theoretical orthodoxy, or some kind of sectarianism, but because they do not seem to us to really enrich the empirical-theoretical "toolbox" that we want to offer the reader (and which we are also building up for ourselves, in a spirit of "continuing education").

REP: *You played an active role in the strike movement of November– December 1995. You were to be seen heading a rally with the rail workers who were in the forefront of the movement, chairing a meeting in 1996 of all the components of the "social movement" (trade unions, campaigning organizations, researchers, and teachers), making a speech in the street during the demonstrations by the unemployed in winter 1997. Reading your books, it would seem that it was scientific reflection on social reality, from* The Inheritors *to* The Weight of the World, *that led you to conduct scientific discourse and political discourse in parallel. Could you analyze that two-track approach?*

PB: I have always conceived my work as inseparably scientific and political. That was true of my years in Algeria, and books like *Travail et travailleurs en Algérie* or *The Uprooting*[5] sought to provide scientific evidence on acutely political situations (rather like the sociologist of

Indian origin who has recently studied the situation of Palestinian refugees in Lebanon) or, more precisely, scientific responses to questions traditionally posed in political terms, such as the question of the economic and social conditions of the emergence of revolutionary consciousness (raised at the time through glorification of the Chinese-style peasant revolution) or, which amounts to much the same, the question of the difference between subproletariat and proletariat. It was also true of the research we did on education shortly before 1968 and which, while contesting the vision of students as a "class" that some student leaders wanted to impose, provided the bases for a critical view of the education system which was taken up by some currents in the student movement. I always had the concern, perhaps a somewhat scientistic one (but I was engaged in a field in which scientificity is an important stake and also, to some extent at least, a condition of political effectiveness), to give myself and to give to others all possible scientific guarantees. So, in 1968, as now with the association *Raisons d'agir*, we endeavored to intervene in the political battles of the day, but with scientific weapons, and I recently rediscovered some stenciled tracts that we produced then on issues that were being debated at the time, such as the American university system, and on possible reforms, such as continuous assessment, which emerged from that typically "reformist" proposition. And I could go on enumerating the activities that would show that interest in politics, or even in political intervention, did not come suddenly and belatedly. The intentions of *The Weight of the World* can be described in the same terms that I used to talk about my research in Algeria.

I have often tackled politically controversial objects, but I have tried to approach them and handle them in the coldest, most scientific way possible. For example, I conducted a survey on consumption—following the most laborious and strict procedures of the methodology devised by INSEE—in resettlement centers in Algeria. There was something rather crazy about questioning the same people—who moreover had almost nothing—countless times about the purchases they had made the previous day, running through all the possible headings: bread, matches, candles.

So I have always known—without always being able to say it out loud, for fear of gratuitously excluding myself from the "scientific community," then dominated by the ideology of "axiological neutrality"—that sociology is through and through political. This does not mean—far from it—that it is inspired by political postulates or that it abdicates all scientific demands in order to advance political causes. I have always been convinced that the most valuable contribution a researcher can make to the political struggle is to work, with all the weapons that science offers at the moment in question, to produce and promote the truth.

What has changed, no doubt, and what makes those who do not know me think that I am the one who has radically changed in the last few years—since the early 1980s, some will say, with the manifesto on Poland that I wrote with Michel Foucault,[7] or, according to others, with the demonstration at the Gare de Lyon in December 1995[8]—is first that my interventions have become more visible, especially for and through the media. But in addition, as you suggest, I have been led by the very logic of my research work to discover things that made it impossible for me to keep silent, or rather, things that I could not keep silent. I am thinking in particular of the long-term consequences, which are now beginning to become visible, of neoliberalism. For a long time, my principle was that when I did not know, or did not know enough, I should keep quiet, and that nothing entitled me to try to impose my feelings of indignation or revolt (which for a long time led me to keep out of the obligatory battles among intellectuals, who, curiously, did not let this prerequisite of previous knowledge stand in their way).

Little by little it became clear to me that even when I did not have all the necessary knowledge, I could not keep silent in the face of the extreme dangers that the policies now being implemented worldwide in the name of economic rationality present for what I see as the most important achievements of our civilization, whether in cultural or social matters, in particular through the systematic efforts made to break down every kind of obstacle to the most brutal logic of the market. Perhaps because I had the sense of, all the same, not being the least well-placed person to know, especially after research such as that which led to *The Weight of the World*, and which had enabled me to encounter the most pernicious effects of neoliberal policies both in Europe and in America, perhaps because I had the conviction that the most terrible dangers, which today are only visible to a scientifically informed eye, will only emerge slowly, in the long run, when it will be too late to resist, I felt obliged to intervene, with all the social force at my disposal, alongside the most lucid and most effective forces of resistance within the social movement.

REP: *You don't limit your critical analysis of policies to France. You have written virulent articles against German monetary policy and the European Central Bank; in your series with Éditions du Seuil, Raisons d'agir, you have published personal pages against "the scourge of neoliberalism" and violent critiques of Anglo-American policies (Keith Dixon's Les Évangélistes du marché); you've lectured on these themes in Germany, in Greece and elsewhere; and you recently wrote an article (in Le Monde diplomatique) on the future of a European social movement. How do you see the role of the committed intellectual? Is it a matter of identifying with those who are forced to struggle and so enhancing their visibility, or do you yourself feel forced to struggle in order to no longer just describe and analyze social reality, but to change it?*

PB: Intervention on an international scale, in Europe and beyond, is a necessity because the policy whose effects need to be countered is no longer confined within the national framework; national governments are more and more simply relays for the forces of the market. One of the most astonishing paradoxes of contemporary politics is the strange effect of the division between *grande* and *petite* state nobility that I described in my book of 1989, *The State Nobility*. We see great officers of the state (Mr. Camdessus, managing director of the IMF, is one of them, along with the Trichets, Tietmeyers, Haberers[9] and Co. who, invested by the state, preach and practice "a smaller state," often at our expense) making themselves the liquidators of the welfare state—in other words, of the *petite noblesse* of the state. We see all these senior civil servants, who owe everything to the state, striving to reduce the scope of the public services, leaving to the frontline civil servants (teachers, youth workers, social workers, hospital staff, police officers) the task of coping at minimum expense with the economic and social consequences (crime, delinquency . . .) of the socially irresponsible policies imposed on them.

REP: *You say in the Prologue to* Sociology in Question *that sociology is "a science that involves social stakes . . . that touches on vital interests" and that "one cannot expect bosses, bishops, or journalists to praise the scientificity of work that reveals the hidden foundations of their domination." Is it your aim to break the "fields" and the field effects, to dismantle the mechanisms of domination in such a way that the "activists" can take possession of a certain way of thinking?*

   You continue to write difficult works, like Pascalian Meditations; *you also want your thinking to have a "nonscientific," directly political use, as the content of the books in your Éditions du Seuil series would tend to show. As early as 1974, you were denouncing in the same sentence the women's fashion magazine* Elle *and* Le Monde *in your contribution to the analysis of fetishism and magic. When and how did you realize the need for a more direct intervention on the role of the media in general?*

PB: I'll limit myself to the journalistic field, because a methodical examination of the relationship between the various relatively autonomous fields—legal, scientific, literary, artistic, or even political—and laypersons (among whom one must each time include the members of the other fields) would require very long and complex arguments. From the point of view from which you are asking, that of activists' access to mastery of the instruments of knowledge produced within the restricted fields, and in particular of analyses of the mechanisms of domination, the journalistic field occupies a strategic position. In broad terms, one can say that the media constitute a twofold screen or obstacle to diffusion of the findings of social science, especially when they may have critical implications. Driven by the aim of intervening in the first person in the construction of the correct representation of the social world—without possessing the necessary minimum of instruments of knowledge—journalists mostly condemn themselves to contributing to the maintenance of the established symbolic order by consciously or unconsciously reproducing the discourse of those who dominate the economic and political worlds or of their spokespersons in the intellectual field; and they cannot envisage changing the role they might play by modestly making themselves the relays and communicators of the work of researchers. Next, they have a kind of de facto monopoly over access to the public sphere: being in a position to block any dissonant or dissident message, they exercise a censorship that is all the more pernicious because it is invisible. One could say, parodying an old formula, that the most urgent task for intellectuals today would be to fight collectively for ownership of their means of production and distribution—in other words, for control of all their means of expression, such as books, newspapers, radio, television, Internet, or cinema (the *Raisons d'agir* series is a minute step in that direction). Many intellectual interventions are nipped in the bud because they cannot attain the public visibility that the slightest court essayist readily obtains from his partners in media connivance.

All this makes the production and communication of a rigorous (and thereby critical) knowledge of the hidden mechanisms of the journalistic field an absolute priority for research, and also for all citizens and all journalists concerned for freedom and democracy: through the parties, the unions, or associations, but also through the education system and the journalistic vehicles that escape the censorship of the field, we need to try to distribute as widely as possible to all citizens the means of exercising their critical vigilance over media discourse and the conditions in which it is produced. (The extraordinary success of the little *Raisons d'agir* books that ventured in that direction is evidence of an enormous social demand that ought to be satisfied, because, as Jacques Bouveresse has said—to *explain* his intervention with the weapons of logic on a terrain normally left to rhetorical manipulations—it is a question of a demand for democracy.)

REP: *The victory of Israel, the Arab defeat, in 1967, marked for the Western consciousness the beginning of a long period in which the Arab-Israeli*

conflict has been at the forefront of the political scene. How did you see the
events of 1967? What did you then know of the Palestinian question itself?
How did you perceive it? Has your thinking been influenced by the subse-
quent debate about the question of Palestine, the emergence of Palestinian
people as an actor on the scene, its aspirations, and the very particular na-
ture of its struggle?

PB: I have always been attentive to the Palestinian question, not least
because I encountered its effects in the Arab countries with which I
was in contact. (How can one not see, for example, that Islamic fundamentalism, a kind of symbolic terrorism that can lead to physical
terrorism, to the great despair of all "enlightened" Arabs—which does
not mean "Westernized" or enslaved to Western values—is fueled by
the permanent affront of the treatment of the Palestinian question?)
It is probably through that channel that I have felt myself concerned,
very directly, by the Arab-Israeli conflict, then by the treatment of the
Palestinians in the various agreements that were supposed to settle
the question, and on which I have always been extremely skeptical and
pessimistic. I have always hesitated to take public stands (although
I have sometimes signed petitions launched by Israeli or American
friends against various forms of oppression of the Palestinians), first
because I did not feel sufficiently competent to offer real insights on
what is perhaps the most difficult and most tragic question of our time
(how does one choose between the victims par excellence of racist violence and the victims of those victims?); and then because this problem, especially for a person like me, known for his sympathies toward
the Arab countries, was surrounded by a host of taboos tending to generate a real symbolic terror.

I do not, course, feel capable of suggesting the slightest solution,
or even of choosing between the various possible solutions. But I think
it is urgent for all the progressive forces in the world to have the courage to transgress the deliberately maintained taboo surrounding the
Israeli-Palestinian problem and address this issue, if only to break the
artificial confrontation between the two protagonists and their American and Arab protectors, who are so tragically unequal. I also think

that, in the interest of the Israelis as much as the Palestinians, they should unequivocally denounce all the abuses of power committed by the Israelis—confiscation of land, violent repression, etc.—and carry on the symbolic struggle both against the effacement of Palestinian history and against the anti-Arab and anti-Islamic propaganda which, in the guise of combating Islamic fundamentalism, permeates the media (and which has as negative consequences in Europe, in relations with immigrants, as in Israel or the United States). Finally, I think—but I am conscious here of going far beyond the limits of my knowledge of the problem—that rather than separating the Israelis and the Arabs (as the Israelis seem to want) in a kind of search for ethnic purity or purification that is perfectly absurd (especially, of course, for the Palestinians, whose territories are reduced to wretched enclaves always subject to the goodwill of the dominant power), it would be better, as Edward Said suggests, to integrate the two peoples or, in order to try to escape from the logic of "communities" (of blood? race? religion?— these foundations are not very *Aufklärung*) to bring together two sets of free and equal citizens in a secular democracy, freed from ethnic and religious criteria and capable of inventing the means of organizing democratic competition (and hence peaceful coexistence) between the interests and ideals that both unite and separate fellow citizens. Utopian, perhaps, but what an example for the Middle East!

REP: *Algeria, Palestine, the Gulf War, Yugoslavia are all questions, conflicts, that concern you currently. You have expressed your thoughts on these subjects on many occasions. You have also done so through a more comprehensive reflection on the American view of the world. Can one speak today of a need for resistance on a global scale? Is a new internationalism possible—and necessary?*

PB: I do think that only a new form of internationalism, radically freed from any kind of imperialism, can stand up to the intrinsically international power of the great multinational corporations and the financial markets, relayed by agencies such as the World Bank or the IMF, which try to impose universally a worldview that is presented as universal, in the name of the authority of economic science. The neoliberal model, which can be condensed into a few fundamental principles (i.e., the economy is a separate domain, governed by natural, universal laws with which governments should not interfere or compromise; the market is the optimal means for organizing production efficiently and fairly in democratic societies; "globalization" requires a reduction of state expenditure, especially in the welfare area, since social entitlements in employment and welfare benefits are expensive and dysfunctional), is in fact no more than the universalization of the particularities of a historical and therefore contingent society, the American one. And these, very briefly, are some of its typical features: a state, which, already reduced to the minimum, has been systematically weakened by the ultraliberal conservative revolution started by Reagan and continued by Clinton (as evidenced by the fact that the monopoly of physical violence, the minimal characteristic of the state according to Weber and Elias, is very imperfectly assured, with weapons on open sale, etc., or the economic withdrawal of the state, in the name of the virtues of *self-help*[10] inherited from the Calvinist belief that God helps those who help themselves); a tradition of "metaphysical individualism," as Dorothy Ross puts it, which reappears at the heart of economic theory; a tendency to exalt the mobility and dynamism of the American social order, which leads to efficiency and productivity being associated with high flexibility and to social insecurity being seen as a positive principle of collective organization, etc. It is a worldview that can be very unattractive to all those who are attached to forms of action that are collective, collectivist, or, if that word is too frightening, solidarist, and that are inherited, not, as is sometimes wrongly said, from the celebrated "Judeo-Christian tradition" but from the European social movement of the 19th century, which, in contrast to the charitable traditions of the churches, invented various forms of secular "solidarism" based either on the state or on associations. Its universal imposition can indeed only be combated by an internationalism based on solidarity among all the "colonized" of all continents—South Americans, Africans, Indians, Koreans, but also, in many respects, Europeans. It is, it seems to me, within the wider framework of collective struggles against the neocolonial strategies of delocalization linked to the growth of direct investment abroad and the quasiuniversal imposition of the iron law of the financial markets, that all the movements of resistance to the "scourge of neoliberalism"—Palestinian, Chilean, Indian, or French—may find the intellectual and material strength they need to impose in reality the solidarities of a truly social economy against all the atomizing forces contained in the neoliberal vision.

EPILOGUE

Remembering Pierre Bourdieu

by Craig Calhoun, 2002

Pierre Bourdieu was the most distinguished European sociologist since Emile Durkheim and Max Weber, and made major contributions to a range of other fields. No one would describe Bourdieu's writings as easily accessible, yet few social scientists in our era have had broader influence. Indeed, Bourdieu exemplified intellectual commitments at the heart of the mission of the SSRC: collaboration across disciplinary lines, internationalism, and bringing social science to bear on public issues. He approached these as we also hope to do in a spirit of scientific rigor, with insistence on both quality and creativity.

After Bourdieu died on January 23, 2002, *Le Monde* delayed publication by several hours so the front page could carry the announcement. It was the lead story on TV news, and ran with expressions of grief and loss from France's president, prime minister, trade union leaders, and a host of other dignitaries and scholars. These continued to flow for weeks, though after a few days they were complemented by attacks from old enemies and pretentious would-be heirs. The media low point came when a *Nouvel Observateur* journalist who had been refused admission to the hospital nonetheless published a first-person account of the supposed deathbed scene.

In all of this we see something of the French intellectual field that Bourdieu himself famously analyzed. We see the intellectual as celebrity, the desire of politicians to appear as men of ideas, and the debasement of intellectual life that journalism can effect even while it ostensibly exalts it. We see also the workings of a scientific field in which scholars struggle for distinction—some by associating themselves with a great man and others by claiming to be important enough that their differences from him actually matter. But not least we see a reflection, however distorted, of an extraordinary intellectual career and the intellectual resources that made it possible.

Born in 1930, Bourdieu was the son of a peasant farmer turned postman in a remote village in the Pyrénées Atlantiques. He was at the top of his class at the Lycée de Pau, the Lycée Louis-le-Grand à Paris, and eventually the Ecole Normale Supérieure, breeding ground of France's intellectual elite. Never allowed the unself-conscious belonging of those with wealth and cultivated accents, he also never confused success with proof of meritocracy. He knew it had been a struggle. His very bodily sense of insertion into an intensely competitive social world was one of the inspirations for his enormously fruitful resuscitation of the Aristotelian idea of *habitus*. His awareness of what his classmates and teachers did not see because it felt natural to them informed his accounts of *doxa* and misrecognition and his grasp of the need to struggle with everyday consciousness in order to "win" social facts. Indeed, Bourdieu's estrangement from the institutions within which he excelled propelled his critical analyses of French academic life, and indeed of the state and capitalism more generally.

Bourdieu's sense of distance from the dominant culture of the Ecole Normale was shared with his contemporaries Jacques Derrida and Michel Foucault. Though the specifics varied, a certain horror at the social environment of the Ecole informed each in a struggle to see what conventional consciousness obscured. Indeed, as Bourdieu often reminded listeners, Foucault attempted suicide as a student. Bourdieu's response, however, was to embrace science and, in opposition to the elitist world of philosophy, specifically social science.

This commitment was crystallized by national service in Algeria during that French colony's horrific struggle for independence. Scarred but also toughened, Bourdieu stayed on as a teacher and became a self-taught ethnographer, proving himself an extraordinarily keen observer of the interpenetration of large-scale social change and the struggles and solidarities of daily life. He conducted research in the Kabyle region and with Berber-speaking labor migrants, addressing themes from the introduction of money into marriage negotiations to cosmology and the agricultural calendar. His first three books, *Sociologie d'Algérie* (1958), *Travail et travailleurs en Algérie* (1963, with

Alain Darbel), and *Le Déracinement* (1964, with Abdelmalek Sayad) were signal empirical contributions to the study of Algeria, colonialism, economic change, and the crisis of traditional agriculture. Working with Darbel and Sayad (an exceptional scholar who remained a close friend until his own death in 1998) helped to inaugurate a pattern of collaboration that characterized Bourdieu's entire career. In a branch of science that has been slow to institutionalize collaboration (compared to, for example, the biomedical sciences), and in a French intellectual field heavily focused on the ideal of the heroic individual genius, Bourdieu developed long-term relationships and a support system for shared intellectual labor. He founded the journal *Actes de la recherche en sciences sociales* and later the European review of books, *Liber*, as well as two research centers. The combination of feudalism and pursuit of celebrity that characterize French academia were in tension with this, of course, even while they helped Bourdieu procure resources. In order to achieve personal autonomy, several of Bourdieu's students and collaborators felt it necessary to go through painful rebellions. A few could not restrain themselves from expressing emotions from their old quasi-Oedipal struggles in newspaper commentary after Bourdieu's death.

Some of the postmortem attacks reflected the *ressentiment* of the lesser for the greater that Nietzsche appropriated the French word to designate. In Bourdieu's case this was compounded by the extraordinary amount of intellectual terrain he covered and thus of space he occupied and shadow he cast. Perhaps most of all, though, there was anger over the extent to which Bourdieu challenged the very system in which he prospered and his unwillingness to turn his own success into an endorsement of that system and thus of all those honored by it. On the contrary, Bourdieu was relentlessly critical of the consecration function performed by educational institutions. Knowing the antagonism this would arouse, he called the first chapter in *Homo Academicus* (1984) "A 'Book for Burning'?"

Bourdieu's studies of universities and intellectual production were partly an extension of his inquiries into education and social inequality (including *The Inheritors* in 1964, *Reproduction in Education, Culture and Society* in 1970, and *The State Nobility* in 1989). Equally, though,

they were central to his pursuit of a reflexive grounding for social science. One could not understand the stances intellectuals took without
understanding both the positions they held within their microcosm
or the place of that intellectual field in the web of symbolic and material exchanges involving holders of different kinds of power and resources. This was no simple determinism, but a demand that social
scientists pay attention to the conditions of their own work—starting
with the very unequal social distribution of leisure to devote to intellectual projects—and objectify their own efforts to produce objective
knowledge of the social world. He challenged, in other words, the common tendency to propound objective explanations of the lives of others
while claiming the right of subjective interpretation for one's own.

Struggling to grasp the subjective and objective together was a leit-
motif of Bourdieu's work. He railed against false antinomies and the
kinds of oppositions that serve less to advance knowledge than to advance careers of those who write endless theses arguing one side or the
other. The point was not simply to choose Weber over Marx or Lévi-
Strauss over Sartre but to escape from imposed categories. "Objective
analysis," he wrote in *Homo Academicus*, "obliges us to realize that the
two approaches, structuralist and constructivist . . . are two complementary stages of the same procedure." Bourdieu applied the lesson
equally in studies of museums and artistic fields and of science itself.
He offered no simple "solution" to the riddle of structure and agency.
He insisted, rather, that the interaction be worked out in analysis of
concrete empirical cases. Only in this way could social scientists do
the necessary, if hard, labor of "conquering and constructing social
facts"—that is, of distinguishing what was really going on from the
received understandings of previous academic knowledge, culture in
general, and everyday preconceptions.

In a review of Bourdieu's great study of the origin of the modern literary field, *The Rules of Art* (1992), Harrison White suggested
that, masquerading behind the appearance of a Parisian intellectual,
Bourdieu was in fact a hard empirical scientist. Indeed, Bourdieu had
little patience for the rejection of science recently fashionable among
self-declared critical thinkers. He thought the "French theory" that
claimed indebtedness to Derrida and Foucault (though it seldom

reached their standards) had "much to answer for." While he shared
the view that simple empiricism was liable to reproduce ideologically
conventional results, he argued that the necessary response was not to
abandon empirical research but to carry out a struggle over the classifications by which knowledge was produced—including by state actors whose classifications pigeonholed human beings for purposes of
their own even as they provided social scientists with apparently neutral data.

Accordingly, Bourdieu wrote few purely theoretical treatises. He
devoted himself, rather, to substantive analyses (and occasionally to
sharp polemics). Only relatively late, in *Pascalian Meditations* (1997),
did he offer a general discussion of his approach to social knowledge:
why it must be related to the conditions of intellectual work, the dispositions of agents, and particular locations in collective and individual
histories, and why this reflexivity did not mandate relativism.

Bourdieu's most famous "theoretical" studies are actually analyses deeply rooted in his field data from Algeria. *Outline of a Theory
of Practice* (1972) and later *The Logic of Practice* (1980) are among the
most influential works to try to overcome the simple opposition between subjective and objective, agency and structure. They join with
Foucault's work of the same period in moving beyond structuralism's
avoidance of embodied subjectivity and with Derrida's effort to recover
epistemology by breaking with the notion that it must be grounded
in the Cartesian perspective of the individual knowing subject. But
they also lay the basis for an empirical science that would address the
practices of knowledge at the same time as it produced knowledge of
social practice.

Bourdieu approached social science itself as a practical activity; it
was no accident that he titled his book of epistemological and methodological preliminaries *The Craft of Sociology* (1968, with Jean-Claude
Chamboredon and Jean-Claude Passeron). The craft worker is always a
lover of knowledge, the craft itself being precisely a store of knowledge,
and yet craft knowledge is never fully discursive; masters teach their
skills, but know-how can never be reduced to instructions and never
escapes its situated and embodied character. "The rules of art," for
example, is (like *habitus*) a phrase that signifies practical knowledge,

like the knowledge of cooking embodied in a grandmother's hands-on guidance rather than a cookbook. Art could never be reduced to following rules, and yet to say it is without strategy or intention or not based on knowledge would be to misunderstand it utterly. Neither is science simply the value-free expression of truth. It is a project, but one organized—ideally—in a social field that rewards the production of truth, including new truths and new approaches to understanding, and not merely performance according to the rules. It is a project that depends crucially on reason—as an institutionally embedded practice—and therefore refuses equally the rationalistic reduction of reason to rules, simple determinism's unreasoned acceptance of the status quo, and the expressive appeal to insight supposedly transcending history and not corrigible by reason.

It was as a scientist that Bourdieu in the last years of his life turned to analyze some of the impacts of neoliberal globalization. He was concerned above all that the social institutions that supported reason—by providing cultural producers with some autonomy—were under attack. Reduction to the market threatened to undermine science; reduction to the logic of television entertainment threatened to undermine public discourse. The problem was not internationalization as such—Bourdieu himself called forcefully for a new internationalism and saw science as an international endeavor. The problem was the presentation of a particular model of globalization as a force of necessity to which there was no alternative but adaptation. He usually called this the American model, annoying Americans who wished to distance themselves from government and corporate policies. Whatever the label, he was referring to the view that institutions that developed out of more than a century of struggle should be scrapped if they couldn't meet a test of market viability. Many of these, including universities, were state institutions. They were far from perfect—as his own work showed—but collective struggles had grudgingly and partially opened them to workers, women, and others. These were social achievements, and to sacrifice them was to step backward whether it was masked by a deterministic analysis of the market or a simple assertion of self-interest by the wealthy and powerful. In his own life, Bourdieu recognized, it was not merely talent and effort that propelled his extraordinary ascent from rural Béarn to the Collège de France, but also state funding.

Bourdieu's polemical writings brought him a wide readership in and beyond the universities but also considerable derision from some academics. The sociologist who had refused the French notion of the philosopher as "omnicompetent intellectual" and criticized Sartre seemed to be taking on a Sartrean mantle. Indeed, Bourdieu became remarkably famous, especially after the movie about him, *Sociology Is a Martial Art*, was a surprise commercial success in 2000–2001. Theater groups staged performances based on his ethnographic exploration of social suffering, *The Weight of the World* (written with twenty-two collaborators). Women approached him on the street and told him—to his evident embarrassment—that their lives were changed by his book *Masculine Domination* (which is a surprisingly abstract text for that subject, and not even one of his best books—though after Bourdieu had left, one of these women told me how "hot" it had made her just to be next to him). As his theory predicted, the media made him all the more a celebrity when he attacked the celebrity-making machine in *On Television* (1996).

Nonetheless, Bourdieu's public interventions were firmly rooted in his sociological analyses. It was precisely his theory of social fields—honed in studies of the religious field, the legal field, and the field of cultural production—that informed his defense of the autonomy (always only relative) of the scientific field from the market. His theory of the multiple forms of capital—cultural and social as well as economic—suggested that these were indirectly convertible, but if they were reduced to simple equivalence, cultural and social capital lost their specificity and efficacy. His early studies in Algeria showed the corrosive impact of unbridled extension of market forces.

In his struggles "against the tyranny of the market" as in his earlier, more academic work, Bourdieu worked tirelessly for the international solidarity of scholars. He edited a book series that played a major role in making international social science—from Erving Goffman to Joseph Schumpeter—available in French translation. *Liber* and *Actes* were published in a dozen languages. He joined forces with Günter Grass, Eric Hobsbawm, Toni Morrison, and Edward Said, not just to support particular public causes but to help develop a new "Internationale" of intellectuals, partially institutionalized in the World Parliament of Writers.

Bourdieu is best known in the United States for his book *Distinction* (1979), an analysis of how culture figures in social inequality and the pursuit of distinction figures in social practice. In his death, it is at once fitting and ironic that Bourdieu was accorded great distinction, and that the struggle should ensue among those seeking to enhance their own distinction by positioning themselves in relation to Bourdieu. But it is worth recalling that *Distinction* was also a response to Kant's third critique. As Durkheim had sought to challenge individualistic explanation of social facts in *Suicide*, so Bourdieu sought in *Distinction* to demonstrate the social organization of judgment and taste.

Bourdieu was accorded the honor of burial in Père Lachaise Cemetery. This famed site in the northeastern corner of Paris is the resting place of a remarkable range of French and international public figures, from the Abbé Sieyès to Gertrude Stein. Among its oldest tombs are those of the famed medieval lovers Abelard and Héloise. Bourdieu is buried between Saint-Simon and Brillat-Savarin, a founder of social science and a founder of gastronomy. Père Lachaise also holds the remains of Bourdieu's great forebears Auguste Comte and Maurice Merleau-Ponty—the latter an underrecognized influence—and of the great historians Jules Michelet and Fernand Braudel. As Bourdieu was engaged with literature and the arts throughout his life, one is pleased to see that the graves of Balzac, Bizet, Chopin, Delacroix, Max Ernst, Modigliani, Molière, Seurat, Oscar Wilde, and Richard Wright are nearby (and one is glad to see Frenchness and internationalism intertwined). Greatness of more "middlebrow" sorts is celebrated as well, with Edith Piaf, Stephane Grapelli, and, of course, Jim Morrison. Maria Callas was buried in Père Lachaise, but after trouble with grave robbers, her body was cremated and her ashes scattered over the Aegean (and but for the cancer that took him, Bourdieu would have delivered the keynote address to an SSRC conference on opera in Florence in May 2002).

On February 3, more than 2,000 people gathered at the Théâtre

Nationale de la Colline in Paris to honor the life and work of Pierre Bourdieu. Speakers came from as far as Japan. They included professors, trade union leaders, artists, and political activists. As I said then, it was a privilege to know Pierre Bourdieu, and an honor to speak in homage to him. I also noted, however, that Bourdieu didn't concern himself much with ceremonies. He had a passion to know and understand, not to receive tributes and honors. Indeed, this is a source of some of the resentment toward him. He gained huge recognition without the formal recognition so important to others. His very transcendence insulted them. In this regard, academics too often participate in a kind of mutual reassurance scheme. Cite me and I'll cite you; praise me and I'll praise you. Be clever and facile but don't be too demanding because most of your colleagues want new understanding less than they want the reassurance that they already know everything worth knowing.

Bourdieu never confused social facts with the preferences of colleagues or the public. He knew the political importance of science, but also that this importance would be vitiated by reducing science to politics. In *Pantagruel*, Rabelais famously said, "Science without conscience is nothing but the ruin of the soul." It is a better line in French, where "conscience" also means consciousness. It is not the sort of line Bourdieu would quote, though, because public appeals to conscience are too commonly justifications for a jargon of authenticity rather than the application of reason. But Bourdieu demonstrated that conscience is not simply an interior state of individuals. It is a social achievement, in both its senses. As such, it is always at risk. Pierre was a scholar and researcher of great rigor and also a man and a citizen with a conscience attuned to inequality and domination. Would there were more.

TRANSLATOR'S NOTE: *ON TELEVISION*

As Pierre Bourdieu explains, this work aims at an audience beyond the usual public for his scholarly works. To make connections to the French situation, for the most part all Anglo-American readers need do is follow Bourdieu's reasoning, supplying their own equivalents from Britain or the United States or, indeed, elsewhere. However, an important element that needs to be mentioned because it is absent from American or British journalism is the extent to which the government intervenes in the operations of all media.[1] A ministry of communication (grouped for some administrations with the ministry of culture) oversees the direct or indirect financial support accorded the print press, radio, and television, regulates their competition, and determines as well the nature and kind of official information made available. (The Service juridique et technique de l'information, which reports directly to the prime minister, is charged with coordinating communications policy and subventions.) Forms of support range from direct subsidies, tax reductions, and postal benefits to promotional campaigns for one or another official policy which are paid for by the government. It is not unheard of for total governmental support to reach 20 percent of income for a newspaper or journal. The goal of this financial intervention is to guarantee economic viability of "serious" opinion journals and reviews by removing them from the hold of the market. Similarly, the governmental supports the production of French television programs by limiting the proportion of foreign (read, American) programs that may be broadcast. (A few years ago, this protectionism brought France into direct conflict with the United States during the negotiations of GATT [General Agreement on Tariffs and Trade].)

Television in particular is subject to governmental controls. The first three television networks, established in 1949 (TF1), 1964 (Antenne 2), and 1973 (FR3, a regional network), were until recently almost entirely government-subsidized and run. Originally absent altogether, advertising was introduced with two minutes per day in 1970, which had become twenty minutes a decade later, and increasingly prominent since. Liberalization of radio and television received its big push in the Events of 1968, when the ORTF (Office de la Radio et Télévision Françaises) went on strike. By the 1980s, begun by Valéry Giscard d'Estaing but primarily under the Socialist François Mitterrand, the government monopoly on programming was eliminated, a cable station was added (Canal Plus), TF1 and La Cinq were privatized, M6 and 7 were created; Channel 7 eventually turned into Arte, which, as its name suggests, is devoted to more or less high-cultural fare, not unlike but of a higher level than public broadcasting stations in the United States.

A further distinction, notably from the American press, is the strongly defined political orientations claimed and proclaimed by the print media in France. The principal national dailies referred to in *On Television* are *Libération* (center-Left), *Le Monde* (center-liberal), *Le Figaro* (right-conservative), *L'Humanité* (the paper of the French Communist Party), and tabloids like *France-Soir*. The prominent weekly newsmagazines on the order of *Time* or *Newsweek* are *L'Express* (center) and *Le Nouvel Observateur* (center-Left). *Le Monde diplomatique*, a monthly journal devoted to foreign affairs, represents liberal (in the Anglo-American sense) currents of reflection. The National Front, the radical right party led by Jean-Marie LePen (whom Bourdieu targets in Part Two of *On Television*), has no comparable news outlet.

As far as official institutions goes, it is not irrelevant that Pierre Bourdieu himself speaks from and with the authority of a peculiarly French institution, the Collège de France, founded in 1543 to counter the conservatism of the Sorbonne. The Collège grants no degrees and gives the professors (who are elected by the other members) exceptional freedom to pursue their research and an especially public venue to present that research. (All lectures are free and open to the public.) Prominent scholars at the Collège have included Louis Pasteur, Henri Bergson, and Marcel Mauss, and closer to the present, Raymond Aron, Michel Foucault, Roland Barthes, and Claude Lévi-Strauss. Bourdieu was elected to a chair in sociology in 1980.

—Priscilla Parkhurst Ferguson

REFERENCES

Part I: On Journalism and Television

Accardo, Alain, with G. Abou, G. Balastre, and D. Matine. *Journalistes au quotidien: outils pour une socioanalyse des pratiques journalistiques.* Bordeaux: Mascaret, 1995.

Accardo, Alain. "Academic destiny," pp. 719–35, in Pierre Bourdieu, et al., *La Misère du monde.* (*Misère*, P. Ferguson et al., trans., Cambridge: Polity Press, 1999.)

Bourdieu, Pierre. *Distinction: A Social Critique of the Judgment of Taste* [1979] trans. R. Nice. Cambridge, MA: Harvard University Press, 1984.

———. "L'Emprise du journalisme," *Actes de la recherche en sciences sociales* 101–102, March 1994: 3–9.

———. "The Institutionalization of Anomie," pp. 238–53, in *The Field of Cultural Production: Essays on Art and Literature.* Ed. Randal Johnson. New York: Columbia University Press, 1993.

———. *The Rules of Art: Genesis and Structure of the Literary Field.* Trans. S. Emanuel. Stanford: Stanford University Press, 1996.

———. *The State Nobility: Elite Schools in the Field of Power.* Trans. L. Clough. Cambridge: Polity Press, 1996.

———. (with Loïc Wacquant). *An Invitation to Reflexive Sociology.* Chicago: University of Chicago Press, 1992.

Champagne, Patrick. "La Construction médiatique des 'malaises sociaux,'" *Actes de la recherche en sciences sociales* 90, December 1991: 64–75.

———. "La Loi des grands nombres: mesure de l'audience et représentation politique du public," *Actes de la recherche en sciences sociales*, 101–102, March 1994: 10–22.

———. "Le Journalisme entre précarité et concurrence," *Liber* 29, December 1996.

———. "The View from the Media," in Pierre Bourdieu et al., *La Misère*. Trans. P. Ferguson, et al. Cambridge: Polity Press, 1999.

Deleuze, Gilles. *A propos des nouveaux philosophes et d'un problème plus général*. Paris: Minuit, 1978.

Fallows, James. *Breaking the News: How the Media Undermine American Democracy*. New York: Vintage, 1997.

Ferenczi, Thomas. *L'Invention du journalisme en France: naissance de la presse moderne à la fin du 19ᵉ siècle*. Paris: Plon, 1993.

Gaarder, Jostein. *Le Monde de Sophie: roman sur l'histoire de la philosophie*. Trans. from the Norwegian by H. Hervieu and M. Laffon. Paris: Seuil, 1995.

Godard, Jean-Luc. "Enquête sur une image." 1972 interview, originally a film entitled "Letter to Jane," pp. 350–362, in *Jean-Luc Godard par Jean-Luc Godard*, ed. Alain Bergala. Paris: Cahiers du cinéma—Éditions de l'Étoile, 1985.

———. "Pour mieux écouter les autres." 1972 interview, pp. 362–367, in *Jean-Luc Godard par Jean-Luc Godard*, ed. Alain Bergala. Paris: Cahiers du cinéma—Éditions de l'Étoile, 1985.

Goulemot, Jean-Marie, and Daniel Oster. *Gens de lettres, Écrivains et bohèmes: L'imaginaire littéraire, 1630–1900*. Paris: Minerve, 1992.

Hoberman, John M. *Mortal Engines: The Science of Performance and the Dehumanization of Sport*. New York: Free Press, 1992.

Homer. *Iliad*. Trans. R. Lattimore. Chicago: University of Chicago Press, 1951.

Lenoir, Remi. "La Parole est aux juges: crise de la magistrature et champ journalistique." *Actes de la recherche en sciences sociales* 101–102, March 1994: 77–84.

Murray, Philippe. "Des Régles de l'art aux coulisses de sa misère." *Art Press* 186, June 1993: 55–67.

Pouthier, Jean-Luc. "L'État et la communication. Le 'modèle français,'" pp. 582–586, in *L'État de la France* 95–96. Paris: La Découverte, 1995.

Sapiro, Gisèle. "La Raison littéraire: le champ littéraire français sous l'Occupation (1940–1944)." *Actes de la recherche en sciences sociales* 111–12, March 1996: 3–35.

———. "Salut littéraire et littérature du salut: deux trajectoires de romanciers catholiques: François Mauriac et Henry Bordeaux." *Actes de la recherche en sciences sociales* 111–12, March 1996: 36–58.

Schudson, Michael. *Discovering the News*. New York: Basic Books, 1978.

Simson, Vyv, and Andrew Jennings. *The Lords of the Rings: Power, Money and Drugs in the Modern Olympics*. London: Simon & Schuster, 1992.

Williams, Raymond. *Culture and Society, 1780–1950*. New York: Columbia University Press, 1958.

Wolton, Dominique. "Culture et télévision: entre cohabitation et apartheid," in *Éloge du grand public: une théorie critique de la télévision*. Paris: Flammarion, 1990.

Part II: Acts of Resistance: Against the Tyranny of the Market

Accardo, A. et al. *Journalistes au quotidien: outils pour une socioanalyse des pratiques journalistiques*. Bordeaux: Le Mascaret, 1995.

Actes de la recherche en sciences sociales, "L'économie de la maison," 81–2, March 1990.

———. "La souffrance," 90, December 1991.

———. "Les nouvelles formes de domination au travail," 114, September 1996, and 115, December 1996.

———. "Histoire de l'Etat," 116–17, March 1997.

———. "Les ruses de la raison impérialiste," 121–2, March 1998.

Bloch, E. *L'Esprit de l'utopie*. Paris: Gallimard, 1977.

Boschetti, A. *Sartre et* Les Temps Modernes: *une entreprise intellectuelle*. Paris: Minuit, 1976.

Bourdieu, P. *Travail et travailleurs en Algérie*. Paris and The Hague: Mouton, 1963 (with A. Darbel, J.P. Rivet, and C. Seibel).

———. *Algeria 1960*. Cambridge: Cambridge University Press, 1979.

———. "Deux impérialismes de l'universel," in C. Fauré and T. Bishop (eds.). *L'Amérique des Français*. Paris: Éditions François Bourin, 1992.

———. "The racism of intelligence," in *Sociology in Question*. London: Sage, 1993.

———. *The State Nobility: Elite Schools in the Field of Power*. Cambridge: Polity Press, 1996.

———. *Méditations pascaliennes*. Paris: Seuil, 1997.

Bourdieu, P. et al. *La Misère du monde*. Paris: Seuil, 1993.

Champagne, P. *Faire l'opinion*. Paris: Minuit, 1993.

———. "Le journalisme entre précarité et concurrence," *Liber*, 29, December 1996.

Charle, C. *Naissance des intellectuals*. Paris: Minuit, 1990.

Dejours, C. *Souffrance en France: la banalisation de l'injustice sociale*. Paris: Seuil, 1997.

Dezalay, Y., and B.B. Garth. *Dealing in Virtue*. Chicago: University of Chicago Press, 1995.

Dezalay, Y., and D. Sugarman. *Professional Competition Power: Lawyers,*

Accountants and the Social Construction of Markets. London and New York: Routledge, 1995.

Dixon, K. "Les Evangélistes du Marche," *Liber,* 32, September 1997, 5–6.

Fallows, J. *Breaking the News: How Media Undermine American Democracy.* New York: Vintage Books, 1997.

Ferry, L., and A. Renaut. *La Pensée 68.* Paris: Gallimard, 1985.

Goffman, E., *Asylums: Essays on the Social Situation of Mental Patients and Other Inmates.* Harmondsworth: Penguin, 1961.

Grémion, P. *Preuves, une revue européenne à Paris.* Paris: Julliard, 1989.

————. *Intelligence de l'anti-communisme: le congrès pour la liberté de la culture à Paris.* Paris: Fayard, 1995.

Halimi, S. *Les Nouveaux Chiens de garde.* Paris: Liber—Raisons d'Agir, 1997.

Liber. "Mouvements divers: le choix de la subversion," 33, December 1997.

Pasche, C., and S. Peters. "Les premiers pas de la Société du Mont-Pelerin ou les dessous chics du néolibéralisme," *Les Annuelles* (L'avènement des sciences sociales comme disciplines académiques), 8, 1997, 191–216.

Salesse, Y. *Propositions pour une autre Europe: construire Babel.* Paris: Félin, 1997.

Théret, B. *L'État, la finance et le social.* Paris: La Découverte, 1995.

Vidal-Naquet, P. *Les Juifs, la mémoire et le présent.* Paris: La Découverte, vol. 1 1981, vol. 2, 1991.

Wacquant, L. "De l'État charitable à l'État pénal: notes sur le traitement politique de la misère en Amérique," *Regards Sociologiques,* 11, 1996.

NOTES

Introduction

1. The most famous of them, Bernard Henri-Lévy, is overtly challenged in "On Television" and implicitly in the piece titled "The negative intellectual," included in the present volume.

2. Bourdieu explained his conception of the collective intellectual in his keynote address to the 1999 meeting of the Modern Language Association (MLA) in Chicago, titled "For a Scholarship with Commitment," and in an interview he gave to the Greek journal *Elephteriotipia* in October 1996, both included in this volume.

3. Gisèle Sapiro and Mauricio Bustamante, "Translation as a Measure of International Consecration: Mapping the World Distribution of Bourdieu's Books in Translation," *Sociologica*, no. 2 (2009), available online at http://www.sociologica.mulino.it/journal/article/index/Article/Journal:ARTICLE:340/Item/Journal:ARTICLE:340.

4. Cass R. Sunstein, "Tube Boobs: Television, a French Sociologist Explains, Dumbs Itself Down," *New York Times*, August 2, 1998.

5. According to the reviewer in *Kirkus Reviews*, March 1998, who nonetheless regretted this discourse sometimes got lost in "postmodernist vocabulary." On the contrary, in the *Boston Review*, summer 1998, Carsten Schinko lamented the "uncharacteristic plain style" of the essay and the fact it was "only 80 pages."

6. "On Television," *Publishers Weekly*, September 2, 1998.

7. The broadcast can be found online at http://www.dailymotion.com/video/xx6kd_pierre-bourdieu-davos-26-janv-2001_news.

8. See, for instance, Pierre Bourdieu, "Les Sous-Prolétaires algériens," *Les Temps modernes* 199 (December 1962), pp. 1033, 1044, 1049–1050. In English, see Pierre Bourdieu, *Algeria 1960*, trans. Richard Nice (Cambridge/Paris: Cambridge University Press/Editions de la Maison des Sciences de l'Homme, 1979).

9. See "The Protest Movement of the Unemployed: a Social Miracle" in this volume.

10. Loïc Wacquant, *Punishing the Poor: The Neoliberal Government of Social Insecurity* (Durham, NC: Duke University Press, 2009).

11. Some of the texts he published on this topic are available in English translation in Loïc Wacquant, ed., *Pierre Bourdieu and Democratic Politics: The Mystery of Ministry* (Cambridge: Polity Press, 2005).

12. Pierre Bourdieu, *The Rules of Art: Genesis and Structure of the Literary Field,* trans. Susan Emanuel (Palo Alto, CA: Stanford University Press, 1996); originally published in French in 1992.

13. See André Schiffrin, *The Business of Books* (New York: Verso, 2000).

14. Bourdieu relies, for this analysis, on Dorothy Ross, *The Origins of American Social Science* (Cambridge, MA: Harvard University Press, 1998).

15. This paper was omitted because Bourdieu decided to write a specific preface for the American edition, in which he summarized its main arguments. However, a translation of the original version was included here for documentary interest.

16. Donald Fisher, "The Role of Philanthropic Foundations in the Reproduction and Production of Hegemony: Rockefeller Foundations and the Social Sciences," *Sociology* 17, no. 2 (May 1983), pp. 206–33; George Steinmetz, ed., *The Politics of Method in the Human Sciences: Positivism and Its Epistemological Others* (Durham, NC: Duke University Press, 2005).

17. Bourdieu's political interventions since the 1960s were collected and presented by Franck Poupeau and Thierry Discepolo in *Political Interventions: Social Science and Political Action,* trans. David Fernbach and Gregory Elliott (London: Verso, 2008).

18. Pierre Bourdieu, "Sartre," *London Review of Books,* vol. 2, 22 (trans. Richard Nice), 20 November–3 December 1980, pp. 11–12. Bourdieu developed the notion of the intellectual field in several papers that I have collected in a volume to be published in 2011 by The New Press.

19. See Dan Clawson et al., eds., *Public Sociology* (Berkeley: University of California Press, 2007).

20. Ibid., p. 51.

21. I would like to thank André Schiffrin and Richard Nice for their comments on this introduction.

Part I: On Journalism and Television

Priscilla Parkhurst Ferguson's translator notes are set in brackets.

1. To avoid producing "finger-pointing" or caricature (effects easily produced whenever recorded interviews or printed texts are published as is), I have had to leave out documents that would have given my argument all its force and—because highlighting pulls them out of a familiar context—would have reminded the reader of similar examples that ordinary observation fails to see.

2. [*On Television* raised a widespread controversy that lasted several months and engaged the most important journalists and columnists from the daily papers, the weekly newsmagazines, and the television stations. During this period the book was at the top of the best-seller list.]

3. [Pierre Bourdieu et al., *La Misère du monde* (Paris: Seuil, 1993), trans. P. Ferguson et al. (Cambridge: Polity Press, 1999). This book contains some seventy interviews with individuals across the spectrum of French society, which are placed within a theoretical, historical, political, and personal context of the interviewer. The work is a multifaceted ethnographic and sociological study by Bourdieu and his team, but it is also a collection of wonderfully evocative (if rather depressing) life stories. It is these narratives that made *La Misère du monde* the best-seller that it became.]

4. [*The State Nobility: Elite Schools in the Field of Power*, trans. L. Clough (Cambridge: Polity Press, 1996). The Grandes Écoles are prestigious, wholly state-subsidized, nonuniversity schools in a number of areas, including engineering (the École Polytechnique), the humanities and science (the École Normale Supérieure), administration (the École Nationale d'Administration), and commerce (Hautes Études Commerciales). Unlike the universities, which admit students on the basis of their high school diploma (the *baccalauréat* examination), the Grandes Écoles admit students after a highly competitive entrance examination.]

5. [*Iliad*, trans. R. Lattimore (Chicago: University of Chicago Press, 1951), 2:212–256.]

6. See James Fallows, *Breaking the News: How the Media Undermine American Democracy* (New York: Vintage, 1997).

7. See Patrick Champagne, "Le Journalisme entre précarité et concurrence," *Liber* 29 (December 1996).

8. This text is the revised and corrected unabridged transcription of two

television programs that were part of a series of courses from the Collège de France. The shows were taped on March 18, 1996, and shown by the Paris Première station the following May ("On Television" and "The Field of Journalism," Collège de France—CNRS audiovisual production). The appendix ["The Olympics"] reproduces an article from a special issue of the *Actes de la recherche en sciences sociales* (founded by Pierre Bourdieu in 1975) on the power of television, which addresses the themes of these two lectures more rigorously.

9. [Jean-Luc Godard, "Pour Mieux écouter les autres," 1972 interview with Jean-Luc Godard, in *Jean-Luc Godard par Jean-Luc Godard*, ed. Alain Bergala (Paris: Cahiers du cinéma—Editions de l'Etoile, 1985), p. 366. The earlier reference is to Godard's extensive analysis of the political subtexts and uses of the widely diffused photograph of Jane Fonda talking to North Vietnamese. "Enquête sur une image," 1972 interview, originally a film entitled "Letter to Jane," in ibid., pp. 350–62.]

10. [Bouygues is the largest French company in commercial and public works construction. The subsidiaries of the holding company cover a wide range of goods and services, including telecommunications. It controls 42 percent of the TF1 television station.]

11. ["The View from the Media," in Pierre Bourdieu, et al., *La Misère*. The French "suburbs" (*banlieue*) correspond to the American "inner city," which is the translation used here.]

12. [Bourdieu here refers to the controversy in France which began in 1989 when Muslim girls, children of relatively recent immigrants from North Africa, were expelled from public school for wearing headscarves (*le foulard* in French, *le hidjab* in Arabic, sometimes tendentiously translated as "veil"). After much debate the then–Minister of Education Lionel Jospin authorized wearing the scarf in class.]

13. [English in the original, as are "fast-thinkers," "talk-show," "news" below.]

14. [Jostein Gaarder, *Le Monde de Sophie: roman sur l'histoire de la philosophie* (Paris: Seuil, 1995), translated from the Norwegian by H. Hervieu and M. Laffon, was a curious and phenomenal bestseller, perhaps luring unsuspecting readers by the subtitle that announces a novel instead of an introduction to philosophic thought.]

15. [Bourdieu refers to well-known and often-seen political pundits and social commentators, journalists and writers as well as academics, all of whom have written numerous books and have multiple connections in journalism and publishing. Alain Minc is an industrialist and

social commentator closely connected to *Le Monde*; Jacques Attali was a prominent adviser to the Socialist President François Mitterrand; Guy Sorman is a journalist and newspaper editor; Luc Ferry is a professor of philosophy at the University of Caen, who writes regularly for *L'Express*; Alain Finkielkraut is a philosopher who teaches at the École Polytechnique; the historian Jacques Julliard, a regular commentator on the radio station Europe 1, is Director of Studies at the École des Hautes Études en Sciences Sociales (the prestigious, nonuniversity institution for teaching and research in the social sciences where Pierre Bourdieu also held an appointment), and is associate editor of *Le Nouvel Observateur*; Claude Imbert is the editor of the middle-of-the-road business-oriented news magazine *Le Point*; Nicolas Sarkozy is an important figure in the conservative RPR (Rally for the Republic) party of President Jacques Chirac. Bourdieu cites Jacques Julliard's diary, *L'Année des dupes* (Paris: Seuil, 1996), for an illustration of how the system works.]

16. [Guillaume Durand hosts a late-night talk show on TF1.]

17. [Since 1990, Jean-Marie Cavada has produced and moderated a talk show on the France 3 television channel. In December 1996 he was appointed as director of the educational channel La Cinquième.

The strike in question was called in November 1995, when the then–conservative prime minister Alain Juppé proposed raising the retirement age for workers on the national railway system. The general railroad strike lasted into December. Juppé eventually withdrew the proposal, leaving the retirement age at fifty.]

18. [Television in France developed comparatively late: in 1963, France had some 3 million TV sets against 12 million in Great Britain. It has since caught up so that by 1984 there were television sets in 93 percent of French households and 94 percent of homes in Great Britain.]

19. [See Raymond Williams, *Culture and Society, 1780–1950* (New York: Columbia University Press, 1958).]

20. [See Pierre Bourdieu, "The Institutionalization of Anomie," in Rahdal Johnson, ed., *The Field of Cultural Production: Essays on Art and Literature* (New York: Columbia University Press, 1993), pp. 238–53.]

21. For example, the long-running show of Bernard Pivot (see note 26). [The American equivalents are found on PBS.]

22. [The Puppets (*Les Guignols*) is a weekly satirical program where prominent political figures are represented by marionettes with exaggerated features and such.]

23. [Bernard-Henri Lévy is one of the most prominent of contemporary

journalist-philosophers, so well known in fact that he is often referred simply as "BHL." Besides his many books and essays, he has written plays and directed films (and has acted in television drama). Lévy has also taken a particularly active stand in favor of Bosnia (see his film from 1992, *La Mort de Sarajevo*).]

24. [Remi Lenoir, "La Parole est aux juges: crise de la magistrature et champ journalistique," *Actes de la recherche en sciences sociales*, 101–2 (March 1994), pp. 77–84; and Patrick Champagne, "La Loi des grands nombres: mesure de l'audience et représentation politique du public," in ibid., pp. 64–75.]

25. [The eminent sociologist and political scientist Raymond Aron (1905–1983) was appointed (in 1958) to the Chair in Sociology at the Sorbonne, originally occupied by Émile Durkheim, and elected to the Collège de France in 1970.]

26. [From 1975 to 1990, Bernard Pivot was the extraordinarily popular host of *Apostrophes*, a book review show on the Antenne 2 television station. An appearance on this show made reputations and all but guaranteed sales. His current program, on France 2, has a somewhat different format and rather less impact.]

27. [Alain Peyrefitte is a well-known writer and essayist, member of the Académie Française, onetime attorney general of France, who is currently also a columnist for the conservative newspaper *Le Figaro*.]

28. [France abolished the death penalty in 1981 under the newly elected Socialist government of François Mitterrand. The National Front is the extreme right-wing party led by Jean-Marie LePen.]

29. This text is an abridged version of a talk given at the 1992 annual meeting of the Philosophical Society for the Study of Sport in Berlin, held in Berlin on 2 October 1992. It was subsequently published in the *Actes de la recherche en sciences sociales* 103 (June 1994), pp. 102–3.

30. "Sponsors were offered a complete communication package based on product category exclusivity and continuity over a four-year period. The programme for each of seventy-five matches included stadium advertising, official supplier's titles, the use of mascots and emblems and franchise opportunities." For £7 million ($14 million) each sponsor in 1986 had the possibility of a share of "the biggest single televised event in the world," with "unparalleled exposure, far in excess of other sports" (Vyv Simson and Andrew Jennings, *The Lords of the Rings: Power, Money and Drugs in the Modern Olympics* [London: Simon & Schuster, 1992], p. 102).

31. The top competitive sports increasingly rely on an industrial technology

that calls on various biological and psychological sciences to transform the human body into an efficient and inexhaustible machine. Competition between national teams and governments increasingly and ever more emphatically encourages the use of prohibited substances and dubious methods of training. See John M. Hoberman, *Mortal Engines: The Science of Performance and the Dehumanization of Sport* (New York: Free Press, 1992).

32. See Pierre Bourdieu, *The Rules of Art: Genesis and Structure of the Literary Field*, trans. S. Emanuel (Palo Alto, CA: Stanford University Press, 1996).

33. For a gross indicator of the real value of different actors of Olympic "show business," the presents distributed by the Korean authorities to different important figures went from $1,100 for IOC members to $110 for the athletes. See Simson and Jennings, *Lords of the Rings*, p. 153.

34. One could, for example, imagine an *Olympic charter* that would define the principles to be followed by everyone involved in the production of both shows (beginning, obviously, with the men who run the Olympic Committee, who are the first to benefit from transgressions of financial disinterestedness they are supposed to enforce). Or an Olympic oath could bind the athletes (prohibiting them, for example, from joining in patriotic demonstrations like carrying the national flag once around the stadium) and those who produce and comment on the images of these exploits.

35. I thought it useful to reproduce this text, which has already been published in *Les Actes de la recherche en sciences sociales*, in which I had set out, in a more tightly controlled form, most of the themes discussed in a more accessible fashion above.

36. See for example the work of Jean-Marie Goulemot and Daniel Oster, *Gens de lettres: écrivains et bohèmes, l'imaginaire littéraire, 1630–1900* (Paris: Minerve, 1992), which gives numerous examples of observations and remarks by writers themselves that constitute a sort of spontaneous sociology of the literary milieu. They do not, however, derive the basic explanatory principle, largely because of their efforts to objectify their adversaries and everything they dislike about the literary world. But the picture that emerges of the functioning of the nineteenth-century literary field can be read as a description of the concealed or secret functioning of the literary field today (as Philippe Murray has done in "Des Règles de l'art aux coulisses de sa misère," *Art Press* 186 [June 1993], pp. 55–67).

37. [Raymond Williams, *Culture and Society, 1780–1950* (New York: Columbia University Press, 1958).]

38. On the emergence of this idea of "objectivity" in American journalism as a product of the effort of newspapers worried about their respectability to distinguish news from the simple narrative of the popular press, see Michael Schudson, *Discovering the News* (New York: Basic Books, 1978). On the opposition between journalists oriented toward the literary field and concerned with style, and journalists close to the political field, and on what each contributed, in the French case, to this process of differentiation and the invention of a "job" of its own (notably, with the advent of the reporter), see Thomas Ferenczi, *L'Invention du journalisme en France: naissance de la presse moderne à la fin du 19ᵉ siècle* (Paris: Plon, 1993). On the form that this opposition takes in the field of French newspapers and news magazines and on its relationship with the different categories of reading and readers, see Pierre Bourdieu, *Distinction: A Social Critique of the Judgement of Taste* [1979] trans. R. Nice (Cambridge, MA: Harvard University Press, 1984), pp. 442–51.

39. As with the literary field, the hierarchy that is constructed according to the external criterion—sales—is just about the reverse of that set up by the internal criterion—journalistic "seriousness." The complexity of this structurally chiasmic distribution (which is also the distribution in the literary, artistic, and juridical fields) is redoubled by the fact that, at the heart of print media or television, each one of which functions like a subfield, the opposition between a "cultural" pole and a "market" pole organizes the entire field. The result is a series of structures within structures (type a:b::b1:b2).

40. It is through temporal constraints, often imposed in purely arbitrary fashion, that *structural censorship* is exerted, almost unnoticed, on what may be said by television talk show guests.

41. If the assertion that "it's out-of-date" or "we've gone beyond that" today so often takes the place of critical argument (and this is true well beyond the journalistic field), this is because the rushed actors have an obvious self-interest in putting this evaluative principle to work. It confers an indisputable advantage to the last-in, to the youngest. Further, because it is reducible to something like the virtually empty opposition between "before" and "after," this kind of assertion obviates the need to prove one's case.

42. All that has to be done is to formulate the problems of journalists (like the choice between TF1 and Arte) in terms that could be those

of journalism. See Dominique Wolton, "Culture et télévision: entre cohabitation et apartheid," in *Éloge du grand public: une théorie critique de la télévision* (Paris: Flammarion, 1990), p. 163. In passing, and to justify how rough and even laborious scientific analysis can appear, let me stress the degree to which adequate construction of the analytic object depends on breaking with the preconstructions and presuppositions of everyday language, most particularly with the language of journalism.

43. The uncertain boundaries of "journalist-intellectual" category make it necessary to differentiate those cultural producers who, following a tradition that began with the advent of "industrial" cultural production, ask of the journalistic professions the *means of existence* and rather than powers (of control or validation) capable of acting on the specialized fields (the Zhdanov effect). [Andrei Aleksandrovich Zhdanov (1890–1948), a loyal Stalinist, member of the Politburo, and general in the Finnish-Russian war of 1939–1940. Bourdieu refers to Zhdanov's political control of the intellectuals in the postwar Soviet Union.]

44. A number of recent battles over modern art are hardly distinguishable, except perhaps by the pretension of their claims, from the judgments that would be obtained if avant-garde art were put to a referendum or, what comes down to the same thing, to an opinion poll.

45. An addendum to "L'emprise du journalisme." *Actes de la Recherche en Sciences Sociales* 101/102 (March 1994), p. 8.

46. "Convicted of the rape and murder, on 13 September 1993, of little Karine, then eight years of age, Patrick Tissier was condemned to life imprisonment followed by a period of supervision of thirty years, at the assize court of Perpignan, Pyrénées-Orientales on 30 January 1998." (*Le Monde*, 2 February 1998.)

47. An intervention at a conference organized by Reporters Without Borders, and published in *Les Mensonges du Golfe* (Paris: Arléa, 1992), pp. 27–32.

48. Cofremca is a leading market-research institute for the media.

Part II: Acts of Resistance: Against the Tyranny of the Market

1. At the risk of increasing the number of breaks in tone and style resulting from the diversity of situations, I have presented this selection of articles and contributions here in their chronological order, so as to make clearer the historical context of remarks which, though they are

not reducible to a given context, make no concessions to the vague and wordy generalities of what is sometimes called "political philosophy." I have added here and there some basic references to enable the reader to explore further the argument that is put forward.

2. From all my collective interventions, in particular those of the Association de Réflexion sur les Enseignements Supérieurs et la Recherche (ARESER), the Comité International de Soutien aux Intellectuels Algériens (CISA), and the International Parliament of Writers (with which I no longer feel affinities), I have chosen only the article published in *Libération*, here entitled "The Status of Foreigners: a Shibboleth," with the agreement of my co-authors, both visible (Jean-Pierre Alaux) and invisible (Christophe Daadouch, Marc-Antoine Lévy, and Danièle Lochak), victims of the censorship quite spontaneously and routinely exercised by the journalists responsible for the so-called *tribunes libres* in the newspapers. Always in pursuit of the symbolic capital associated with certain names, they do not like articles signed with the name of a group, or bearing several names—this is one of the obstacles, and a significant one, to the constitution of a collective intellectual—and they tend to remove the names they do not recognize, either after negotiation or, as happened there, without consultation.

3. *Actes de la Recherche en Sciences Sociales* 90 (December 1991), special issue "La souffrance"; Bourdieu et al., *La Misère du monde*.

4. Alluding to the author's book *The State Nobility: Elite Schools in the Field of Power*.

5. The practice whereby civil servants move to positions in the private sector.

6. François Mitterrand (president of France, 1981–1995) was often praised for his *"fidélité en amiti,"* and a number of personalities appointed to important posts were, according to the newspapers, chiefly noted for being his "personal friends."

7. *effets d'annonce* in the original, produced when a minister reduces his political action to the ostentatious announcement of spectacular decisions which often have no effect or no follow-up—Jack Lang has been cited as an example.

8. The Rennes Congress (15–18 March 1990), the scene of heated disputes between the leaders of the major tendencies within the Socialist Party, Lionel Jospin, Laurent Fabius, and Michel Rocard.

9. The amnesty that was granted, in particular, to the generals of the French army in Algeria who attempted a putsch against de Gaulle's government.

10. See Bourdieu et al., "L'économie de la maison," *Actes de la Recherche en Sciences Sociales* 81–82 (March 1990).
11. Socially analogous to the "inner cities" but in France implying peripheral housing estates.
12. As generated and taught in the institutes of political science ("Sciences-Po"), in particular the one in Paris.
13. Allusion to Ferry and Renaut, *La Pensée 68.*
14. Vidal-Naquet, *Les Juifs, la mémoire et le present.*
15. Philippe Sollers, French author, founder and editor of the journal *Tel Quel.*
16. Edouard Balladur, conservative politician (RPR), former prime minister, candidate in the presidential election of 1995 against Jacques Chirac and Lionel Jospin.
17. Graduates of the École Nationale d'Administration, an elite school training France's top civil servants.
18. As prime minister, Balladur had as his minister of the interior Charles Pasqua, the author of a particularly repressive law on immigration.
19. Philippe Sollers regularly contributes a column of literary criticism in *Le Monde*, part of a circuit of literary mutual admiration.
20. Sollers is a great admirer of the works of Guy Debord (author of *La Société du spectacle*) and a frequent participant in all kinds of TV programs.
21. Sollers is the author of a book entitled *Théorie des exceptions.*
22. *les candidats républicains*, i.e., excluding the overtly racist Front National.
23. General Secretary of the French Communist Party.
24. Leader of one of the ecology parties; minister of the environment in the Jospin government.
25. Cf. note 18.
26. Shibboleth, a decisive test by which a person's capacity can be judged.
27. Bourdieu, "Deux impérialismes de l'universel."
28. This was Charles Pasqua—cf. note 18.
29. The wearing of the "veil" at school aroused strong protests from a number of "intellectuals" who saw it as a threat to the secular principles of French state schooling.
30. This was Paul Ricœur.
31. Grémion, *Preuves, une revue européenne à Paris*, and *Intelligence de l'anti-communisme.*
32. Dixon, "Les Evangélistes du Marché"; Pasche and Peters, "Les premiers pas de la Société du Mont-Pélerin ou les dessous chics du néolibéralisme."

33. Cf. Bourdieu et al., "L'économie de la maison."
34. In particular, Edgar Morin and Jean Baudrillard.
35. Wacquant, "De l'État charitable à l'État pénal."
36. Cf. Bourdieu, "The racism of intelligence."
37. Intellectual journal associated with "Christian personalist" thinking and the focus of intellectual support for the Juppé reforms.
38. I borrow a number of these suggestions from Yves Salesse, *Propositions pour une autre Europe: construire Babel.*
39. Johnny Halliday, interviewed by Daniel Rondeau.
40. On these complicities, see Halimi, *Les Nouveaux Chiens de garde.*
41. See for example the excellent analyses presented in Accardo et al., *Journalistes au quotidien; outils pour une socioanalyse des pratiques journalistiques.*
42. The French bishops have collectively expressed their "repentance" over the attitude of the French hierarchy during the German occupation.
43. Kelkal is the name of a young Algerian, a member of a terrorist network, who was shot by the police.
44. Bourdieu, *Travail et travailleurs en Algérie*; Bourdieu, *Algeria 1960.*
45. By Bernard Henri-Lévy, in *Le Monde.*
46. This is a reference to Khalida Messaoudi, co-author (with Elisabeth Schemla) of *Une Algérienne debout: entretiens* (Paris: Flammarion, 1995).
47. August Walras (1800–66), French economist, was one of the first to attempt to apply mathematics to the study of economics.
48. E. Goffman, *Asylums.*
49. On all these matters, see the two issues of *Actes de la Recherche en Sciences Sociales* devoted to "The new forms of domination at work" (114, September 1996, and 115, December 1996), and especially the introduction by Gabrielle Balazs and Michel Pialoux, "Crise du travail et crise du politique" (114, pp. 3–4).
50. Dejours, *Souffrance en France.*

Part III: Firing Back: Against the Tyranny of the Market 2

Richard Nice's translator's notes are set in brackets.

1. I have not supplied references to all the works mentioned in these talks. They were aimed at a general audience of interested citizens in various countries. While that target audience has little use for bibliographical details, academics who want such information already know where to find them.

2. [See Pierre Bourdieu, "The Corporatism of the Universal: The Role of Intellectuals in the Modern World," *Telos* 81 (Fall 1989): 99–110.]

3. [Pierre Bourdieu, "The Scholastic Point of View," *Cultural Anthropology* 5, no. 4 (November 1990): 380–91, and *Pascalian Meditations* (1997; Cambridge: Polity Press, 2000), chap. 1 and 2.]

4. [Pierre Bourdieu et al., *The Weight of the World: Social Suffering in Contemporary Society* (1993; Cambridge: Polity Press, 1997).]

5. Contribution to Raisons d'agir–Loccumer Kreis colloquium, Loccum, Germany, 16–17 October 1999.

6. Cf. Dorothy Ross, *The Origins of American Social Science* (Cambridge, MA: Harvard University Press, 1998).

7. Although it is possible to achieve high productivity by combining high flexibility with strong social guarantees, as is the case in some economies embedded in societies with a different tradition, such as Denmark.

8. Gary Becker and George J. Stigler, "De Gustibus Non Est Disputandum," *American Economic Review* 67, no. 2 (1977): 76–90.

9. Adolf A. Berle and Gardiner Means, *The Modern Corporation and Private Property* (1933; New Brunswick, NJ: Transaction, 1991).

10. [For Bourdieu, the "left hand" of the state is the "set of agents of the so-called spending ministries which are the trace, within the state, of the social struggles of the past, as represented by the ministries of labor and social rights, education, public housing, and health." They are opposed to the "right hand" of the state, represented by the ministries of finance and budget (Pierre Bourdieu, *Acts of Resistance* [Cambridge: Polity Press, 1999], p. 2) as well as the repressive arm of the state (police, courts, prison, military).]

11. Pierre Bourdieu, *The Rules of Art: Genesis and Structure of the Artistic Field* (1992; Cambridge: Polity Press, 1998).

12. Michael Baxandall, *Painting and Experience in Fifteenth-Century Italy: A Primer in the Social History of Pictorial Style* (New York: Oxford University Press, 1988).

13. Karl Polyani, *The Great Transformation: The Political and Economic Origins of Our Time* (1947; Boston: Beacon Press, 2001).

14. Pierre Bourdieu, *Algeria 60: Economic Structures and Temporal Structures* (Cambridge: Cambridge University Press, 1977).

15. Claude Lévi-Strauss, *Race et histoire* (1955; Paris: Gallimard, 1987).

16. Oliver Williamson, *Markets and Hierarchies: Analysis and Antitrust Implications* (New York: The Free Press, 1975).

17. Cf. François Chesnais, *La Mondialisation du capital* (Paris: Syros,

1994), and M. Freitag and E. Pineault, eds., *Le Monde enchaîné* (Montréal: Éditions Nota Bene, 1999).

Part IV: Interviews and New Acts of Resistance

1. *Sociologie de l'Algérie* (Paris: PUF, 1958). (English translation: *The Algerians* [Boston: Beacon Press, 1962]).
2. Date of the "Algiers putsch," the military coup against the Fourth Republic.
3. In English in the original.
4. In English in the original.
5. *Le Déracinement* (English translation forthcoming, Polity Press).
6. The National Institute for Statistics and Economic Studies.
7. France was one of the main supporters of Solidarnosc. The events in August and September 1980 immediately gained the interest of the French media. Trade unionists started to collaborate with their Polish colleagues, for instance, by setting up exchange programs or by introducing Solidarnosc to international trade unions. Organizations of solidarity were founded and started to collect food, clothes, and drugs. After the proclamation of martial law in Poland, this grew into a mass movement, involving many layers of the French population. Both workers and intellectuals (Foucault, Bourdieu, etc.) were drawn to the idea of a "second Left"—an alternative to the old and radical socialism.
8. On 12 December 1995, during the social movement (train strike), Bourdieu made a famous speech: "Combattre la technocratie sur son terrain, discours aux cheminots grévistes," Paris, Gare de Lyon.
9. Jean-Claude Trichet, then governor of the Bank of France; Hans Tietmeyer, president of the German Bundesbank, 1993–99; Jean-Yves Haberer, former chairman of Crédit Lyonnais and Crédit National.
10. In English in the original.

Translator's Note

1. See Jean-Luc Pouthier, "L'Etat et la communication; le "modèle français,'" pp. 582–86 in *L'Etat de la France* 95–96 (Paris: La Découverte, 1995).

PERMISSIONS